Working for the Common Good

Concepts and Models
for Service-Learning
in **Management**

Paul C. Godfrey and Edward T. Grasso, volume editors

Edward Zlotkowski, series editor

STERLING, VIRGINIA

Originally published by AAHE

**Working for the Common Good: Concepts and Models for Service-Learning in Management
(AAHE's Series on Service-Learning in the Disciplines)**
Paul C. Godfrey and Edward T. Grasso, *volume editors*
Edward Zlotkowski, *series editor*

About This Publication
This volume is one of eighteen in AAHE's Series on Service-Learning in the Disciplines.

Stylus Publishing, LLC
22883 Quicksilver Drive
Sterling, VA 20166-2102
Tel.: 1-800-232-0223 / Fax: 703-661-1547
www.Styluspub.com

ISBN 978-1-56377-021-0
ISBN (18 vol. set) 978-1-56377-005-0

Contents

About This Series

by Edward Zlotkowski

The following volume, *Working for the Common Good: Concepts and Models for Service-Learning in Management*, represents the 15th in a series of monographs on service-learning and the academic disciplines. Ever since the early 1990s, educators interested in reconnecting higher education not only with neighboring communities but also with the American tradition of education for service have recognized the critical importance of winning faculty support for this work. Faculty, however, tend to define themselves and their responsibilities largely in terms of the academic disciplines/interdisciplinary areas in which they have been trained. Hence, the logic of the present series.

The idea for this series first surfaced late in 1994 at a meeting convened by Campus Compact to explore the feasibility of developing a national network of service-learning educators. At that meeting, it quickly became clear that some of those assembled saw the primary value of such a network in its ability to provide concrete resources to faculty working in or wishing to explore service-learning. Out of that meeting there developed, under the auspices of Campus Compact, a new national group of educators called the Invisible College, and it was within the Invisible College that the monograph project was first conceived. Indeed, a review of both the editors and contributors responsible for many of the volumes in this series would reveal significant representation by faculty associated with the Invisible College.

If Campus Compact helped supply the initial financial backing and impulse for the Invisible College and for this series, it was the American Association for Higher Education (AAHE) that made completion of the project feasible. Thanks to its reputation for innovative work, AAHE was not only able to obtain the funding needed to support the project up through actual publication, it was also able to assist in attracting many of the teacher-scholars who participated as writers and editors. AAHE is grateful to the Corporation for National Service–Learn and Serve America for its financial support of the series.

Three individuals in particular deserve to be singled out for their contributions. Sandra Enos, former Campus Compact project director for Integrating Service With Academic Study, was shepherd to the Invisible College project. John Wallace, professor of philosophy at the University of Minnesota, was the driving force behind the creation of the Invisible College. Without his vision and faith in the possibility of such an undertaking, assembling the human resources needed for this series would have been very difficult. Third, AAHE's endorsement — and all that followed in its wake

— was due largely to then AAHE vice president Lou Albert. Lou's enthusiasm for the monograph project and his determination to see it adequately supported have been critical to its success. It is to Sandra, John, and Lou that the monograph series as a whole must be dedicated.

Another individual to whom the series owes a special note of thanks is Teresa E. Antonucci, who, as program manager for AAHE's Service-Learning Project, has helped facilitate much of the communication that has allowed the project to move forward.

The Rationale Behind the Series

A few words should be said at this point about the makeup of both the general series and the individual volumes. Although management — with its predominantly private-sector focus — might seem an unusual discipline with which to link service-learning, "natural fit" has not, in fact, been a determinant factor in deciding which disciplines/interdisciplinary areas the series should include. Far more important have been considerations related to the overall range of disciplines represented. Since experience has shown that there is probably no disciplinary area — from architecture to zoology — where service-learning cannot be fruitfully employed to strengthen students' abilities to become active learners as well as responsible citizens, a primary goal in putting the series together has been to demonstrate this fact. Thus, some rather natural choices for inclusion — disciplines such as anthropology and geography — have been passed over in favor of other, sometimes less obvious selections, such as management. Should the present series of volumes prove useful and well received, we can then consider filling in the many gaps we have left this first time around.

If a concern for variety has helped shape the series as a whole, a concern for legitimacy has been central to the design of the individual volumes. To this end, each volume has been both written by and aimed primarily at academics working in a particular disciplinary/interdisciplinary area. Many individual volumes have, in fact, been produced with the encouragement and active support of relevant discipline-specific national associations.

Furthermore, each volume has been designed to include its own appropriate theoretical, pedagogical, and bibliographical material. Especially with regard to theoretical and bibliographical material, this design has resulted in considerable variation both in quantity and in level of discourse. Thus, for example, a volume such as Accounting contains more introductory and less bibliographical material than does Composition — simply because there is less written on and less familiarity with service-learning in accounting. However, no volume is meant to provide an extended introduction to service-learning *as a generic concept*. For material of this nature, the reader is referred to such texts as Kendall's *Combining Service and Learning: A Resource Book for Community and Public Service* (NSEE, 1990) and Jacoby's *Service-Learning in Higher Education* (Jossey-Bass, 1996).

I would like to conclude with a note of thanks to Paul Godfrey and Ed Grasso, coeditors of the present volume. Their sense of professional and social responsibility has given us a text that points to exciting new possibilities in business education.

March 2000

Preface

by Charles Wankel

The Academy of Management's Management Education and Development (MED) Division endorses this Management service-learning monograph as an excellent vehicle for management departments around the world to see ways to enhance student learning by joining management theory with experience, and management analysis with action

Service-learning prepares business students to see new dimensions of relevance of their coursework. It provides structures for students to establish caring relationships with others that validate their humanity. Service-learning is an important way for management faculty to help their departments, schools, and universities to better fulfill their missions and visions.

This volume is an excellent way to get involved.

Charles Wankel is chair of the Management Education and Development (MED) Division of the Academy of Management. He also is associate professor of management at St. John's University, in New York City.

Introduction

by Paul C. Godfrey and Edward T. Grasso

The moral virtues we do acquire by first exercising them. The same is true of the arts and crafts in general. The craftsman has to learn how to make things, but he learns in the process of making them. So men become builders by building, harp players by playing the harp. By a similar process we become just by performing just actions, temperate by performing temperate actions, brave by performing brave actions.

— Aristotle

Service-Learning and Management Education

Corporate decisions that opt for improving the bottom line while creating negative consequences for other stakeholders (e.g., employees, the natural environment) have resulted in heavy criticism of both corporations and the management teams that run them (Korten 1996). Many factors enter into the tendency of managers to focus only on the financial performance of a business, one among them being the professional training (and resulting mind-set) of the individual business manager. This volume takes root in the idea that a key component of the "managerial mind-set" prevalent in American business today originates in, and is perpetuated through, business school education. Business schools do more than merely train technical professionals in management; they also communicate a set of values regarding economic rationality and human worth that become the foundation of the managerial mind-set. It is our contention that service-learning represents an important vehicle both for preparing excellent technical managers and for instilling a mind-set that makes decisions based on more than merely bottom-line criteria.

The term "service-learning" was coined in the late 1960s in developing a Southern Regional Education Board program. The membership of the board defined service-learning as "the integration of the accomplishment of a needed task with educational growth" (Sigmon 1994). Now, some 30 years later, service-learning is coming of age, and its value in preparing students for citizenship roles in their communities is being recognized (Gray et al. 1996).

Over the last three decades, many educators, students, and community leaders have joined together in redefining and, more important, implementing service-learning. Their rationale for combining traditional classroom practices with community service has been threefold. First, such a combination leads to more effective teaching and learning. Second, it leads to more effective collaboration between the campus and the community. Third, it attempts to prepare people for more effective participation in the communities in which we lead our lives (Kupiec 1993). In 1990, the National and Community Service Act characterized service-learning as having four components:

1. Students actively participate in organized service experiences that meet actual community needs and that are coordinated in collaboration with the school and community.

2. These experiences are integrated into the students' academic curriculum, and/or structured time is provided for them to think, talk, or write about what they did and saw during their actual service activity.

3. Students have opportunities to use newly acquired skills and knowledge in real-life situations in their own communities.

4. These experiences help to foster the development of a sense of caring for others. (adapted from Cohen 1994)

Management educators have for years incorporated internships and cooperative education units into their programs as a means of providing students with experiential education grounded in the "real world." Such familiar experiential ventures have much to recommend them; however, traditional internships and cooperative education programs cannot serve as surrogates for service-learning, because, for the most part, they do not require (or often even allow for) the community placements and the rigorous reflective process that connect town and gown (see Trent, Grasso, and Roby 1996). However, rigorous reflection on experiences gained through service is a hallmark of the service-learning approach. Ross (1989) identifies the following as essential elements of that reflective process:

• recognizing a problem or dilemma,

• responding to that dilemma by recognizing both its similarities to other situations and its unique qualities,

• framing and reframing the dilemma,

• experimenting with the dilemma to discover the consequences and implications of various solutions,

• examining the intended and unintended consequences of an implemented solution, and evaluating that solution by determining whether or not those consequences are desirable.

This volume is designed to help management faculty, and those who manage them, to catch the vision of the service-learning movement. In many ways, it continues the work begun in a special issue of the *Journal of Business Ethics* in 1996 (vol. 15, no. 1). That issue features an excellent overview of the potential role of service-learning in management education by Edward Zlotkowski (editor of the AAHE series of which this volume is a part), followed by program-related essays that provide readers with cogent and compelling suggestions for going forward (Kolenko et al. 1996). Much like what follows in this volume, the *Journal's* nine featured programs cut a broad swath across the field of management education. Included are descriptions of individual courses and a program-level course in an MBA program — initiatives at Research I institutions as well as small undergraduate teaching colleges. Indeed, the power of that special issue comes directly from its breadth and diversity. As the issue's guest editor, Denis Collins, notes:

> *By the end of this special issue you will know how some educators have integrated service-learning projects in their undergraduate classes, internship programs, graduate classes, orientation week, across the business school curriculum, and across the university curriculum. (1996: 4)*

Volume Overview

The design of the volume that follows also aims at breadth and diversity. We explore service-learning not only in a variety of different settings but also at different curriculum levels, thereby providing as many readers as possible with a meaningful starting point for their own service-learning efforts. We have also sought to make available more theoretical/contextual material, as well as a guide to additional resources. Thus, the volume falls into several complementary parts. Part 1 lays a general moral and pedagogical foundation for the service-learning approach, suggesting at the same time several different philosophical rationales. Parts 2 and 3 consist of various case studies that illustrate how management educators are currently using service-learning in their work. These illustrations make clear the power of service-learning at all levels of management education: introductory undergraduate, advanced undergraduate, graduate, and executive. It concludes with an annotated bibliography designed to provide readers with several additional "access points."

We launch Part 1 with an essay by someone outside the academy. Judith Samuelson, director of the Aspen Institute's initiative for social innovation in business, offers a unique perspective on the need for service-learning. The Aspen Institute is a private, not-for-profit organization working with many of the nation's leading foundations to improve the social performance of business organizations. Samuelson discusses the history of business education and the problems facing business education in the 21st century, and suggests that service-learning can aid business schools in their attempt to integrate into their educational programming the broad context and impact that business has on contemporary society. Simply put, we lead off with this essay in order to provide evidence of concern for improving corporate social performance from significant groups not within the academy proper. While Samuelson's language may resonate more with the experiences of those in the town rather than those wearing the gown, her powerful call for more attention to social welfare within business education represents a timely, even critically important, message.

Paul Godfrey's essay further develops Samuelson's general theme as he argues that the private sector will only control the social agenda so long as it proves itself a worthy steward of the power to improve society. He argues that service-learning pedagogies provide a mechanism for management educators to combine our traditional worship of the market with solutions to problems of social justice and ecological sustainability. Especially noteworthy is Godfrey's attempt to outline concrete benefits for students in learning skills of civic participation as well as organizational management.

Sandra Waddock and James Post also explore the kinds of concerns Godfrey raises. Their starting point is that much corporate behavior shows little real concern for moral authority; indeed, they argue that the idea of corporate social responsibility is all but dead. Management education has contributed to its demise because the overriding mind-set in business education has been that managerial activity is a "private good" — pursued for the enhancement of personal and private wealth. They argue that business education needs to focus on management as a "public good" — with ramifications for the common wealth of the community as well as the private wealth of shareholders and managers. They then argue that service-learning provides an excellent vehicle for shifting the management education paradigm in this direction.

If the first three chapters focus on broad moral and social considerations, Amy Kenworthy's chapter provides a wholly pragmatic argument for adopting service-learning. Kenworthy believes that putting students in consultancy relationships with local community organizations represents perhaps the best way to embed the skills of traditional management education in these students. Service-learning projects give them an opportunity for sustained, professional experience in difficult and complex situations. Kenworthy argues that exposure to these complex, at times seemingly intractable, problems can help business students gain an understanding of both how to manage complexity and what role business professionals can play in solving social problems.

Grace Ann Rosile and David Boje conclude this part with a postmodern view of service-learning. We have included this essay both because of the substance of Rosile's and Boje's instructional experience and because the waves of postmodernism continue to challenge our assumptions about education. Service-learning offers Rosile and Boje the best pedagogy to expose students to a variety of organizational forms, and to the different management styles that effectively run those forms. It allows them to force students out of their comfort zones in order to look critically at many of the underlying assumptions that make up modern management.

Parts 2 and 3 of this volume consist of six pedagogical essays. The first three essays detail service-learning at the level of individual courses. Each author of these essays details the integration of service-learning into specific management courses and includes course syllabi. The strength of these essays collectively lies in the broad band of students their courses expose to service-learning — from an introductory management course to an MBA capstone course. We asked each author, in the process of working with this material, to be sure to include his or her own reflections so as to provide the reader with more than a clinical description of the course under consideration.

In the first essay, James Davis and John Michel describe how service-learning enhances their MBA-level corporate policy and strategy course at Notre Dame. What is especially interesting, given that the authors teach at a church-affiliated university, is the way in which Davis and Michel seem to favor an approach to service-learning that stresses its instrumental benefits in developing skills over its moral/social dimension.

Next, Gaylen Chandler details his success in integrating service-learning into an entry-level management course taken by undergraduates in the College of Business at Utah State University. He describes both the positive educational outcomes for the students and the positive service outcomes for client organizations and the community in general. Chandler also surfaces a third kind of service-learning benefit: the way in which such work reflects positively on the business school and the university at large.

Finally, Sue Campbell Clark relates her experiences in integrating service-learning into an upper-division human resource management course at the University of Idaho. While she delineates how service-learning is used in the course and how service-learning enhances her students' learning, a special strength of her essay rests in her account of how service-learning has affected her as a teacher.

The next three chapters highlight program-wide or institution-based service-learning efforts. Again, these essays testify to the variety of ways in which service-learning can reach important student cohorts within a business school. Larry Michaelsen and his colleagues describe a comprehensive service-learning–based program at the University of Oklahoma called the Integrated Business Core. They suggest that students who enroll in the Integrated Business Core are better able to view organizations from an interdisciplinary perspective, are better able to communicate effectively with others, and are better able to solve unstructured problems.

Christine Lamb and her colleagues from the College of Business at Montana State University at Bozeman detail the role of service-learning in a program that uses service both as a first-year foundational experience and as a final-semester capstone experience. This essay provides perhaps the clearest sense of service-learning's dynamic aspects; indeed, Montana State uses its service-learning program to help students understand how much they have learned while in business school.

Marilyn Taylor concludes the volume's series of program-based essays with a description of the recently established Initiative for a Competitive Inner City (ICIC) and its service-learning–related component: the University Alliance Network at the Bloch School of Business and Public Administration at the University of Missouri at Kansas City. The Bloch School's Executive MBA program provides a potential model for service-learning that ICIC could encourage throughout the country. The unique value of Taylor's essay lies in showing how service-learning can be effectively used in the most prized and fastest-growing segment of the business school market — executive education.

In concluding our review of the volume's featured courses and programs, we should, in fairness, note that there are many excellent service-learning programs that we have not had space to include. Two programs in this category especially stand out: the service-learning program at Bentley College (an undergraduate business college) and the global leadership program at the University of Michigan (in the MBA program). Since both of these programs are described in some detail in the *Journal of Business Ethics* special issue mentioned above, we felt confident that they would nonetheless remain accessible to those interested in the programs we have profiled.

Three Final Questions

As we conclude this introduction, we step back from the details of the chapters that follow and highlight three questions raised by them that will present challenges for service-learning in management education in the new millennium. First, should service-learning courses and programs focus on the instrumental value of service-learning as a pedagogy or on its intrinsic value in building a better society? Our experience with this volume, and in other settings, suggests that many faculty recognize the strong instrumental benefits of service-learning. As Kenworthy argues in Part 1, service-learning provides perhaps the most "bang for the buck" in terms of helping students learn management skills in a complex environment.

While this may be true, we would nonetheless like to suggest that the instrumental/intrinsic divide may represent an unnecessary or even false dichotomy. Certainly service-learning projects result in significant opportunities for skills development. But these opportunities can be simultaneously supplemented with discussions, readings, and reflective exercises that force each student also to ask larger questions about the role of businesses in society and, more specifically, about his or her own role in both business and society.

Second, should service-learning be located in individual courses or should it be an institution-wide initiative? Obviously, this question will be answered in a variety of ways, depending on the values, strengths, and histories of various institutions. Still, we cannot pass off the question with a noncommittal "it depends on where you are," because the level at which service-learning occurs carries with it pragmatic choices that influence its success.

Service-learning at the level of individual courses carries two major advantages. First, the instrumental learning is more focused and hence richer. Course instructors work with students and agencies to provide service that uses a specific set of skills (e.g., negotiation skills, compensation planning skills, etc.). Programmatic, or institution-wide, service-learning initiatives tend to be broader in focus and application, and students often use existing or general skills (e.g., hard work) in their activities rather than developing new skills. Second, service-learning courses are easier to start than service-learning programs. Courses usually begin with committed faculty members willing to invest the extra time, energy, and network resources needed to make service-learning a reality. Individual instructors typically do not have to negotiate with others about the nature of their projects and require little coalition building to support their ideas. By necessity, initiating service-learning at the program or institutional level involves far greater start-up costs and far greater risks of initial failure.

However, the primary advantage of service-learning at the program or institutional level is its sustainability. Once such a program has taken off, it has the constituency and the stable resource base to survive and prosper. Although sustaining service-learning at the program level may require greater resources and skill specialization (e.g., dedicated and qualified staff as well as faculty), the fact that one individual in the service-learning coalition leaves the institution does not mean the program's very survival is threatened. This is in sharp contrast especially to the initiatives of maverick professors who take a department's commitment to service-learning with them when they leave.

The third question gets at a core difference between business education and other fields within the academy: Which students should be involved in service-learning? When one compares Gaylen Chandler's program with Marilyn Taylor's, key differences emerge. Chandler can plan his service-learning projects for a "captive" student population. Beginning business students are typically full-time students with few (if any) primary outside commitments. Taylor's Executive MBA students enjoy no such luxury; many of them shoehorn their MBA studies into already full schedules and lives. Thus, the contents of the projects must diverge as well. Taylor's students can make vastly different contributions to the community than can Chandler's. Looking into the future and seeing the growth of nondegree-related executive education and the increasing diversity among student populations in terms of experience, entering knowledge, and extracurricular commitments, we believe that course design, administrative support, and faculty commitment will all have to deepen in order to make service-learning projects meaningful across a broad spectrum of students.

We conclude this introduction by reaffirming our own personal commitment to service-learning. We use it in our courses and encourage its use throughout our institutions. To us, it represents a powerful way to connect the theories of management with the realities of day-to-day life, and with the complexities of a postindustrial world. Service-learning also allows us to satisfy our desire to have a more significant impact on the lives of both our students and our communities. We encourage you to find — in a spirit of trial and experimentation — the chapters that most interest you. We hope that the next publishing foray into service-learning in management education will fill several volumes in its own right. We close by returning to the words of Aristotle: "The moral virtues we do acquire by first exercising them."

References

Cohen, J. (1994). "Matching University Mission With Service Motivation: Do the Accomplishments of Community Service Match the Claims?" *Michigan Journal of Community Service Learning* 1(1): 98-104.

Collins, D. (1996). "Closing the Gap Between Business Students and the Poor: An Introduction to the Volume." *Journal of Business Ethics* 15(1): 1-4.

Gray, M., S. Geshwind, E. Ondaatje, A. Robyn, S. Klien, L. Sax, A. Astin, and H. Astin. (1996). *Evaluation of Learn and Serve America, Higher Education: First Year Report, Volume 1.* Los Angeles, CA: Higher Education Research Institute, UCLA.

Kolenko, T., G. Porter, W. Wheatley, and M. Colby. (1996). "Critique of Service-Learning Projects in Management Education: Pedagogical Foundations, Barriers, and Guidelines." *Journal of Business Ethics* 15(1): 133-142.

Korten, D. (1996). *When Corporations Rule the World.* San Francisco, CA: Berrett-Kohler.

Kupiec, T.Y., ed. (1993). *Rethinking Tradition: Integrating Service With Academic Study on College Campuses.* Denver, CO: Education Commission of the States/Campus Compact.

Ross, D.D. (1989). "First Steps in Developing a Reflective Approach." *Journal of Teacher Education* 40: 22-30.

Sigmon, R.L. (1994). "Linking Service With Learning." Washington, DC: Council of Independent Colleges.

Trent, Donna M., Edward T. Grasso, and Christopher J. Roby. (1996). "Management Education Through Service-Learning." In *Proceedings of the International Association for Business and Society Annual Conference,* pp. 663-667.

Business Education for the 21st Century

by Judith Samuelson

> *What is most important is that management realizes that it must consider the impact of every business policy and business action upon society. It has to consider whether the action is likely to promote the public good, to advance the basic beliefs of our society, to contribute to stability, strength, and harmony.*
>
> — Drucker 1955: 342

> *Business education must be concerned not only with competence but also with responsibility, not only with skills but also with the attitudes of businessmen. . . . Business schools have an obligation to do what they can to develop a "sense of responsibility" and a high standard of business ethics in their graduates.*
>
> — Gordon and Howell 1959: 111

Perhaps the most striking feature of our time is the prominence of business and its influence on culture, social values, and civic life. Unprecedented growth in equity markets, business consolidations, corporate contributions to political campaigns, and "consumerism" are all factors in the ascendance of business as an institution. The explosion of global capitalism[1] — worldwide flows of investment capital and exchange of goods in excess of budgets of nation states — provides a platform for business as a social force around the world. Other equally important factors are disillusionment with government and the failure of other social institutions — especially the family, religion, and education — to regulate the balance between self-interest and the collective interest.

To those concerned with negative social, economic, and environmental consequences of industrialization, the growth in power and influence of business presents both challenges and opportunities. On the one hand, business is under attack from community, labor, and environmental advocates for business practices that, while "profitable," are socially costly and ultimately damaging to the business environment itself. As multinational corporations expand into emerging markets around the globe, issues of corporate responsibility and the risks of failing to consider the long-term social impacts of business decisions and operations are becoming more evident. The practices in question span environmental, capital investment, and human resource policies. They include the growing wage gap between top-level managers and workers, the use of child labor and substandard conditions in emerging markets, and a wide assortment of environmental and developmental policies that have harmful health or social effects or that undervalue the long-term costs of consuming nonrenewable resources.[2]

At the same time, work practices that artfully address real business problems while making important contributions to dealing with complex social issues are growing in number. Examples in the United States include Marriott's program to link low-wage workers to supportive services such as child care and transportation, McDonald's training program for at-risk minority youth, Pathmark's retail expansions in inner cities, and numerous creative approaches to economic development and conservation that utilize market forces and community-based solutions.

In 1994, as director of the Ford Foundation's social investment program, I began working with colleagues on an initiative that recognized the growing importance of business as a social institution and potential partner. The Corporate Involvement Initiative was organized to explore the nature of successful public-private partnerships in the area of community and economic development, and to better understand the ways in which corporations might be supported and encouraged to apply functional business resources and competencies to complex social problems. To date, this Initiative has made grants to more than a dozen business and industry associations and training and community development organizations that are pursuing promising business activities and economic development partnerships. For example, the Initiative encompasses a portfolio of action-learning projects in specific industries — banking, insurance, and information technology to name a few — in order to develop private-sector solutions to "social" problems that affect business's ability to expand markets in the inner city and build the skills of entry-level workers.

Members of the Ford Foundation Initiative's development team had themselves followed career paths that combined public or nonprofit work experience, private-sector work in finance or consulting, and a business degree. In my case, a master's degree from the Yale School of Management facilitated the transition from lobbying and legislative work in Sacramento, California, to commercial banking in the garment center of New York City. For me, the work at Ford was an opportunity to examine how the private and nonprofit worlds collide in culture and values, as well as to examine theories of the business rationale for social innovation and investment through business.

In 1996, we began investigating possible connections between this work and formal business education. Research projects were funded at the University of Pittsburgh (Wood 1997) and Students for Responsible Business[3] to begin mapping the existing activities at and course content of business schools insofar as they related to community and economic development. In addition, we conducted our own interviews to explore the environment of business schools and the barriers they found to elevating — through teaching, research, and experiential education — discussion of the role of business in society. In person and through focus groups, we met with more than 200 academics, administrators and deans, nonprofit leaders, and business executives to begin painting a picture of the current landscape of management education. In 1998, we launched another venture — the Initiative for Social Innovation Through Business (ISIB) — to focus additional attention on the social implications of management and executive education. Although the Ford Foundation provided the initial support for this project, it now operates out of the Aspen Institute, an organization that promotes value-based leadership through seminars and dialogue (see the profile at the end of this chapter).

The mission of the ISIB is to bring together innovative thinkers and leaders from business, academia, and the social sector to develop new and better ways to address complex social issues, to influence future leaders by encouraging and motivating business educators and business schools to expand their research and curricula, and to test new approaches to the role of business in society.

Why Business Education?

"Professional" business education is essentially a postwar phenomenon, having evolved from more narrowly conceived vocational and specialized industry training during the 1930s and 1940s. Since the 1950s, we have seen dramatic growth in formal business education. At the end of the 1950s, only 125 U.S. colleges and universities offered master's degrees in business administration, with Harvard and NYU representing 25 percent of the national total. No doctoral degree programs in business existed. Today, 900 American graduate-level business schools produce approximately 90,000 graduates, representing 23 percent of the postgraduate degrees granted annually in U.S. higher education. More than 100 business schools offer doctorate degrees.

Internationally, we are also witnessing a dynamic change in business education as established schools around the world grow in reputation and new programs enter the field to serve emerging markets. Some are challenging assumptions about how best to prepare students and managers for the global business environment.

Such institutional and programmatic growth has been accompanied by important changes in the content of management education. The Ford Foundation and the Carnegie Foundation are often credited with putting these changes in motion. From 1954 to 1966, Ford invested $35 million in business schools in an effort to move the field "from a romantic view of business as a subjective art, one requiring judgment rather than the accumulation of knowledge," to a more rationalist view, consistent with that of other professions (Schossman, Sedlak, and Weschsler 1987: iii).

The results of this effort were dramatic but mixed. George Leland Bach, former dean of the School of Industrial Administration at the Carnegie Institute of Technology and one of the chief architects of the Ford Foundation's program, observed as early as 1966:

> *Today the results seem somewhat unbalanced. . . . The revolution in business education, subject matter–wise, has centered around [the] increasing use of rigorous, quantitative-mathematical methods for managerial decision making and control. Clearly there has been too little attention in the business schools to a parallel development of the behavioral sciences and to the rapidly changing environment in which business operates.*

Lately, these words have taken on new urgency. The quality of business education and its relevance to the "real world" have been much discussed and analyzed. Thomas Piper, coauthor of *Can Ethics Be Taught?* writing on the basis of his experience developing an ethics program at Harvard, has described the need for business schools to help business leaders understand the "intensifying complexity of an interdependent global economy and ecology, and the power of the business corporation to [affect] social welfare and the environment, both positively and negatively" (Piper, Gentile, and Parks 1993).

The position that business leaders have an obligation not only to their stockholders but also to their employees, customers, and the public at large goes back several decades to a seminal report, sponsored by the Ford Foundation to assess and guide the Foundation's investment in business schools (Gordon and Howell 1959). Stakeholder theory and emerging work in the field of social auditing continue to evolve today as key conceptual frameworks for understanding business success in the context of all affected parties — the community, workers and managers, suppliers, the environment, and shareholders. Yet despite the evolution of such frameworks, recent growth in equity markets has seen an increasing focus in business theory and practice on short-term financial returns, or the financial "bottom line," at the expense of other measures of success and impact. Indeed, in many business schools today, stakeholder theory is largely ignored by or subordinated to a paradigm that assumes corporations, especially publicly traded companies, exist solely to maximize shareholder return.[4] Study of business ethics — and even general management studies — continues to give way to more specialized and technical educational interests. The effects of business on society and the social context in which business operates are deemed at best of marginal importance.

Thus, despite the fact that by now business schools have largely attained the stature of "professional" education, they do not fare well when compared with professional schools in other fields — e.g., law, medicine, and engineering — that exist (at least in theory) to serve, with science as their foundation (Gordon and Howell 1959). While business education arguably has advanced in its development of management as a "science," almost no one would argue that business schools promote "service" in the broad definition. Gordon and Howell have directly addressed this "question of personal goals and professional standards of business education":

> There is no clearly agreed and generally accepted standard of professional conduct for business as a whole. Some minimum standards of honest dealing are embodied in the law; beyond this, businessmen, like all other members of society, subscribe in varying degrees to the traditional moral standards of Western civilization. In entering on a business career, one does not undertake to live up to a Hippocratic Oath or otherwise to meet clearly stated standards of professional conduct. . . . But a business enterprise can have a complex set of objectives, only one of which is profits for the owners. Are the businessman's goals of service and his standards of conduct to be geared solely to the objectives of the firm, whatever they may be? (Gordon and Howell 1959: 70)

The Role of Service-Learning in Management Education

In today's environment, amid pressure from employers to enhance the technical and financial skill of graduates, how does a business school attempt to integrate the broad context and impact of business into the educational experience it provides? One important approach that is now the focus of discussion and experimentation is service-learning.

In the workplace, community service or voluntarism has been valued for its positive effect on employee motivation, for the opportunity it affords to better understand the community and the customer, and for the developmental challenge of applying business skills to complex social problems. Analogously, in educational settings, service-learning invites business students to use their "hands as well as their heads" — and thus can be a powerful teaching tool. A case example is the innovative MBA orientation program at the University of Michigan Business School, which places groups of students in community organizations and projects in order to provide them with exposure to specific social issues and to develop in them qualities of leadership as well as team work skills. Also relevant in this regard is the Yale School of Management's highly successful student-managed Internship Fund, which subsidizes summer work experiences in nonprofit and community organizations, and thus facilitates application of newly acquired analytical skills and organizational theory to a broad range of management challenges — while all the time underscoring the critical role of the non-profit sector. Summer interns working in that sector are subsidized by class-mates with more lucrative summer positions — thus allowing all to take some "ownership" of the program. The school matches student pledges, and the Internship Fund and related fundraising activities provide much of the management school's social "glue." As some of the essays in this volume tes-tify, still other business schools integrate consulting opportunities with com-munity ventures or inner-city businesses into their undergraduate and/or MBA curricula.

If, on the one hand, service-learning requires students to apply business analysis to real problems in a live setting — something rarely achieved with standard case materials — it also allows critical connections to values and leadership to emerge from this work. Finance students who tackle the bud-get of a soup kitchen are exposed to the challenge of running a small busi-ness and to the connections that exist between elective service and morale. Human resources candidates working with poorly skilled welfare recipients explore the difficulties single mothers face when they attempt to enter the workforce. Management students confronted with the nonprofit reality of "living on a shoestring" receive a lesson in leadership and in the art of mak-ing things happen through teamwork even in the face of restricted resources.

Perhaps I should at this point stress that in advocating broad-gauged, values-based management education, ISIB does not itself distinguish sharply between service-learning and a broader, more general context of experiential education. Instead, it seeks out innovative ways to connect the analytical skill–focus of management education with both the social context and the social "footprint" of business. Ideally, from our perspective, MBA stu-dents should have an opportunity to develop and hone business skills in a number of ways, including applying them to very real social problems — problems that surface in the neighborhood of the university, in the inner city, or in the developing world. Why? Because we believe that these skills, context, and values are required of successful business leaders today and will only become more important for future business leadership.

Education for Business Leaders in the 21st Century

The need for strong values-based leadership in the business sector is obvi-ous to environmentalists, social innovators, and entrepreneurs engaged in the full spectrum of problems that confront the government and nonprofit sectors. Business leaders, in turn, have begun to realize the importance of direct involvement in social and environmental issues that limit the ability of business to attract and retain skilled workers and to develop worldwide markets for their goods and services. To secure the right to operate around the globe, business will need to create value for communities, employees, and investors alike. Business leaders will need to be both willing and able to engage the firm directly in social and environmental issues of consequence and, in doing so, to build effective partnerships with other businesses as well as with public and nonprofit organizations.

In order to prepare business managers to operate within this new paradigm, it is essential to engage the debate about business education — undergraduate, MBA, and executive programs — and to experiment with ways to bring the social impact and social environment of business into the curriculum. After years of attempting to capture the imagination of faculty and students in the teaching of "ethics" and "social responsibility," globalization forces us to consider new models. The critical social and environmental issues facing business leaders and societies worldwide require bold new approaches to teaching and research rooted in the "felt needs" of managing a business, and linked to understanding both business strategy and risk management. In order for future business leaders to function effectively in a complex global market, business schools will need to illustrate the business case for combining management technique and social innovation. One of the distinct advantages of service-learning and programs that support service activity is their ability to infuse the social context of business throughout the business education experience, and with greater immediacy than is possible through traditional coursework limited to ethical dilemmas and moral decisions rooted in philosophy.

In short, this challenge of effective management in global companies may, in part, be met by beginning to acquaint future business leaders with the problems faced by the communities in which they will do business, the vital importance of the nonprofits that work in those communities, and the need for public-private partnerships to increase the likelihood of advancing the highest-quality solutions to the shared problems of business and society.

Notes

1. A characteristic of globalization is the fact that the largest of these firms, "multinationals," no longer identify as strongly with their country of origin or headquarters city. As Rosabeth Moss Kanter points out in her 1995 book *World Class*, globalization changes the requirements for business as well as communities, raising questions about the meaning of "community" in a global economy.

2. Books and articles published in recent years that chronicle the community impacts and social and environmental effects of globalization and contemporary business practice include *One World Ready or Not* by William Greider, *Building a Win-Win World* by Hazel Henderson, Kanter's *World Class*, and *When Corporations Rule the World* by David C. Korten.

3. Students for Responsible Business (SRB) is a network of more than 1,300 business students and alumni across North America. SRB's mission is to create a new generation of leaders who use the power of business to transform society. The organization was founded in 1993 and is based in San Francisco.

4. The financial view of the firm is appealing, in part, because of the desire for measurable outcomes and performance. Profits are to the firm what the gross national product is to the country — shorthand for measuring progress and financial success. Redesigning Progress, a nonprofit "actiontank" created to improve measurement of progress in society, points out that many of the real long-term costs to society of business practice and economic "progress" fall outside contemporary metrics. Neither accounting profits nor the GNP, for example, measures the significant and long-term costs of environmental degradation or chronic unemployment.

References

Bach, George Leland. (1966). "Lessons From Business Education." Memo to Marshall Robinson.

Drucker, Peter. (1955). *The Practice of Management*. New York, NY: Harper & Row.

Gordon, Robert Aaron, and James Edwin Howell. (1959). *Higher Education for Business*. New York, NY: Columbia University Press.

Kanter, Rosabeth Moss. (1995). *World Class: Thriving Locally in the Global Economy*. New York, NY: Simon & Schuster.

Korten, D.C. (1996). *When Corporations Rule the World*. West Hartford, CT: Kumarian Press.

Piper, Thomas R., Mary C. Gentile, and Sharon Daloz Parks. (1993). *Can Ethics Be Taught?* Boston, MA: Harvard Business Press.

Schossman, Steven, Michael Sedlak, and Pat Weschsler. (1987). "The 'New Look': The Ford Foundation and the Revolution in Business Education." GMAC Occasional Papers.

Wood, D.J. (November 1997). "Field-Mapping: Business School Approaches." Unpublished report to the Ford Foundation.

The Aspen Institute

Founded in 1950 by Chicago industrialist Walter Paepcke, the Aspen Institute was envisioned as a place where world leaders might gather to pause and reflect on the underlying values of their culture. Paepcke, chair of Container Corporation of America, was particularly concerned with business leaders' knowledge of and perspective on the core values and ideas necessary to lead a democratic society. Convinced that these values — justice, equality, beauty, the rights of the individual — were best represented in the writing of great classical and modern philosophers, he sought to create a forum in which businessmen could be exposed to such thinking. "It could be asserted," said Paepcke, "that men so exposed to basic issues, social, economic, and religious, might not merely remain business leaders but become leading citizens."

With the help of Time Inc. founder Henry Luce, University of Chicago president Robert Hutchins, and philosopher Mortimer Adler, Paepcke created the Executive Seminar, which remains the core offering of the Aspen Institute. Leaders from business, government, academia, labor, and the arts gather around a seminar table in Aspen for a week to discuss the essential values of life as found in the works of some of the world's greatest thinkers — Plato, Aristotle, Jefferson, Madison, Martin Luther King, Jr., Vaclav Havel, to name a few — and how one achieves the necessary balances among liberty, equality, community, and efficiency.

These discussions are also a part of the Institute's 17 Policy Programs, which again, use informed, civil dialogue as the basis for examining crucial policy issues in such diverse areas as defense and arms control, rural economic development, education, the changing workforce, and most recently the role of the corporation in society.

Headquartered in Washington, D.C., with facilities in Aspen, Colorado, and on Maryland's Eastern Shore, the Aspen Institute's non-partisan approach and emphasis on civil dialogue have involved it in such projects as the International Commission for the Balkans, a group of international leaders charged with examining the interrelated conflicts in the area and proposing long-term approaches to establishing regional stability; and the 1997 Bipartisan Congressional Retreat, where members of the U.S. House of Representatives met to discuss ways to foster an environment in which vigorous debate and mutual respect could coexist.

Values-based leadership has been the focus of the Aspen Institute, the home for the Initiative for Social Innovation Through Business (ISIB), since its founding.

A Moral Argument for Service-Learning in Management Education

by Paul C. Godfrey

> [In the United States] compared [with] other nations, the power to deter-
> mine the national agenda was fairly evenly, if not perfectly, divided among
> elitist managers. The arrangement, however, disguised the essential
> dynamics of American rulership, wherein the contest among elitists was
> over the matter of moral authority. Put another way, this contest concerned
> which institutions or subgroups of their leaders were to be first among
> equals. . . . Historically, the location of that power changed cyclically,
> depending on the political atmosphere. . . . The site of moral authority
> depended to a great extent on whether public opinion and voting behavior
> favored strong government intervention or autonomy of the private sector.
> . . . Shifts between these sectors occurred regularly as a reaction of one
> against the excesses of the other.
>
> — Scott 1992: 2-3

As the 20th century has drawn to a close, the private sector appears to hold the moral authority to set the social agenda for the United States. What began in the early 1980s as the Reagan Revolution has blossomed into numerous attempts to restructure the role of government in American life. Welfare reform and Social Security reform (including serious calls for the privatization of the Social Security program) stand as representative issues that highlight the shift in favor of the private sector. The doubling in the mid 1990s of the value of the Dow Jones industrial average evidenced a contin-ued confidence in the ability of American industry to compete in world mar-kets. Events outside the United States further enhanced the moral ascen-dancy of the private sector. The collapse of the Soviet Union and the flower-ing of market-based democracies behind much of the former Iron Curtain and the emergence of the Asian Tigers as economic powerhouses solidified and deepened the belief that private-sector capitalism is best suited to set the moral agenda for the world's societies.

Scott's observation about the pendulum motion of the seat of moral authority offers a salutary reality check for those enamored with market capitalism as a moral agent. The weight of moral authority will again swing in the direction of the public sector if the private sector proves an unworthy steward of that authority. Critics of the private sector abound today, and their arguments paint a compelling picture of a decreased quality of life, environmental degradation, and social decay arising from intrinsic characteristics of market-based economies. Daly and Cobb (1994) present an academy-based elaboration of the moral hazards of unbridled neoclassical capitalism. Korten (1996) offers the layman much of the same fare: a searing indictment of the morality of major multinational corporations. The continuing ability of the private sector to set the agenda for the United States (and by implication for much of the world) depends on the extent to which individual private managers and business organizations can deliver an improved standard of living while avoiding excesses of greed, overconsumption, ecological degradation, and the vicissitudes of the business cycle.

The fundamental purpose of this essay is to help the private sector find a way to blend the positive power of the market with nonmarket moral concerns. Since this essay is not morally neutral, I feel an obligation to expose my own assumptions and biases at the outset. The arrows of critique of the capitalist system find many appropriate targets: that unbridled capitalism places individual rights and satisfactions above community interests (Daly and Cobb 1994), and that the market mechanism may possess allocative efficiency but not necessarily justice or fairness (Korten 1996). However, that the moral pendulum currently favors the private sector is for me a good thing, and my concern as a management educator and researcher is to provide managers and organizations with the skill sets and mind-sets necessary to be effective stewards of society's moral authority: that is, to enjoy the fruits of capitalism while actively seeking justice, fairness, and ecological sustainability. I concur with the assumptions undergirding a growing body of literature — that there is nothing in the market mechanism that intrinsically opposes justice, fairness, or ecological sustainability (see Hosmer 1994, 1995 and Jones 1995 for the argument around ethics in general, and Hart 1995, 1997 and Shrivastava 1995 for examples of the argument around ecological sustainability).

Consistent with my advocacy of the private sector, I believe that business schools in general, and management educators in particular, have a vital role to play in improving the private sector's collective ability to address many of our most pressing social needs. Management education, for good or ill, influences management practice by encoding key moral and behavioral tenets into undergraduate and MBA curricula. Hence, management educators can inculcate habits of strong moral behavior (evidenced by increased concern for others) among the next generation of business leaders. Management educators also possess important knowledge bases and skill sets, can activate important stakeholder networks (e.g., alumni, colleagues, students), and can mobilize institutional efforts to act as a bully pulpit for social causes (Porter 1995).

Specifically, I argue that the pedagogy known as service-learning provides a mechanism for management educators to combine our traditional worship of the market with solutions to problems of social justice and ecological sustainability. Service-learning can provide management students with a more complete set of skills, principles, and knowledge to become effective stewards of society's moral and social resources. To advance this argument, I first provide a detailed description of what service-learning is. I next argue that service-learning enhances the ability of private-sector managers to be effective stewards of society's moral authority. My experiences as a practitioner of service-learning provide anecdotal examples and evidence of many of the claims I advance.[1] The essay concludes by placing service-learning within a larger moral context.

Service-Learning

In its simplest formulation, "service-learning combines traditional classroom and laboratory experiences with significant experiences in field placements where pertinent social issues are being played out" (Bonar et al. 1996: 15). Jacoby offers a more complete definition:

> Service-learning is a form of experiential education in which students engage in activities that address human and community needs together with structured opportunities intentionally designed to promote student learning and development. Reflection and reciprocity are key concepts of service-learning. (1996: 5)

Stanton (1990: 65) notes that service-learning "is more of a program emphasis, representative of a set of educational, social, and sometimes political values, rather than a discrete type of experiential education." Fundamentally, service-learning parts company with much of traditional business education in that it does not seek, nor claim, value neutrality. Ten principles of good practice in service-learning follow (on the next page).

Ideally, service-learning courses seamlessly integrate students' community service experiences with the academic knowledge being considered. For example, a business policy class could effectively integrate community service by helping a local food bank systematize its policies for food collection and distribution. A human resources class could integrate service-learning by helping a local crisis line develop and implement a training program for new volunteers. Finance students could use service-learning to help either individuals or local agencies with budget planning materials and training. The key notion here is that service-learning does not merely append community service onto the curriculum, but instead integrates community service within the curriculum.

Service-learning also includes both reciprocity and reflection among its key elements. Reciprocity ensures that student learning is accomplished

Benchmarking Principles for Service-Learning Activities

An effective and sustained program:
1. Engages people in responsible and challenging actions for the common good.
2. Provides structured opportunities for people to reflect on their service experience.
3. Articulates clear service and learning goals for everyone involved.
4. Allows for those with needs to define those needs.
5. Clarifies the responsibilities of each person and organization involved.
6. Matches service providers and service needs through a process that recognizes changing circumstances.
7. Expects genuine, active, and sustained organizational commitment.
8. Includes training, supervision, monitoring, support, recognition, and evaluation to meet service and learning goals.
9. Ensures that the time commitment and learning is flexible, appropriate, and in the best interests of all involved.
10. Is committed to program participation by and with diverse populations.

Source: The Wingspread Principles (Kendall and Associates 1990)

through meaningful community service so that both parties involved benefit. It implies that service-learning programs partner with local community agencies or service providers, that students work with these groups to help solve problems identified by the community (Kendall et al. 1990). Thus, service-learning does not create projects to highlight the academic subject du jour, but instead focuses on projects that meet and solve human needs and problems: "Through reciprocity, students develop a greater sense of belonging and responsibility as members of a larger community" (Jacoby 1996: 7).

As for reflection, it may include student journals, reflective essays, portfolios, oral interviews, and other pedagogical tools that force students to consider what their experiences mean to them. Reflection works to ensure that service-learning results in education, not merely in experience (Giles 1990; Jacoby 1996; Kendall et al. 1990). Thus, not only would human resource students design and implement a training program for new volunteers at a community action agency, but each student would also write a reflective essay about his or her experiences in the course. Reflective essays compel students to go beyond the traditional analysis that usually surrounds projects (What went well? What could be improved on?) and pushes them to deal with a synthesis and evaluation of the experience in light of their own values and goals (What did I learn? How am I different now?). In other words, one objective of reflection is to help students to internalize experience rather than merely to evaluate it.

Service-learning, as a branch of experiential education, sinks its theoretical roots in the work of David Kolb (1984). Kolb's experiential learning model builds on notions of education based on cognitive knowledge transfer. It does so by postulating that learning occurs in one of four distinct ways. People learn by *concrete experiences* with the real world, by *reflective observation* of their own (and others') lived experiences, by an *abstract conceptualization* of theoretical concepts and models (the focus of cognitive pedagogies), or by *active experimentation* that seeks to discover cause-and-effect relationships or to determine which solution of many proves most viable. Service-learning finds a base of legitimacy in Kolb's model because it assumes that significant and important learning takes place through a combined process of concrete experience and reflection on that experience.

Giles (1990) draws on the educational philosophy of John Dewey to support service-learning. Dewey believed in the "primacy of experience" as a source of learning because the immediacy and closeness of experience to the individual facilitates an "organic connection between education and personal experience" (Dewey 1938 quoted in Giles 1990: 258). Not all experience produces positive learning, however. Two criteria allow experience to educate an individual: (1) the principle of continuity, which links present experience with future experience; and (2) the principle of interaction, which balances the learner's subjective/internal elements and the external/objective elements of the experience (Giles 1990). Connecting community service to management coursework enacts the principle of continuity; the service projects allow students to apply course skills and concepts in real organizational settings — something they see themselves doing throughout their careers. The reflection component creates opportunities for interaction between the objective, formal nature of the course and project and students' own subjective thoughts, impressions, and feelings.

Service-learning proponents argue that many important skills can best be learned by doing (Bonar et al. 1996). Effective communication skills can be taught by means of abstract concepts or experimental role plays; however, mastery of communication comes only through actually communicating. Thus, while organizational behavior classes can teach listening and communication skills in the abstract (e.g., Cherrington 1994), mastery of these skills comes only through application. Service-learning acknowledges the importance of cognitive and theoretical skills, and provides students with a deep and meaningful context in which to practice them. In this fashion, a service-learning class does not differ from any experiential pedagogy. There are, however, other skills that can be acquired only through active community service. These include the skills of responsible citizenship (Bonar et al. 1996).

The foundations of the American democratic system rest on the philosophical pillar of the social contract and a participatory citizenry (Lempert 1996). Citizens have traditionally been understood as possessing many characteristics, among them their being "caring members of a moral community who share certain values and feel common responsibilities toward one another" (Boyte and Farr 1997: 37).

Effective participation by citizens translates into an informed citizenry and an activist citizenry (Lempert 1996). Responsible citizenship requires that individuals have the skills to acquire knowledge about important social phenomena (e.g., the unemployment rate among Native Americans in our community is 19%) and about the data that define those phenomena (hard data, such as education levels, skill sets mastered, proximity of available jobs, etc., and distinctly soft data, such as life-style patterns or family structures among Native Americans in our community). Informed citizens have abilities to go beyond sound bites and uncover the deep causal web that perpetuates many social problems. Stated differently, informed citizens understand that isolated facts extracted from social situations and relations are meaningless (Follett 1924). Responsible citizenship also involves learning advocacy skills — knowing how and when to act as an advocate for someone who cannot advocate his or her own position. Finally, citizenship skills involve the ability to show concern for others, particularly those who differ from us in some important respect. While each of these activities may have a cognitive or abstract component (e.g., there may be generic advocacy strategies), perfection of these skills comes only through experience.

Service-learning sinks its moral roots deeply in the Judeo-Christian tradition as well as in the secular moral and ethical philosophy of the Western tradition. Both the Old and the New Testaments are replete with injunctions to care for the poor and needy, typified by Moses's instructions to his people: "If there be among you a poor man of one of the brethren within any of thy gates in thy land which the Lord thy God giveth thee, thou shalt not harden thine heart, nor shut thine hand from thy poor brother: But thou shalt open thine hand wide unto him, and shalt surely lend him sufficient for his need, in that which he wanteth" (Deuteronomy 15:7-8).

The ethical theories of traditional Western philosophy provide an analogous secular foundation for service-learning. The writings of the German philosopher Immanuel Kant are illustrative. Kant devised a categorical imperative, a maxim that would always produce moral action. He formulated this maxim as "Act in such a way that you always treat humanity, whether in your own person or in the person of any other, never simply as a means, but always at the same time as an end" (Kant 1956: 96). A more contemporary philosopher, Emanuel Levinas, has argued this moral imperative of concern for others in different language: "It is I who support the Other and am responsible for him. . . . Responsibility is what is incumbent on me exclusively, and what, humanly, I cannot refuse. This charge is a supreme dignity of the unique. I am I in the sole measure that I am responsible" (1985: 100-101). Thus, concern for and action on behalf of others are the ultimate criteria on which our morality should be judged.

In summary, the "learning" component of service-learning grounds itself in the theory that much of what can be learned can best be learned through experience, while its "service" component holds that service-learning's benefits go beyond the mere acquisition of technical skills of analysis, communication, and problem solving. Service-learning carries its own moral authority because service to others is a fundamentally moral act. Thus, service-learning becomes a powerful pedagogical tool in helping private-sector managers enhance their abilities to properly steward the authority that society grants them. It is to an extended discussion of how this takes place that I now turn.

Service-Learning and Moral Management

Service-learning, as practiced within management education, enables moral management by (1) enhancing management students' technical capabilities, (2) enhancing students' abilities to act as good citizens and strengthening their desires to do so, and (3) involving business school faculty, alumni, and institutions in an ongoing process of service to the community. Managers who have the skills to negotiate increasingly complex business and economic environments represent the *necessary* condition for the private sector to maintain its moral authority; indeed, if the private sector cannot thrive in its own environment, the time and energy needed to become a community-wide moral agent will not be forthcoming. Responsible citizenship skills and abilities constitute the *sufficient* condition. No matter how effectively managers run their own firms and increase their economic prosperity, unless the private sector turns sufficient attention to solving pressing social problems, the pendulum of moral authority will swing back toward the public sector. The involvement of business school faculty, alumni, and institutional support units represents a serendipitous additional benefit in this overall process. Since business schools operate in the interstice between the public and private sectors, they can bring resources of knowledge, skill, and clout to bear on critical social issues (Porter 1995).

Technical Capabilities

Service-learning enhances the technical skills of students by virtue of giving them a concrete experiential base for skill application. Hence, it blends theory and practice in a unique way. Lempert (1996) describes the value of experiential education: "The success of an economics course is not measured in one's ability to draw a graph but one's ability to manage a small business or farm successfully and to understand the workings of the economy through experience" (76). My own service-learning course engages second-year business graduate students. The focus of the course requires them to use their expanding business skill sets in planning, designing, and implementing a community service project. The service project allows them to practice skills in marketing, finance, interviewing and data collection, analysis, and both oral and written communication. Because they develop and design their own projects, they have an opportunity to make real strategic decisions and trade-offs about what is feasible versus what is possible. They also gain skills in client-consultant interactions, as well as in determining a client's true needs and in developing a customized solution to those needs. In this way, service-learning provides students with opportunities commensurate with those of courses requiring more-traditional field study or consulting.

However, even in skills application, service-learning tends to go beyond other kinds of field study classes, because it allows students to apply skills in new domains. Most of my students' work involves not-for-profit organizations. Working in this environment, they see with greater precision the commonalties of all organizations and many of the unique elements of for-profit and not-for-profit organizations. For example, accounting students learn that not-for-profit organizations face many of the same control and reporting requirements as their for-profit counterparts; indeed, not-for-profits may face a greater demand for control and accountability because they are viewed by many in the community as "public trusts."

Not-for-profits often operate within different time frames; the lack of intense market competition means that these organizations sometimes move more slowly, and more conservatively, than their for-profit counterparts. Many not-for-profits also possess a different decision-making structure, one involving a much greater amount of stakeholder input and buy-in than occurs in more-hierarchical, for-profit firms. While organizational characteristics such as competition, speed, and risk taking are what attract many of our students to corporate careers in the first place, service-learning exposes them to competent managers who espouse, and enjoy, an alternative value system. It exposes them to an organizational form that, because of its very foreignness, provides them with a "ground" to more accurately understand the "figure" of for-profit organizations. Reflecting on the organizational differences (and similarities) between not-for-profit agencies and their for-profit counterparts opens the door to a deeper and richer understanding of the world of organizations, and to the actions of people within them.

Service-learning also provides students with intimate access to bureaucratic processes and the difficulties many organizations have in resolving moral dilemmas. Traditional internships and other experiential learning exercises shield students from the intense conflicts inherent in most organizations. The moral dimension of service-learning projects means that students will be exposed, most likely, to these conflicts more or less directly. For example, my students usually believe that the lack of support enjoyed by some agencies in our community results from either indifference or malice on the part of local businesses. They often want to approach these businesses for support or assistance. When they do so, what they come to realize is that most businesses, and many individuals, are already invested in the community in some form or other, and that these organizations cannot fund (with time or money) every good cause. Businesses with limited resources have to make real (and real tough) choices about their approach to social involvement. In this way, students gain a greater appreciation both of the willingness of the private sector to become involved and of the importance to businesses of focusing their efforts on a few worthwhile projects rather than attempting to provide blanket, blank-check support for all causes.

Just as service-learning exposes students to alternative organizational forms, so it also exposes them to a diverse set of stakeholders. Meaningful service-learning courses expose students to clients, volunteers, agency administrators, and government regulators or agencies. Valuable management insights can occur when students are given an opportunity to analyze and reflect on the different agendas, skill sets, and demands of different stakeholder groups. In this way, service-learning personalizes the concept of the "stakeholder" and helps students see the legitimacy of each competing stakeholder's claim. Indeed, one of the richest experiences students have is exposure to the perspectives of their own peers. Since graduate students have typically worked together in case analysis or project teams, their service-learning experience can shed new light on what it means to belong to a group or team.

Another way in which service-learning enhances technical skills development is by giving students projects based in real time and demanding real outcomes. Indeed, service-learning invites students to work in a highly charged environment. Unlike term papers, exams, or case discussions, service-learning projects are usually negotiated primarily by the students and their clients. It is the client who imposes the deadline, and it is the client who must be served by the project's deliverables. Because the students themselves have negotiated the project and its deadlines, their level of commitment to completing it and to its professional nature usually exceeds their commitment to its academic requirements. Further, ideal service-learning projects have real human outcomes. If the training program is not completed on time, or is not coherent and understandable, the ability of the agency to help its clientele is noticeably and tangibly affected. The nature of service-learning projects, then, not only allows students to apply technical and business skills but also provides an environment conducive to high motivation and effort.

In some instances, service-learning provides students with exposure to long-term, difficult, and even intractable problems. Longevity, difficulty of solution, and intractability are characteristics of many of the problems these students will face as business managers, and early exposure to strategies for approaching problems of this nature improves students' managerial capacities. As they become involved with the basic service mission of the agencies they are helping, they become aware of the deeply embedded, socially complex nature of many social problems. Exposure to the diverse individuals served by many community service agencies helps students understand that most social problems do not spring from a single cause: Each individual has an important and compelling story surrounding the sources of his or her problem, and this, in turn, impacts the nature of possible solutions. When students have sustained exposure to people experiencing some type of hardship, their capacity to recognize and understand the nuances and complexities of those hardships becomes greater. In this way, service-learning promotes deeper knowledge about social issues and problems.

The ability to recognize, structure, and understand complex, deep-seated social phenomena is a critical management skill. When our students leave business school, most move on to help firms uncover and solve their own complex, deep-seated business problems. Service-learning provides students with exposure to this kind of problem. Furthermore, as business increasingly is called on to become more socially responsible, managers desperately need moral paradigms beyond the morality of the market, particularly to counteract the strong pressures exerted by considerations of personal gain in the corporate world.

In summary, some of the skills identified here can be acquired through experiential education strategies that do not involve service-learning. However, because service-learning typically forces business students to deal with problems outside the traditional arena of *business* organizations, the skills development such problems promote reach deeper into students' repertoires, and the managerial and personal insights they provide become more meaningful.

Responsible Citizenship Skills

Service-learning courses enhance students' citizenship skills primarily by placing them in the middle of some of our society's most intractable problems. Students are exposed to the raw data generated by real people found in shelters, soup kitchens, and agency offices, or by the ecological consequences of past and current economic activities. They come face to face with pollution, the underserved, the abused and battered. Working in a direct-care environment, students are also able to place clients (human or environmental) within a meaningful social context; indeed, continued interaction with such clients allows students to gain firsthand knowledge of the causal underpinnings of social and environmental distress. For example, students learn firsthand that homelessness and illiteracy are not merely motivational problems but have social causes beyond the control of individual victims.

Exposure to those raw data and working through temporary or permanent social difficulties benefit students in several important ways. For example, students from middle- or upper-middle-class suburban environments gain awareness of the scope and magnitude of societal problems. A group of women students in one of my classes chose to work at the local Women and Children in Crisis Center. One student was shocked to discover that some of the women at the shelter came from prosperous economic and social backgrounds; indeed, she discovered the thinness of the veil separating those living in luxury from those living in crisis. Her comment was, "There but for the grace of God go I." This was not merely a trite acknowledgment of her own good fortune but a deep insight regarding the closeness of each of us to the problems others experience. With increased awareness of the scope and magnitude of these problems, students become more sensitive to both the systemic causal structure of these problems and the deep human and social costs incurred by people in crisis.

The most powerful learning occurs, however, through humanization of the problems students encounter. Homelessness no longer exists as a statistic but has real faces and stories. Humanization causes preconceived notions and stereotypes to fall, to be replaced by concrete experiences and real data. This applies to agency staff as well as to agency clients. A group of MBA students chose to work with the local food provider. Their operating assumption was that the agency directors could not be very competent or skilled; otherwise, they would have found "real" work in the private sector. Eventually the students came to appreciate the high level of competence, the deep knowledge, and the skill possessed by the agency director. As such stereotypes fall and students put a face on the statistics that catalogue social problems, their willingness to care increases. And a willingness to care precedes a willingness to act.

Humanizing social issues may prove the greatest benefit to service-learning students, particularly in management. The traditional management curriculum focuses on very instrumental views of human beings. Economics-based courses, such as finance or strategy, build from the theoretical foundation of Homo economicus, which postulates that human beings are individual utility maximizers and that interactions with other human beings occur only to help maximize the utility of the self. The "softer" disciplines in management fare no better. Human resource management becomes strategic human resource management because of the underlying assumption that people are a means to competitive advantage. One tangible benefit of involvement in meaningful community service is exposure to human situations with no instrumental value: Dealing with problems such as homelessness or abuse gives students an excellent opportunity to view people as intrinsically valuable.

Students learn citizenship advocacy and problem-solving skills by becoming part of the solution to society's problems. When service-learning works, students actively participate in the solution of real and pressing problems. A colleague of mine at the University of Utah, Peter Martin, has his traffic engineering students engage in neighborhood traffic management projects (Martin 1997). In the course of a single term, students gather data on traffic patterns, analyze that data and generate possible solutions, and attend neighborhood meetings to discuss the proposed solutions with impacted neighbors. These student projects become grist for the mill of community decision making, and these students have an opportunity to have real influence on the solution to neighborhood problems. Well-run service-learning courses force students to go at least one step beyond the traditional case study mode of making recommendations and presenting them to a professor, for they bring students face-to-face with real decision makers and those whose lives will be impacted by those decisions. Such interfacing with individuals whose lives will be directly affected helps students to understand the consequential nature of their work.

Service-learning builds citizenship skills because it exposes students, particularly business management students, to a moral paradigm other than that of wealth creation. So much of the bottom line of management education concerns the economic bottom line that students take in a strong dose of the fundamental ethic of capitalism: Wealth creation and market mechanisms can solve the majority of social ills. Or, at the very least, market mechanisms can help me insulate myself from intractable social problems. Service-learning provides a strong counterpoint to this ethic, since it is built around a concern for justice and compassion for others (attributes that students themselves come to appreciate as requisite elements of a good life). Direct exposure to those marginalized by the market allows students to count the real costs of things such as market failures, inequitable wealth creation and distribution, and "externalities." Just as management education makes students effective and knowledgeable citizens of the marketplace, service-learning helps them become citizens of the broader community.

Finally, service-learning helps students create behavioral intentions to continue to serve their communities. Much of our academic coursework in ethics, stakeholder analysis and management, organizational behavior, and corporate social responsibility works to change students' cognitive approaches to dealing with problems. Cognitive training may have powerful effects on the attitudes of students toward their moral roles as managers; however, cognitive training often lacks a solid link with behavior. Discussing the ethical ramifications of homelessness for business differs in kind and degree from tangible contact with and service on behalf of homeless people. The reflective essay component of effective service-learning courses provides students with an opportunity to integrate their previous experiences (actual behaviors) with evolving attitudes about their roles in the community and thus to create intentions to continue prosocial behaviors after they have graduated.

Empirical research on the effects of service-learning on future behavior is now beginning to appear. Markus, Howard, and King (1993) report results of testing done on students taking a service-learning political science course. They found that those students involved in service-learning felt better about their performance in the course, had learned to apply course concepts in different situations, and were more aware of the larger social issues involved. A more recent study jointly conducted by the University of California-Los Angeles and the Rand Corporation attempted to measure the effect of service. Students who participated in some form of service were "significantly more likely than nonparticipants to be committed to participating in community action programs, influencing social values, in helping others in difficulty, promoting racial understanding, influencing the political structure, and involvement in environmental cleanup" (Gray et al. 1996: 49).

Business School Involvement

Finally, we should consider the ways in which service-learning increases the likelihood that business school faculty will themselves engage in community-based civic initiatives. Since the "key partners in . . . academically anchored [service-learning] experiences are the professor and the business students" (Kolenko et al. 1996: 134), for this pedagogy to work effectively, faculty must become at least somewhat current on the issues their students will encounter. Community service agencies are, of course, the other critical unit in service-learning, and faculty must be knowledgeable about these agencies in order to provide useful guidance. Helping students perform meaningful service involves knowledge of and involvement with the agencies the students are attempting to help. Effective grading of project work and reflective essays requires that faculty have a common reference point with their students.

When service-learning really works, faculty find themselves reflecting on their own moral agency and position within the communities in which they work and live. Effective teaching in a service-learning environment requires that faculty engage in serious introspection on critical social problems, *and earnestly seek their own reconciliation with these issues*. If instructors have experienced the "There but for the grace of God go I" phenomenon, their attitude toward service, and their commitment to service-learning, will deepen and become a motive force in their own academic work.

Like students, faculty gain most when they allow social issues or problems to become humanized. Many business school faculty, particularly those with strong economics backgrounds, view problems in aggregate terms, i.e., the human element factored away in the aggregation process. For these faculty, service-learning provides a powerful alternative to data collection and interpretation. Our sophisticated and sometimes very accurate models based on aggregate data and underlying causal structures become richer, deeper, and more meaningful as we become aware of the human beings behind the data and the actual costs those human beings incur as they struggle with social problems. Clearly, such involvement forces us to sacrifice some of our "scientific objectivity"; however, the potential gains in deep knowledge, and in commitment to making a difference, serve to counterbalance this loss.

While individual service-learning courses can and do occur under the direction of single faculty members, the adoption of broader, school-wide service-learning initiatives requires an investment in staff and administrative infrastructure. Staff involvement benefits the community in two distinct ways. First, staff members bring their own unique skills, knowledge bases, and resources to bear in working with agencies and their clients. Community service truly benefits from economies of scale; the more people who become involved, the greater the number of potential actions that can be taken, and the greater number of lives that can be benefited. Second, the presence of staff and infrastructure ensures continuity in service-learning efforts and continuous involvement by the campus community in the life of the larger community. The pressing issues and challenges facing our communities did not arise during the course of a semester, nor will they be adequately addressed over the course of a single semester. When service-learning becomes the raison d'être for staff and institutional infrastructure, an institutional momentum and trajectory builds for continuous involvement and a commitment to working on otherwise intractable problems.

The preceding sections of this essay have made the case that service-learning provides critical skills for future private-sector managers to (1) be more effective in their economic roles and (2) be more involved, more informed, and more effective in their roles as citizens. It is through increased effectiveness in these two areas that the private sector can discharge its moral responsibility as steward of the social agenda.

Final Considerations

I would like to conclude by touching upon two issues notably absent from what has been discussed so far: first, the idea that service-learning enhances the prestige of business schools, and second, a deep description of how one begins and continues using service-learning.

My own experience indicates that service-learning enhances the prestige and reputation of a business school in several ways. Alumni, members of the central university administration, and recruiters all have spoken glowingly about my school's efforts to embed service-learning options within the curriculum. All college deans desire evidence of good works for inclusion in annual reports, brochures, and submissions to business school rating organizations. Service-learning gives institutions tangible evidence that they are seriously fulfilling their lofty professional mission statements. Alumni feel a certain pride when they see their institution active in its local community. Recruiters appreciate community service efforts because these efforts show not only initiative but also exposure to diversity on the part of students.

Given that service-learning has such a relatively strong payoff, why not deliberately capitalize on it? First, this seems to put the cart before the horse. Programs that are run in order to enhance an organization's prestige have different agendas from programs designed to serve local communities according to the latter's needs and interests. Indeed, service based on its instrumental value to the business school risks violating the reciprocity covenant so essential to service-learning. Marketing service-learning as a mechanism for building "brand equity" would mean that service-learning would serve primarily the school, and not the community. One reality that my students come face to face with in their work is the willingness of many people to give community agencies what those people *think* the agencies need or what they *want* to give them; however, few are willing to uncover the deep, unmet needs of the agencies themselves.

Motive matters in service-learning, at least the type of service-learning I myself practice. Doing service-learning primarily to advance my own or my institution's interests creates deep ethical problems. I am reminded of Christ's admonition to his followers: "Take heed that ye do not your alms before men, to be seen of them: otherwise ye have no reward of your father which is in heaven" (Matthew 6:1). The philosopher Martin Buber echoes this admonition, but from a different tradition. The center of Buber's ethical system is the relationship between human beings. Moral and uplifting relationships occur between two people, viewed as distinct beings and total personalities, not as objects (Buber 1970). In Buber's terminology, I must view others as a You or a Thou (implying a certain divine heritage) and not as an It (implying any instrumentalism in our relationship). Engaging with another person as a means of satisfying my own ends forces me into an "It" relationship with that person; what primarily matters is that that person satisfy my needs, desires, or aspirations, not what that person himself or herself may be concerned about. While the principle of reciprocity mandates that both parties must benefit, the risk of one party (a business school) entering a service-learning relationship with instrumental motives starts the collaboration off on a bad footing.

A second issue deserving some attention concerns service-learning's downsides and potential risks. Kolenko et al. note that

> . . . the most critical barrier to service-learning projects often resides in the faculty ranks. Many faculty members will resist or flatly refuse to participate in service-learning projects or programs. Some may be philosophical-

ly opposed to academia involving itself in such projects. Nontenured facul-
ty quickly pick up such signals and may become skeptical and reluctant to
participate given the pressures of balancing publishing and teaching
responsibilities. (1996: 137)

Faculty apathy, or active resistance, creates enormous pressure to stop service-learning initiatives before they get off the ground. As I announced my own service-learning intentions to a senior colleague, he asked why I would want to waste my time on such an undertaking when there existed several exciting traditional opportunities to exploit. It would be naive to believe that an educational commitment based on moral grounds would help faculty close ranks in support of service-learning; however, without an underlying moral commitment to assist real people living in real communi-ties, it is unlikely that service-learning programs can generate the momen-tum needed to overcome faculty inertia.

Service-learning, especially without a supporting institutional infra-structure, requires additional work by faculty members, and not always at convenient times. Put simply, service-learning means faculty will spend more time on teaching and related activities and less time doing traditional research. For faculty already overwhelmed by research and university ser-vice demands, service-learning may threaten to create a time-management crisis. Indeed, even when schools establish a supporting infrastructure and individual faculty time commitments decrease, the overall institutional commitment will most certainly increase. The bottom line is that doing effective service-learning is not a costless activity, and those who think service-learning will bring a quick, low-cost boost to a school's reputation are almost certain to be disappointed.

But temporal demands are not the only pitfall; sometimes there are either unsatisfactory students or unsatisfactory projects. Unsatisfactory students (those who lack commitment, integrity, or fundamental skills) can tarnish the local reputation of a school very quickly. In community service, as in most areas of life, negative experiences tend to be remembered longer than positive ones. Unsatisfactory projects have the reverse effect — they sour students on the concept of service-learning. Such projects engage stu-dents either in meaningless work (such as making photocopies) or in proj-ects that exceed their levels of expertise and commitment. Informal student networks spread word of bad experiences, and the "grapevine" effect can dampen enthusiasm and enrollment in other service-learning courses.

My point in discussing this downside of service-learning is clearly not to discourage its widespread implementation but rather to caution that service-learning requires a genuine commitment on the part of faculty, staff, and administrators. That commitment must be deep both in terms of will-ingness to serve the local community and in terms of willingness to remain in the community service arena for the long term.

Finally, I should comment on the fact that this essay has not attempted to provide a detailed description of exactly what service-learning courses should look like or how one can go about beginning and sustaining them. It has not done so for two reasons. First, service-learning is a flexible pedagogy capable of providing an effective educational experience in a variety of formats. Stanton (1990) emphasizes that service-learning is more a values orientation and a program than a unique type of pedagogy. Effective service-learning may be only a small part of a course offering, or it may involve an entire syllabus. The specific amount and type of service depend on course objectives and the instructor's design choices.

Second, excellent resources already exist to help faculty plan and implement service-learning initiatives. They include the Campus Compact Center for Community Colleges, an association of community colleges committed to fostering service-learning. Located in Mesa, Arizona, the center is an excellent resource for all wishing to become involved in service-learning. Another excellent resource is the National Society for Experiential Education (NSEE), located in Alexandria, Virginia. This group includes individuals from K-16 educational institutions, community agencies, and private foundations. NSEE has a strong "special-interest group" (SIG) in service-learning — a group that provides many networking opportunities. Still a third important resource is the national Campus Compact, operating out of Brown University in Providence, Rhode Island. Currently, the national Compact boasts a membership of more than 600 colleges and universities committed to developing programs related to civic engagement.

I began this essay by arguing that service-learning represents a strategy for helping the private sector maintain the moral authority to set the social agenda. This moral authority is a multidimensional phenomenon that combines an ability to deliver increased prosperity and an improved standard of living together with justice, fairness, equity, beauty, and elevation of the human condition in more than merely material ways. The strength of the private sector and a market economy has always been their ability to increase prosperity and the standard of living for many parts of the population. Their weakness lies in their lack of inherent mechanisms to consider concerns such as justice, fairness, beauty, etc. Indeed, the excesses of the private sector have often led to outcomes and processes that are manifestly unjust, unfair, inequitable, and indifferent to beauty and all noneconomic factors affecting the human condition. While the public sector fares less well in generating prosperity, it fares better in its ability to foster justice, fairness, equity, and beauty. Herein lies the key to the movement of the moral pendulum. *If* the private sector can couple its ability to provide economic prosperity with an ability to foster justice, fairness, equity, and beauty, it *may* be able to maintain its moral authority indefinitely.

I close by offering a hypothesis. Markets have typically been viewed as excellent generators of prosperity but poor guardians of justice (Daly and Cobb 1994). Perhaps this has less to do with the intrinsic features of the market and more to do with the moral orientations of its key participants. Put simply, when managers are steeped in the logic and morality of market efficiency, these concerns leave no room for justice, equity, and beauty. Hence, my hypothesis: If there can arise a generation of managers with a dual training — a training that understands the logic of the market as well as the morality of justice and compassion — then this generation of managers can provide us with a lasting, just, and compassionate kind of prosperity. I submit that service-learning represents a powerful mechanism that can give future managers this dual training and thus could eventually provide enough data points to test my hypothesis. I believe my hypothesis would pass such a test, and that we would all be enriched by the test itself as well as its outcome.

Note

1. My service-learning course at Brigham Young University, MBA 641, Private Enterprise and Community Service, offers second-year MBA students, as well as graduate accounting and organizational behavior students, the opportunity to share their acquired knowledge with the local community. Learning focuses on critiques of the neoclassical microeconomic paradigm that undergirds most training in the business school. We read Daly and Cobb's For the Common Good and spend class time discussing where their critique of economic theory is on and off the mark, and the viability of their recommendations for making the world truly more concerned with justice, equity, and beauty. We also consider Judeo-Christian calls for community involvement, and seat those within a business context.

The service focus in the course is a service project. Operating in small groups, the students are responsible for identifying, designing, and carrying out a project for a local community group, using their emerging skill sets as businesspeople. The class has worked with the local food and care coalition, a school for at-risk adolescent males, and a crisis center for women and children, as well as having planned on-campus service activities.

References

Bonar, L., R. Buchanan, I. Fisher, and A. Wechsler. (1996). Service-Learning in the Curriculum. Salt Lake City, UT: Lowell Bennion Community Service Center.

Boyte, H.C., and J. Farr. (1997). "The Work of Citizenship and the Problem of Service-Learning." In Experiencing Citizenship: Concepts and Models for Service-Learning in Political Science, edited by R.M. Battistoni and W.E. Hudson, pp. 35-48. Washington, DC: American Association for Higher Education.

Buber, M. (1970). *I and Thou,* translated by Walter Kaufman. New York, NY: Charles Scribner's Sons.

Cherrington, D.J. (1994). *Organizational Behavior.* 2nd ed. Boston, MA: Allyn & Bacon.

Daly, H.E., and J.B. Cobb. (1994). *For the Common Good.* Boston, MA: Beacon Press.

Dewey, J. (1938). *Experience in Education.* New York, NY: Collier Books.

Follett, M.P. (1924). *Creative Experience.* New York, NY: Peter Smith.

Giles, D.E. (1990). "Dewey's Theory of Experience: Implications for Service-Learning." In *Combining Service and Learning: A Resource Book for Community and Public Service,* edited by J.C. Kendall and Associates, pp. 257-260. Raleigh, NC: National Society for Internships and Experiential Education.

Gray, M., S. Geshwind, E. Ondaatje, A. Robyn, S. Klien, L. Sax, A. Astin, and H. Astin. (1996). *Evaluation of Learn and Serve America, Higher Education: First Year Report, Volume 1.* Los Angeles, CA: Higher Education Research Institute, UCLA.

Hart, S.L. (1995). "A Natural Resource–Based View of the Firm." *Academy of Management Review* 20: 986-1014.

————. (January-February 1997). "Beyond Greening: Strategies for a Sustainable World." *Harvard Business Review:* 66-77.

Hosmer, L.T. (1994). "Strategic Planning as If Ethics Mattered." *Strategic Management Journal* 15 (special issue): 17-34.

————. (1995). "Trust: The Connecting Link Between Organizational Theory and Philosophical Ethics." *Academy of Management Review* 20: 379-403.

Jacoby, B. (1996). "Service-Learning in Today's Higher Education." In *Service-Learning in Higher Education,* edited by B. Jacoby and Associates, pp. 3-25. San Francisco, CA: Jossey-Bass.

Jones, T.M. (1995). "Instrumental Stakeholder Theory: A Synthesis of Ethics and Economics." *Academy of Management Review* 20: 404-437.

Kant, I. (1956, orig. 1785). *Groundwork for the Metaphysic of Morals,* translated by H.J. Paton. New York, NY: Harper Torchbooks.

Kendall, J.C., and Associates, eds. (1990). *Combining Service and Learning: A Resource Book for Community and Public Service.* Raleigh, NC: National Society for Internships and Experiential Education.

Kolb, D.A. (1984). *Experiential Learning.* Englewood Cliffs, NJ: Prentice-Hall.

Kolenko, T.A., G. Porter, W. Wheatley, and M. Colby. (1996). "A Critique of Service-Learning Projects in Management Education: Pedagogical Foundations, Barriers, and Guidelines." *Journal of Business Ethics* 15: 133-142.

Korten, D.C. (1996). *When Corporations Rule the World.* West Hartford, CT: Kumarian Press.

Lempert, D.H. (1996). *Escape From the Ivory Tower.* San Francisco, CA: Jossey-Bass.

Levinas, E. (1985). *Ethics and Infinity*, translated by R.A. Cohen. Pittsburgh, PA: Duquesne University Press.

Markus, G.B., J.P.F. Howard, and D.C. King. (1993). "Integrating Community Service and Classroom Instruction Enhances Learning: Results From an Experiment." *Educational Evaluation and Policy Analysis:* 410-419.

Martin, P. (1997). Presentation at a monthly meeting of the Salt Lake Valley Service-Learning Network.

Porter, M.E. (May-June 1995). "The Competitive Advantage of the Inner City." *Harvard Business Review:* 55-71.

Scott, W.G. (1992). *Chester I. Barnard and the Guardians of the Managerial State.* Lawrence, KS: University of Kansas Press.

Shrivastava, P. (1995). "Ecocentric Management for a Risk Society." *Academy of Management Review* 20: 118-137.

Stanton, T. (1990). "Service-Learning: Groping Toward a Definition." In *Combining Service and Learning: A Resource Book for Community and Public Service,* edited by J.C. Kendall and Associates, pp. 65-67. Raleigh, NC: National Society for Internships and Experiential Education.

Transforming Management Education:
The Role of Service-Learning

by Sandra Waddock and James Post

How is it that prominent business leaders of the 1990s such as Jack Welch (General Electric) or "Chainsaw" Al Dunlap (Scott Paper and Sunbeam) have, without apology, dismissed thousands of employees irrespective of the human and community consequences? What legitimizes the efforts of Bill Gates and his Microsoft colleagues to "crush" competitors such as Netscape? Why does profitability and "shareholder value" dominate management thinking in publicly held corporations? Why do brilliant young people flock to e-commerce companies where the thrill of innovation is coupled with the promise of fabulous riches? How is it that some of the elements of a "good life," such as education and health care, do not exist for millions of American citizens and billions of people world-wide? Where is public outrage with unethical behavior and social inequity?

The answers to such questions have a common thread: Business is about economic decisions; corporate social responsibility is dead; knowledge and skill pay off in personal wealth; and social issues are for government and communities to resolve. This is the private good/public good paradigm in action, and it is *wrong*.

Deans, faculty, accreditation agencies, and managers themselves have powerful reasons to rethink the "private good" paradigm of management education and build anew the case for management as a *socially* useful activity. In the private good paradigm, management education emphasizes self-interest, externalizing all possible costs and pursuing competitive gain for the firm without much regard for bystanders. It is a given that firms operate in hypercompetitive environments (D'Aveni 1994) where winners take all and an ideology of maximizing wealth for one stakeholder (the shareholder) prevails. Private goods — the wealth and power gained from business operations — accrue to smart managers, rich owners, and the corporations they control. The dominant values in this paradigm are those of efficiency (or "economizing") and power aggrandizing (Frederick 1995).

We believe this private good paradigm is too narrowly conceived to allow for healthy organizations and healthy societies in the long term. No enterprise can continue to function over an extended period of time without support from society, which depends, in turn, on meeting the legitimate expectations of a large, diverse group of societal stakeholders. Management education needs to embrace a public purpose, which incorporates the civilizing aspects of community, internalizes social costs, and accepts responsibility for long-term ecological and community well-being, as well as for the production of goods and services.

If management education is without public purpose, if it is understood only in terms of adding to private wealth rather than *common wealth*, it misses the point that society benefits from sound management principles and techniques. Every society struggles to strike a balance among three important spheres of human activity: economic, political or governmental, and community or civil society. Each is necessary and integral to the others, and each is also supported by the natural environment that underpins all human life (see, e.g., Capra 1995; Wilber 1996) and must ultimately be used in sustainable ways. Each has priorities and goals that must be balanced for long-term health (see the table opposite).

Employers, donors, foundations, and government agencies at the local, national, and international levels need a system of management education that trains today's students for tomorrow's responsibilities. Those responsibilities will increasingly involve integration of values in all spheres of human life as well as the natural environment. In the aggregate, educators train those who will frame and execute policies relating to every basic need of human beings on the planet. Doing this wisely and well is the essential mission of management education. Public legitimacy ultimately rests on a collective societal assessment of how well this is done.

Students, families, and sponsors have a great stake in a system of management education that effectively trains students for jobs, prepares them for useful lives, and cultivates professional careers that add value to society. For management education to "work" as a system, it must satisfy this range of individual, organizational, and societal aspirations. It must perform a socially useful role that balances the concerns of today's businesses for "effective" managers, the personal concerns of individuals for career and skill development, and societal concerns for individuals who will understand the importance of preserving and cultivating our cultural, political, and ecological well-being.

Integrating the private and public goods perspective in management education requires that the education process engage the "whole person" (mind, heart, body, spirit) in the task of learning how to manage. When this integration takes place, for example, emotions can no longer be divorced from decisions, social impacts will be internalized, and wisdom can be fostered. One way of fostering wisdom through management practice is through community-based learning or service-learning. Service-learning fosters civic engagement that makes mind, heart, body, and spirit part of an integrated action learning process (see, e.g., Fleckenstein 1997; Kohls 1996; Zlotkowski 1996).

A Public and Private Goods View of Management Education's Purposes

Sphere of Activity	Value(s) Added for Stakeholders
Private Goods for Primary Stakeholders	
Economic sphere	Wealth and profits for owners
	Salaries and wages for employees
	Goods and services for customers
	Contracts and profits for suppliers
Public Goods for Citizens in Societies	
Political sphere	Freedom and democracy
Civil society sphere	Community, relationships, civility
Ecological sphere	Sustainability

Recent Reforms

In the early 1980s, Hayes and Abernathy (1980) charged that management education was leading the way to economic decline through an overly analytical emphasis and excessive short-term focus on quarter-to-quarter results. By mid decade, high-level studies of the entire management education enterprise were under way. Porter and McKibbin (1988), in a widely read report, concluded that intractable problems afflicted the entire management education enterprise.

Foremost among the problems were lack of "real-world" connections between classrooms and the life of people in organizations, limited and out-of-date technology, and institutional lack of focus. Porter and McKibbin provided a long list of specific criticisms, including insufficient emphasis on encouraging "vision" in students, weak integration of knowledge across functional areas, and the need for technology investments. Topical criticisms included too great an emphasis on quantitative analytical techniques and too little attention to managing people, communications, the external (legal, social, political) environment of business, international dimensions of business, entrepreneurial topics, and ethics. The authors concluded that the central question facing all schools and faculty was whether "drift" or "thrust" (the subtitle of the report) would characterize management education in the 1990s. The report challenged the academic establishment to become relevant, focused, and energized.

Judged against this long list of criticisms, management schools in the 1990s produced a mixed record of results. Serious investments by faculty and administrators yielded some significant improvements, along with notable failures. The heavy financial investments in technology, for example, succeeded in putting more technology in the hands of students and faculty. This was a relatively easy target at which to "throw money" for a variety of reasons. Meanwhile, the task of changing attitudes and behaviors was more difficult (in part because such change includes changes in faculty attitudes and behaviors), resulting in less visible and consistent progress. If, in short, we can identify a number of important achievements, we can also identify an even longer list of challenges that remain unmet. Major successes would include:

- the development of *team-learning* concepts and the creation of meaningful ways to train students to be effective team members;
- a *more integrated delivery* of the management curriculum;
- an emphasis on *entrepreneurial studies* and creation of new businesses;
- the introduction of a *global outlook* and perspective to many courses;
- the rapid introduction of *technology* and some progress in devising new ways to enhance education through technology-supported learning

processes.

Foremost among continuing problems — directly related, we believe, to the above-mentioned private good philosophy — are:

• *Detachment from consequences:* For the most part, managers are still trained to solve one problem at a time, rather than understand the whole system of which the problem is a part (Senge 1990). Students are still taught "measures without meaning" and see few of the negative effects of business decisions, as if numbers could tell the whole story. Ethics, responsibility, and accountability still receive too little attention in management education.

• *Short-term focus:* Managers still learn that organizations live by short-term results. Revenues, expenses, profits, and losses are calculated by the year, the quarter, and, with new technology to assist, virtually by the minute. Vision is still markedly lacking in management education. Thinking through the political, community, and ecological consequences of corporate actions is too frequently discounted, or simply avoided, as not "relevant" to business decisions, since the "results" that count are defined by the private good of maximized shareholder wealth.

• *Need for balanced reporting:* The trade-off between near-term and long-term results is multiplied manyfold by trade-offs between quality and cost, price-value strategies, customer service, and customer cost. Few organizations have yet developed effective balanced scorecards that also account for the social and ecological costs, consequences, and trade-offs of organizational life. Despite the popularity of balanced scorecard language (see Kaplan and Norton 1995), much of the manager's attention is devoted to satisfying only one stakeholder, the owner. The multiple stakeholders (and associated "multiple bottom lines") to which companies are also accountable in a public good model are given short shrift.

• *Individual and team skills:* A decade of haranguing by business leaders has produced a strong emphasis on team skills and concepts, including leadership, facilitation, and being a team player. However, individual ethical obligations are sometimes subordinated to team consciousness, and individual responsibility can easily become a casualty of "groupthink" education aimed at wealth maximization. On occasion the faculty's mental model of students, typically unquestioned in management courses, is that they are without personal efficacy, destined to be nothing more than "instruments of the corporation" (as one of our students aptly phrased it!) — a sad commentary on the dehumanizing and decivilizing approach of the private good approach to management education.

• *Concepts of wealth and capital:* Recognition of the value of human resources (human capital), reputation (social capital), ecological resources, and intangibles remains at an early stage of development. Although rhetoric about the triple bottom line of social, financial, and ecological performance is increasing, few businesses yet take it seriously enough to account for their activities publicly or to incorporate broader conceptions of wealth into their financial reports. Broader vision, social consciousness, and civic engagement in understanding multiple bottom lines and wealth beyond financial wealth are still important needs in management education.

The Needs

The global economy places significant demands on current and future managers. Among them are the need for managers to be team players *and* individual contributors, a capacity to employ much better written and oral communication skills, and a growing need to enhance both personal awareness and interpersonal skills. Managers also need to be comfortable with individuals and work groups of diverse backgrounds, to develop skills in dealing with multiple stakeholders who bring conflicting and even controversial demands to the enterprise, and to deal with constantly intensifying public and government scrutiny.

Future managers will need a significantly broadened managerial perspective that encompasses *civic engagement* together with *analytical rigor*. By this, we mean that managers will increasingly be expected to use their "left brain" as well as their "right brain," to use their emotional intelligence along with their rational intelligence, to rely on sound intuition as well as sound analysis. Few of the skills that are needed lend themselves to traditional (passive) classroom learning experiences or knowledge transfer; even fewer lend themselves to the "either/or" mind-set that says there is only one "best way" to do things. More analysis, more rigor, and more atomization of knowledge will simply not be sufficient for managers who must cope with the demands of the global village and its attendant political, social, ecological, and economic realities. Managers will need to develop new skills at using a "win/win," "both/and" logic that allows for the integration of whole persons, communities, and societies. These are the requisite skills for what Boyte and Kari (1996) call the "public work" of democracy and citizenship.

Diana Bilimoria, editor of the *Journal of Management Education*, recently called for a "diasporic shift" that would redirect management education away from the classroom toward "real-world learning" (Bilimoria 1998). A big part of that shift involves providing students with the opportunity to enhance their understanding of the roles, relationships, and interconnections that exist in society. This will enhance student understanding of societal needs and nurture their capacity for civic engagement. To some, this perspective is vital if tomorrow's businesses are to operate successfully within the interconnected, but vulnerable, global village whose ecological resources are increasingly strained.

What is important in this educational scenario is moving students from being passive to active learners, and more fully engaging their spirits (i.e., emotional, psychological, and moral commitment and energy) as well as the cognitive capacities prioritized in more-traditional learning approaches. Future managers will need to be prepared for major responsibilities associated with creating and sustaining meaningful work, for themselves and others, within both the large and the small enterprises, the for-profit and not-for-profit settings where they will work. Melding private and public goods, they will have to master the collaborative skills needed to successfully partner in the interstices among the economic, political, and civil society sectors, as well as the competitive skills inherent in the private good model. In short, the managers of the future will need a kind of education very different from the one traditionally provided in schools of management.

Service-Learning as Antidote

Service-learning, action learning, and work-based learning offer powerful experiential alternatives to the exclusive classroom model. They have the capacity to more fully engage the whole person in the fundamental management challenge of "making something work better." As we have seen, there are compelling social, as well as pedagogical, reasons for changing the paradigm of management education toward more active engagement in society. It is not that "teach and tell" methods are completely ineffective; that is *not* true. Classroom presentation and discussion continues to be the dominant framework of interactive learning activity. But service-learning (and its experiential siblings) provides a powerful, and often defining, dimension to a student's education. It introduces the "x factor" that is missing in the classroom — the realism of specific people and social needs.

Although there are many formats and types of service-learning activity, we focus here primarily on community-based projects in which students apply business concepts, techniques, or skills in community settings (see Kolenko et al. 1996 for a summary). The formats with which we are most familiar involve student teams that actively use accounting, information management, leadership, strategic planning, organizational development, marketing, operations, finance, and other bases of knowledge to perform a value-adding task for the client organization. Direct delivery of services (e.g., volunteers at a shelter or food distribution center) are different from the kinds of projects that ask students to take skills learned in the classroom and apply them in ways that *add value* for a client organization.

There are several reasons to favor these types of service-/community-based learning activities as a means of broadening the perspective of students, and transforming the thinking of future managers, about the value of management knowledge as "public work." Consider these examples, drawn from projects undertaken at our respective universities.

Service-learning engages the whole person. A participant in a leadership development program designed a welfare-to-work program that exposed him to local welfare recipients struggling to obtain gainful employment, and to the community agencies that help these individuals. The participant, an administrator with a business background who worked at a local bank, became interested in pursuing a sociology degree to learn more about coping with social problems.

Service deepens the entire learning process. Student members of one MBA project team were astonished to realize the mission complexity of a regional Red Cross program. The team was tasked to design a "balanced scorecard" for the regional organization. In doing so, they experienced firsthand the diversity of societal problems and the necessary trade-offs such agencies address on a daily basis.

Service provides an unparalleled opportunity for reflection. Typical courses are concerned with delivering content; courses with service-learning projects, in contrast, provide rich opportunities for students to reflect on their community-based activities in journals, in small-group in-class sessions, and in other venues. In all of our classes, students have reflected on the opportunity to interact with others, to understand their problems, and to think about how management can make things better.

Service links theory to practice. Theory and practice enrich all participants' understanding of what works and why it does so. The MBA team that undertook the balanced scorecard project found it had to adapt the scorecard concept, originally designed for profit-making companies, to meet the needs of a nonprofit agency. Once adapted, however, it was a very useful tool for the agency's staff.

Service provides a socially useful contribution to the community in the short term. Involvement with the community, whether in a course-specific task, such as the balanced scorecard project, or in providing a generic service (e.g., in serving food to the homeless) provides resources to the community — resources that in some cases would not otherwise be available.

Service assists the community in the long run. Service-learning has the potential to open future managers' eyes to the needs of communities; it can also inspire activities that continue to benefit the community. For example, the welfare-to-work program referred to above is, at this writing, in its third iteration. Red Cross national headquarters has shown interest in using the balanced scorecard methodology developed by a student team. In both instances, the "system" will work a bit better because of the efforts of students involved in the service-learning projects.

By engaging students with local communities, service-learning helps students understand and take responsibility for their own learning *and* for the consequences of their decisions. It moves them toward the proposition that *management is a public good* and away from thinking that their knowledge should be used only in pursuit of private benefits.

Learning experiences that closely tie theory to practice focus not only on the muck and mire of real-life decision-making processes but also on the quagmire of dealing with the political, ethical, and social *implications* of business decisions on the real *lives* of stakeholders affected by those decisions. In this sense, service-learning integrates what is learned in the classroom with "real-world" experiences (e.g., Kenworthy 1996; Tucker et al. 1998; Zlotkowski 1996). When students have to deal with the societal, communal, and human ramifications of managerial decisions — as they do when they engage in service- and action learning — they can no longer view their roles as managers as separate from those of other actors in society.

One MBA team, for example, undertook a corporation-based project that helped the company establish a coalition of other companies to work in partnership with community agencies attempting to prevent domestic violence. In the course of this project, the team realized that domestic violence also affected the *company's* performance because of its impact on attendance, tardiness, and employees' capacity to perform their work while under stress from real or perceived abuse. Team members moved from seeing domestic violence as a purely "social problem" to one that did affect, and should concern, the firm. They began to see how the costs of domestic violence were actually internalized in the company rather than simply remaining outside the organization's boundaries.

Furthermore, when students understand how the less-privileged members of a society live, and the struggles they routinely face, it is possible for management faculty to meaningfully pose academic questions in an entirely new context: What is a "good society"? What must we manage to get there? How can my activities make a difference? How do we make things better? To experience what a layoff means to a community in human terms or to witness the struggle of those in poverty often produces a changed heart, spirit, and mind. At our universities, many undergraduate students participate in service-learning programs that expose them, some for the first time, to poor and diverse people. The results are impressive. As the former head of Boston College's pioneering service-learning program once said, students are not just "informed" but "transformed." Having experienced the struggles of others directly, they have an appreciation for what it means to be in that situation or to work with an organization that tries to address those issues. Their horizons are broadened, their eyes are opened, and their capacity for active learning is expanded. We ourselves have seen the often invoked "win-win-win" outcome actually occur: The community wins, the student wins, and the faculty wins by having more active and engaged students.

Service-Learning in the University of the Future

We have argued that (1) management education is a "public good," not a private good practiced solely for personal benefit; (2) universities in general — and business/management schools in particular — should use service-learning as a pedagogy to link management skills and competencies to make things better in the community; and (3) the educational value of service-learning operates at the personal, organizational, and community levels. As a pedagogy, service-learning enables students, faculty, and community to shape an exchange of ideas and experience that can result in "win-win-win" outcomes for students, universities, and communities.

Hence, service-learning meets three key tests for the future of management education: legitimacy, performance, and outcomes. Engagement in the community certainly meets the critical test of real-world learning. It helps students develop an aptitude for — and an *attitude toward* — applying their managerial knowledge to organizations and situations that need, and can benefit from, that expertise. In doing so, it engages the "full person," and enhances an individual's ability to meet the performance test because there is a real client — organization or individual — with real needs that must be met. Indeed, it represents a client-centered, not a professor-centered, educational process. Such a process cannot help but broaden perspectives, however subtly, and reveal truths beyond those of economics alone. If, as we have argued, future managers/citizens must learn to use their analytical and organizational competencies for the "common wealth," as well as private wealth, service-learning must be seen as a powerful vehicle of that learning.

But it is clear from our experience and that of our students that service-learning also helps to change the practices of management educators in their classrooms. Students who take management tools and skills into the community bring back observations, impressions, and reflections that can enrich everyone's classroom experience. Both aspects of the exchange are valuable.

The modern university faces many challenges in the 21st century, not least of which is the test of public credibility. To be credible, universities must be prepared to change some of the things they do and some of the ways in which they do them. In this new millennium, teaching, research, and public service cannot, nor will, retain all the forms they have had in the past. Through appropriate community-based work, students can learn to function more effectively, to serve their stakeholders in more complete and effective ways, to understand far better their decisions — even to gain wisdom. For at some level, our responsibility as educators is to cultivate not only skills and knowledge but also *wisdom*. In the words of Russell Ackoff, whose ideas have challenged managers and management educators for 40 years, "Wisdom is the ability to perceive and evaluate the long-run consequences of behavior. It is normally associated with a willingness to make short-run sacrifices for the sake of long-run gains" (Ackoff 1999).

For management education to retain its relevance and its integrity, it must take its vision into a society that is diverse, complex, and desperately in need of improvement. Management does add value to social institutions. Good management does so through the private goods and services it produces, and through the public goods of community and civility, freedom and democracy, and the ecological and community sustainability that societies need to survive and prosper long term. To argue, as we have, that *management is a public good* is not to say it cannot also provide private benefits. It is, however, to say that management knowledge cannot be *only* a private good. It is to say that managers are citizens with public responsibilities. Service-learning can teach that lesson early in a person's life. It is a lesson we hope lasts a lifetime.

References

Ackoff, Russell L. (1999). "On Learning and the Systems That Facilitate It." *Reflections* 1(1): 14-24.

Bilimoria, Diana. (1998). "From Classroom Learning to Real-World Learning: A Diasporic Shift in Management Education." *Journal of Management Education* 22(3): 265-268.

Boyte, Harry C., and Nancy N. Kari. (1996). *Building America: The Democratic Promise of Public Work.* Philadelphia, PA: Temple University Press.

Capra, Fritjof. (1995). *The Web of Life.* New York, NY: Anchor Doubleday.

D'Aveni, Richard. (1994). *Hyper-Competition: Managing the Dynamics of Strategic Maneuvering.* New York, NY: Free Press.

Fleckenstein, Marilynn P. (1997). "Service-Learning in Business Ethics." *Journal of Business Ethics* 16(12/13): 1347-1351.

Frederick, William C. (1995). *Values, Nature, and Culture in the American Corporation.* New York, NY: Oxford University Press.

Hayes, R.H., and W. Abernathy. (July-August 1980). "Managing Our Way to Economic Decline." *Harvard Business Review:* 66-77.

Kaplan, Robert S., and David P. Norton. (January-February 1992). "The Balanced Scorecard — Measures That Drive Performance." *Harvard Business Review:* 71-79.

Kenworthy, Amy L. (1996). "Linking Business Education, Campus Culture, and Community: The Bentley Service-Learning Project." *Journal of Business Ethics* 15(1): 121-131.

Kohls, John. (1996). "Student Experiences With Service-Learning in a Business Ethics Course." *Journal of Business Ethics* 15(1): 45-57.

Kolenko, Thomas A., Gayle Porter, Walt Wheatley, and Marvell Colby. (1996). "A Critique of Service-Learning Projects in Management Education: Pedagogical Foundations, Barriers, and Guidelines." *Journal of Business Ethics* 15(1): 133-142.

Porter, Lyman, and Lawrence E. McKibbin. (1988). *Management Education and Development: Drift or Thrust Into the 21st Century?* New York, NY: McGraw-Hill.

Senge, Peter. (1990). *The Fifth Discipline.* New York, NY: Free Press.

Tucker, Mary L., Anne M. McCarthy, John A. Hoxmeier, and Margarita M. Lenk. (1998). "Community Service-Learning Increases Communication Skills Across the Business Curriculum." *Business Communication Quarterly* 61(2): 88-99.

Wilber, Ken. (1996). *A Brief History of Everything.* Boston, MA: Shambala Publications.

Zlotkowski, Edward. (1996). "Opportunity for All: Linking Service-Learning and Business Ethics." *Journal of Business Ethics* 15(1): 5-19.

Management Students as Consultants:
A Strategy for Service-Learning in Management Education[1]

by Amy L. Kenworthy-U'Ren

Recent shifts in prevailing worldviews . . . are encouraging the diasporic movement of learning <u>beyond</u> *the spatial and temporal walls of the management education classroom. [emphasis added]*

— Bilimoria 1998: 265

The educational landscape is changing at a rapid pace. As a result, institutions of higher learning are experiencing what Bilimoria (1998) has termed a diasporic shift in the expectations of, and demands on, the pedagogies employed. This shift challenges universities and colleges to expand their resource pool — to offer students educational experiences *beyond the walls* of the traditional classroom. Service-learning provides a framework for university administrators and faculty members to ground students' educational experiences in rigorous, text-based coursework while moving student learning *beyond* the classroom and *into* the community.

The goal of this chapter is to provide management faculty with a framework for extending student learning into the community via the integration of service-learning into the curriculum. The format for this integration is best labeled "student as consultant." According to this format, management students engage in real-world, concrete, professional, semester-long consulting experiences designed to enhance concepts and skills learned in the classroom. I call this perspective the "exposure and understanding" argument for service-learning integration (Kenworthy 1999). This perspective exposes students to real-world issues in their local communities (e.g., homelessness, violence, poverty) and then challenges them to think through the complexities of these issues, their short- and long-term implications, and the potential for business/community partnerships capable of addressing them. Whereas all service-learning courses are designed to engage students in real-world service experiences, the service-learning pedagogy described in this chapter is designed *specifically* to expand students' views of business and their roles as future business professionals.

The chapter is organized as follows: First, to contextualize this perspective, I share my observations as a service-learning practitioner. Second, I explore the meaning of service-learning specifically within the context of management education. Third, I describe conceptual support for service-learning integration in higher education. Fourth, I outline the ways in which service-learning consulting projects address recent calls for change in management education. Finally, I summarize the responsibilities of university administrators and faculty members involved in service-learning projects, and conclude with a few personal reflections.

Instructor Observations and Student Reflections

My experiences as a service-learning practitioner have been overwhelmingly positive. I am convinced that my students both *learn* and *retain* more through service-learning consulting projects than they would from any other pedagogical approach. As far as I can see, there is no substitute for students using what they have learned in the classroom to concretely impact real-world organizations. Students benefit in three ways: (1) They actually apply classroom concepts and skills, a further step toward retaining the knowledge and skills required to perform well in the future; (2) they produce a tangible product that can be used by an organization, an affirmation of their successful application of what they have learned in the course; and (3) they work with and learn from a community organization, in this way learning about community issues while contributing positively to community groups around them.

Here are a few excerpts from my students' reflective papers (categorized by learning topic):

Assisting the community:

> It was amazing to see that what caused me to be motivated at first, a grade, did not really matter as our project was coming to a close. What mattered was that our brochure had to fulfill its purpose and inform older adults on how to get help if they needed assistance. Knowing that my efforts could help them caused me to do my best to make our brochure a success. Upon receiving the final brochure from the printing press, I realized that our work would make a difference in someone's life and that we had made a fine brochure. — G.R.

Teamwork:

> I benefited from this project in many ways and developed and utilized a variety of skills. Obviously it was essential to be an effective member of a team. This is becoming increasingly important in the business world, and developing these skills as an undergraduate is extremely helpful. This project is closer to a real-world assignment than any other I have been given in school. I learned some real-world challenges that a consultant must face, especially dealing with clients and team members. We were also put into a situation we knew nothing about, had no past results to use, and had

somewhat ambiguous roles. This situation fostered teamwork, creative thinking, and problem solving — all essential skills in the business world. This project had a tangible final product that yielded a sense of accomplishment for all members of the team. — J.H.

Sensitivity/diversity:

A minor conflict arose when we were planning the introduction of our presentation. We were debating whether we should do role playing or state facts as an introduction. I thought that role playing might be too risky because we might offend someone in the audience. Nobody can know for sure if someone in the audience has been a victim of crime or violence in his or her past. Therefore, I argued that cautious measures had to be taken and it might be safer to simply state facts. Other group members were dead set on role playing, so we compromised. We agreed that we would do role playing but that it would be sensitive and kept very ambiguous (one female and one male victim sharing their stories). — J.G.

Effective communication:

One major principle that I learned from the final group consulting project was how to interact with an organization while providing a service. It was imperative here to understand the importance of effective communication with the organization and within the group. In class we learned that effective communication can be curtailed by certain factors such as filtering, conflicting role demands, and increased transmission time. It was important not to confuse any delayed responses from our agency representative with problems associated with the brochure. — A.E.

Real-world learning:

I have greatly enjoyed my role as consultant and as a student in this organizational behavior class. The reason I enjoyed the consulting project so much is because it provided me with the opportunity to put my classroom knowledge into effect. Learning about topics such as organizational culture is much different from actually experiencing these subjects in the real world. — B.A.

Real-world value:

The most motivating factor during our entire project was the fact that we were actually producing something real and something of value. Although we never talked about how much "value" this project had, we all knew that it had a lot. — A.O.

It is important to note that these excerpts are representative of an overwhelming majority of student comments. Students today need to be challenged, to be active, and to apply what they are learning. Service-learning projects meet all of these requirements while either establishing or reinforcing the importance of business/community relationships and partnerships.

Service-Learning and Management Education

For those to whom the factors differentiating service-learning from other forms of experiential education are still not completely clear, the following may be useful. *Experiential education* encompasses a number of pedagogical strategies. A list of these would include, but not be limited to, internships, case studies, text-based team projects, in-class simulations, exercises, and role plays. Like service-learning, each of these strategies is designed to enhance students' understanding of topics covered in a course. In addition, each involves students in the learning process at a level beyond abstract conceptualization. Finally, each of these approaches challenges students to create linkages between conceptual material and more concrete experiences, again, a feature of service-learning. However, despite these similarities, there exist several key differences.

Service-learning provides students with a nontraditional, service-oriented social context for management education. It challenges them to confront, sort through, and excel in the dynamic, chaotic, nonlinear environment of a community-based organization. Real-world learning takes place as they simultaneously assume the role of professional consultants producing "goods" that will, in fact, be used. The responsibilities inherent in such *real-world accountability* to people and organizations in genuine need of one's services clearly separate service-learning from other forms of experiential education — even from traditional internships, where student contributions can often be more accurately described as "useful" rather than "needed." Genuine need creates a "personal emotional intensity" for students — one that is not often found in traditional classroom situations (Mello 1997: 185).

To be sure, service-learning can be viewed from many different perspectives. A definitional debate has gone on for years (Giles and Freed 1985; Stanton 1990) and stems, in part, from the simple fact that service-learning has been appropriated by faculty across a wide range of disciplines. Thus, service-learning projects in, for example, social work or teacher education may reflect a very different set of educational objectives from projects in management. Furthermore, variations arise not only across disciplines but also within disciplines (compare in this regard Godfrey's approach to service-learning, described elsewhere in this volume, with the one presented here).

My own approach would emphasize academic rigor and the integration of real-world course projects where students produce tangible, professional products for use in the local community as they *work with* and *learn from* organizations designed to serve community needs (Kenworthy 1996). This implies that the projects undertaken should be meaningful (i.e., important, worthwhile, deserving of commitment) to four constituencies: participating students, the sponsoring faculty member(s), their host institution, and their community partners. In addition, all project goals should include enhancing students' understanding of local communities and their needs, developing the students' professional skills, and uncovering actual and potential connections between businesses and those local communities (Kenworthy 1999). To illustrate how these aims can actually be embodied in the curriculum, a description of a service-learning consulting project in an undergraduate negotiations course has been included at the end of this article.

Support for Service-Learning Integration

Two types of conceptual support for service-learning integration can be identified. The first involves its theoretical foundations. The second revolves around current "calls" for changes in management education and the ways in which service-learning represents a pedagogical response to such "calls."

Theoretical Foundations

David Kolb's (1984) "learning cycle" model provides theoretical support for active learning and experientially based education.[1] Kolb (1984) defines learning as "the process whereby knowledge is created through the transformation of experience" (38). Using this definition, we see an emphasis on the *process* of learning, not on its outcomes or content (McEwen 1996). In addition, we see an emphasis on *continuous learning* — the argument that learning should not terminate with the end of a class period or with the end of a course. Finally, the term "experience" leads us to understand learning as an interactive phenomenon, involving both the learner and his or her external environment.

Kolb identifies four stations in the overall learning process and four related learning style preferences: (1) concrete experience, (2) reflective observation, (3) abstract conceptualization, and (4) active experimentation. Service-learning projects provide learning opportunities for individuals who favor active (concrete experience, active experimentation) as well as reflective (reflective observation, abstract conceptualization) styles. Students who favor active learning styles have an opportunity to learn from their concrete experiences. Alternatively, students who prefer reflective learning styles benefit from the reflective component integral to all service-learning projects (i.e., journals or written assignments where students draw connections between the service project and the skills learned in the classroom).[2] Thus, incorporating service-learning into university curricula offers students, in contrast to traditional classroom learning, a full range of learning-style opportunities.

Calls for Change

Over a decade ago, Porter and McKibbin (1988) issued one of the most important recent calls for change in management education. Their report, commissioned by the American Assembly of Collegiate Schools of Business, provided a detailed analysis of current criticisms leveled at business schools, especially with respect to management education. Service-learning clearly addresses two of their main concerns: deficiencies in the breadth of much contemporary management education and the importance of engaging the external environment.

Porter and McKibbin describe much management education as surprisingly "narrow" (316). However, in and through service-learning consulting projects, students gain exposure to, and understanding of, a broad section of the social environment. The protective walls of the classroom, artificial circumscription, and linear progression through course material are invariably left behind when students venture out into the community. Indeed, service-learning projects often force students to deal with such real-world logistical issues as changes in schedules, layers of bureaucracy, mixed feedback, and last-minute additions to projects. Furthermore, they must often address emotional issues related to the problems dealt with by community organizations (e.g., homelessness, abuse, poverty, crime, health issues). Such situations help them develop insight into the complexities of their local communities, expanding their "narrow" technical education by exposing them to the external environment and a range of outside influences (i.e., community issues).

Student exposure to such influences certainly has increased since the Porter-McKibbin (1988) report first appeared. However, the report's recommendations go beyond breadth of student experience and exposure to the external environment. The report also calls for efforts to address:

- a deficiency in leadership skills;
- insufficient development with respect to managing people;
- insufficient diversity across educational missions and goals.

Service-learning also addresses all of these issues — some more than others, depending upon variables such as the project environment, the course focus, and the interests of the instructor. However, the net result is that students are able to profit from a fully integrated, socially complex, real-world experience with organizations that genuinely need their services.

Administrative Requirements Defined

Administration of service-learning initiatives falls into two more or less distinct categories: the faculty member's role and university administrator's role. Each role is critical to successful service-learning course integration.

The Faculty Role

A management educator's role in a service-learning project is conceptually similar to the hub of a wheel (see the figure that follows). The spokes of the wheel represent the faculty member's relationships with each of the involved constituencies. The rim represents the relationships among these constituencies. Although the rim is what actually allows the wheel to move the vehicle forward, the wheel would collapse without the hub. Service-learning constituents often develop relationships on their own, but in the end it is the faculty member who is responsible for the successful design, operation, and completion of any service-learning project (Kenworthy 1999).

Defining the faculty member as the crux of a service-learning project does not overstate his or her role. In essence, he or she has primary responsibility for dealing with complexities that are political, social, and logistical in nature. The political complexities stem from the university's responsibility to its constituencies: (1) realizing promises made to community organizations (i.e., usable goods/deliverables), (2) providing quality learning experiences for its students (i.e., well-planned projects with committed partners in the community), and (3) upholding its reputation as a community-responsive institution of higher learning. Each of these obligations falls directly on the shoulders of a faculty member when she or he accepts the challenge of teaching a service-learning course. In the first place, she or he must maintain productive relationships both within and across the university's walls. Second, she or he must be prepared to run what is essentially a series of planned events (where the number of events equals the number of student project teams) in dynamic, chaotic environments.

This constellation of multifaceted responsibilities, coupled with the inexorable instability and dynamism found in service-learning projects, tends to limit the number of faculty members who are both interested in service-learning and good at it. Indeed, teaching an effective service-learning course is a difficult task. Since this approach is grounded in a commitment to active learning where students must first accept and embrace responsibility for their own education before that education can take place, faculty using this approach cannot simply "transfer" knowledge to their students

The Service-Learning Faculty Member as the
"Hub of the Wheel"

STUDENTS

THE FACULTY
MEMBER

COMMUNITY
MEMBERS

UNIVERSITY
ADMINISTRATORS

(Aldrich 1997; Cameron 1997). Faculty as well as students find that the bar has been raised for what counts as success.

In this way, service-learning requires of faculty both a personal sense of humility (Fukami 1997) and a personal desire for continuous learning (Nord 1996). It requires that they accept the fact that there is no right way — no expert solution — no conclusive answer (Weick 1997) to the kinds of questions raised by community involvement. In the end, the most successful service-learning faculty members are those who lead, not those who dictate (Hambrick 1997). But not all faculty are comfortable exchanging the relative safety of monologue for the risks of multilayered and multisided dialogue.

The Administrator Role

Kolb (1984) calls educational institutions "the curators of social knowledge" (161). University administrators serve as the gatekeepers of these institutions and, as such, are responsible for deciding how knowledge will be shared and what learning will be supported. Their decisions invariably affect the emergence and development of service-learning within their respective institutions; therefore, their support is pivotal to its success.

There are a number of models of service-learning implementation, ranging from a comprehensive institutional program (e.g., Bentley College in Waltham, Massachusetts) to utilizing the support of a service-learning center for select courses (e.g., University of Utah, University of North Carolina–Chapel Hill) to efforts concentrated on a single faculty member and/or a single course (e.g., University of Wisconsin–Madison). (For an overview of current service-learning initiatives in different kinds of institutions, see Enos and Troppe 1996 and Zlotkowski's 1998 *Successful Service-Learning Programs*.)

However, regardless of the model adopted (school-wide or single course), there are three fundamental reasons why institutional support for any service-learning initiative is important. First, faculty development (i.e., training, resource acquisition) is critical to successful service-learning initiatives, as it is to any effective teaching method. As Porter and McKibbin (1988) note, "If teaching is going to be improved, attention must be given to the measurement of performance, the structure of incentives, and the training and development of faculty" (160). Providing faculty with templates derived from successful courses as well as incentives and recognition within the promotion and tenure system are all important aspects of institutional support (Morton and Troppe 1996). Without such support, faculty initiative is minimal at best, at worst something to be opposed. Porter and McKibbin (1988) reference the importance of this issue when they note that:

> Critics charge that the quality of teaching is adversely affected by the
> absence of adequate incentives for effective teaching, causing professors at

many schools to concern themselves principally with research and scholar-ly activity, to the detriment of their teaching responsibilities. (152)

This reference to scholarly activity leads directly to the second reason why institutional support is necessary for effective service-learning integration. Institutional recognition encourages faculty not only to develop effective service-learning courses but to write about them. Calls exist across the disciplines (this monograph series being just one example) for theoretical and empirical research on service-learning initiatives. Faculty members, particularly junior members, need reassurance that publishing in this area represents a valued form of scholarly activity. This issue of what constitutes acceptable scholarship goes, of course, well beyond the domain of service-learning and speaks to the importance of recognizing quality pedagogical research in general. For those business schools that do choose to support service-learning, there exist several forums for management educators to share their work (e.g., *Journal of Management Education,* a forthcoming collection of articles on learning and education to be published by the Academy of Management, the annual National and International Organizational Behavior Teaching Conferences).

One final topic related to administrative support concerns questions of liability. These may arise in conjunction with (1) negligence on the part of the faculty member, students, or service site, (2) injuries incurred during a service experience, (3) legal issues associated with mandatory service, (4) transportation requirements, and (5) intentional misconduct. The Nonprofit Risk Management Center, based in Washington, DC, publishes a series of booklets on legal liability, risk management, and insurance issues related to community-service programs. One of its booklets is a guide to legal issues associated specifically with service-learning projects.

Beyond liability issues, service-learning programs must also deal with a variety of other kinds of barriers and challenges. Kolenko et al. (1996) provide a useful discussion of many of these. Their discussion includes sections on faculty responsibilities, curricular issues, barriers to successful integration, and, finally, "guidelines to maximize service-learning success" (139). (The January 1996 issue of the *Journal of Business Ethics,* of which that article was a part, was entirely devoted to business school–based community involvement/service-learning projects, and is to be highly recommended.)

Conclusion

The purpose of this paper is not to try to convince faculty to abandon traditional pedagogies; rather, it is to advocate the selective implementation of service-learning into the curriculum as a valuable new resource. I believe that the two broad pedagogical approaches at issue here — traditional class-room-based learning and service-learning consulting projects — are ultimately complementary. Neither would be wholly effective without the other (Schultz 1990). One of the primary benefits of service-learning, in the form of students serving as management consultants, is that it allows them to "attach significance to what they are doing" (Hambrick 1997: 246). They gain exposure to community issues even as they develop concepts and skills introduced in class. Thus real-world experience and theoretical rigor come together to produce what I personally consider to be the highest possible quality education — an education that allows students to produce something of value to others *and* to themselves.

I would like to conclude this chapter with a personal reflection. Service-learning lets me, as an instructor and a community member, finish each course feeling good about my work, my class, and the projects my students have undertaken. I am always proud of their capabilities, the challenges they overcome, and the learning that takes place both for them and for me. Through service-learning, I am continually learning about them, the community, and myself. Sponsoring a service-learning course never fails to be both physically and emotionally demanding. In the end, however, I see the justification for my hard work in students' reflections on their learning. Frequently they share with me powerful insights, experiences, thoughts, and questions related to any number of course topics — complex questions and thoughts that would most likely never have arisen in a traditional classroom setting. As a result, I remain a strong advocate for the consulting-based "exposure and understanding" approach to service-learning, despite its demands. Exposing our students — and ourselves — to the challenges of understanding real-world issues and needs in settings where what we do can make a measurable difference seems to me pedagogical strategy worthy of widespread attention.

Acknowledgments

I would like to thank Howard Aldrich and Benson Rosen, two champions of active learning and two very gifted writers, for providing me feedback on this chapter. I would also like to thank Edward Zlotkowski, Jim Ostrow, Jeannette MacInnes, and Edward Wondoloski for helping me develop my vision for management education; they have influenced me immeasurably.

Notes

1. Kolb's learning cycle has its origins in the work of John Dewey (1938), Kurt Lewin (1951), and Jean Piaget (cf. Kolb 1984: 23-25).

2. Reflective components are what separate service-learning projects from more-traditional volunteer experiences. Service-learning projects draw connections between service experiences and actual learning; this is typically accomplished through written and oral reflective assignments at preservice, midservice, and postservice points.

References

Aldrich, Howard E. (1997). "My Career as a Teacher: Promise, Failure, Redemption." In *Researchers Hooked on Teaching*, edited by R. Andre and P.J. Frost, pp. 14-26. Thousand Oaks, CA: Sage.

Bilimoria, Diana. (1998). "From Classroom Learning to Real-World Learning: A Diasporic Shift in Management Education." *Journal of Management Education* 22: 265-268.

Cameron, Beverly J. (1997). "Learning to Teach: An Ongoing Process." In *Researchers Hooked on Teaching*, edited by R. Andre and P.J. Frost, pp. 160-177. Thousand Oaks, CA: Sage.

Dewey, John. (1938). *Experience and Education*. New York, NY: Macmillan.

Enos, Sandra L., and Marie L. Troppe. (1996). "Service-Learning in the Curriculum." In *Service-Learning in Higher Education: Concepts and Practices*, edited by B. Jacoby and Associates, pp. 156-181. San Francisco, CA: Jossey-Bass.

Fukami, Cynthia V. (1997). "Struggling With Balance." In *Researchers Hooked on Teaching*, edited by R. Andre and P.J. Frost, pp. 3-13. Thousand Oaks, CA: Sage.

Giles, D., and J. Freed. (March 1985). "The Service-Learning Dimensions of Field Study: The Cornell Human Ecology Field Study Program." Paper presented at the National Conference on Service-Learning, Washington, DC.

Hambrick, Donald C. (1997). "Teaching as Leading." In *Researchers Hooked on Teaching*, edited by R. Andre and P.J. Frost, pp. 242-254. Thousand Oaks, CA: Sage.

Kenworthy, Amy L. (1996). "Linking Business Education, Campus Culture and Community: The Bentley Service-Learning Project." *Journal of Business Ethics* 15: 121-131.

———. (December 1999). "Management Students as Consultants: An Alternative Perspective on the Service-Learning 'Call to Action.'" *Journal of Management Inquiry* 8(4): 379-387.

Kolb, David A. (1984). *Experiential Learning: Experience as the Source of Learning and Development*. Englewood Cliffs, NJ: Prentice-Hall.

Kolenko, Thomas A., Gayle Porter, Walt Wheatley, and Marvelle Colby. (January 1996). "A Critique of Service-Learning Projects in Management Education: Pedagogical Foundation, Barriers, and Guidelines." *Journal of Business Ethics* 15(1): 133-142.

Lewin, Kurt. (1951). *Field Theory in Social Sciences*. New York, NY: Harper & Row.

McEwen, M.K. (1996). "Enhancing Student Learning and Development Through Service-Learning." In *Service-Learning in Higher Education: Concepts and Practices*, edited by B. Jacoby and Associates, pp. 53-91. San Francisco, CA: Jossey-Bass.

Mello, Jeff. (1997). "Teaching in the Real World." In *Researchers Hooked on Teaching*, edited by R. Andre and P.J. Frost, pp. 178-196. Thousand Oaks, CA: Sage.

Morton, K., and M. Troppe. (1996). "From the Margin to the Mainstream: Campus Compact's Project on Integrating Service With Academic Study." *Journal of Business Ethics* 15: 21-32.

Nord, Walter R. (1996). "Research/Teaching Boundaries." In *Rhythms of Academic Life*, edited by P.J. Frost and M.S. Taylor, pp. 83-90. Thousand Oaks, CA: Sage.

Porter, Lyman W., and Lawrence E. McKibbin. (1988). *Management Education and Development: Drift or Thrust Into the 21st Century?* New York, NY: McGraw-Hill.

Schultz, S.K. (1990). "Learning by Heart: The Role of Action in Civic Education." In *Combining Service and Learning: A Resource Book for Community and Public Service, Volume 1*, edited by J.C. Kendall and Associates, pp. 210-224. Raleigh, NC: National Society for Internships and Experiential Education.

Stanton, T. (1990). "Service-Learning: Groping Toward a Definition." In *Combining Service and Learning: A Resource Book for Community and Public Service, Vol. 1*, edited by J.C. Kendall and Associates, pp. 65-67. Raleigh, NC: National Society for Internships and Experiential Education.

Weick, Karl E. (1997). "The Teaching Experience as Learning in Public." In *Researchers Hooked on Teaching*, edited by R. Andre and P.J. Frost, pp. 283-300. Thousand Oaks, CA: Sage.

Zlotkowski, Edward. (1998). *Successful Service-Learning Programs: New Models of Excellence in Higher Education*. Bolton, MA: Anker.

Negotiations Course Project Description

The required group project has been designed as an opportunity for you to use the concepts you will learn in this course by applying them to a real-world organization. Groups of 3 or 4 students will serve as consultants for a local educational organization. Students are expected to negotiate their way to an effective group experience – this "team" project has been incorporated based on the increasing use of teams in the business world. Each group will produce a "tip sheet" on conflict resolution. These "tip sheets" will subsequently be printed in bulk and used by the organization.

This project will benefit everyone in a number of ways:

(1) the organizations you are working with will receive a usable product designed to meet a current organizational need,

(2) each of you will attain consulting experience applying negotiation theories to real-world conflict situations,

(3) each group member will obtain a copy of the final product that can be attached to/referenced in his/her resume portfolio.

Each group member will write a short (5 pp.) assessment of this project to be turned in with their final "tip sheet." Peer- and organizational contact person-evaluations will be administered and incorporated into project grades.

A Postmodern Service-Learning Pedagogy:
The Story of the Greenback Company

by Grace Ann Rosile and David Boje

Service-learning using the Greenback Company postmodern pedagogy has created the most intensely "real" and exciting educational experiences of our careers. Ironically, it is exactly this concrete realism that makes these experiences such rich opportunities for understanding and applying theory. This paper will first briefly explain postmodernism and postmodern pedagogy, and then describe a semester-long service-learning approach called "the Greenback Company." It concludes with a discussion of the theoretical implications of this postmodern service pedagogy, as well as a discussion of why service projects are central to this learning process.

Postmodernism and Postmodern Pedagogy

What is postmodernism? Our colleague Bob Dennehy once remarked that being asked to briefly explain postmodernism is like being asked "Where do babies come from?" An appropriate answer can be quite lengthy, and a brief answer is likely to leave many "misconceptions." In other words, to be postmodern is to resist definition, to embrace undecidability. Nevertheless, we will first try to suggest a few features of postmodernism, and then we offer from the Greenback approach a few examples that we think demonstrate a postmodern — as opposed to a modernist — approach to pedagogy. We will even go so far as to present a table summarizing some of these postmodern/modern differences. In doing so, we recognize that such an exposition is a decidedly unpostmodern perpetuation of dualisms. Indeed, we acknowledge that this presentation is itself a modernist interpretation of postmodernism. However, we will balance this nod to analytic foundationalist modernism with the more favored postmodern medium, the multivocal local narrative of the marginalized.

With this prelude, we suggest that a postmodern perspective may be summarized by reference to four characteristics (Rosile and Boje 1996a: 235): Postmodernism is (1) self-reflexive, (2) deconstructionist, (3) nontotalitarian/nonuniversalist, and (4) decentered. The following is a discussion of these characteristics as they contrast with premodern and modernist perspectives. We should note, moreover, that while premodern, modern, and postmodern can be considered eras, the view here is that all three are perspectives, linked in an ongoing struggle for dominance. Thus, while we see today the increasing influence of a postmodern perspective, it is likely that modernism (or "late modernism") will remain for some time the dominant paradigm, with fewer (but still visible) vestiges of premodernism apparent.

Postmodernism is self-reflexive. While modernists believe that increased knowledge leads to progressive betterment, postmodernists self-reflexively call this belief the "progress myth." Postmodernism questions the value of progress, and asks who is benefited and who is marginalized by modernist progress. Premodernism would value order and conformity over progress.

For some, postmodernism is almost synonymous with deconstruction. Deconstruction involves demystifying the way in which that which is perceived as "reality" or "truth" is constructed. Magicians Penn and Teller have been called postmodern because they perform magic tricks and then reveal to the audience the secret of how the trick or illusion has been created.

Deconstruction is not a state; it is a continual process. The nature of any construction is such that it is constantly in a state of deconstructing itself. This state of constantly deconstructing change is also why objective reality is always just beyond our reach, is always put off or "deferred," is always different (Derrida 1978) from our experience of it. The postmodern world is composed of deconstructing constructions. In premodern times, humanity discovered god, a powerful force controlling the universe. In modern times, humanity discovered reason as a means of dominating the universe. We agree with Binzagr and Manning's combining of self-reflexivity and deconstruction to define postmodernism as "that moment when humanity discovered it can reinvent itself" (1996: 251).

Postmodernism is nontotalitarian/nonuniversalist. From a modernist perspective, knowledge is power. To postmodernists, power is knowledge (Foucault 1980). Those at the top of our scientific "disciplines" use their power to define what constitutes acceptable knowledge (Fox 1989), what is considered "good research." Premodernism looks for truth to be revealed by god through clergy and monarchy. The modernist project relies on reason to uncover universal truths and create knowledge (or "enlightenment"). Postmodernists question both the existence and knowability of absolute truth. Such a stance is sometimes described as "relativist." Critics complain that postmodernists take their relativism and skepticism to such an extreme as to lead to paralysis; however, Rosenau (1992: 14-17) identifies a version of "affirmative" postmodernism. This more closely resembles the approach taken by the present authors. The postmodernism presented in this paper justifies taking action not because of the moral superiority of truth but because of a contextualized preference, a self-conscious valuing. We agree with Binzagr and Manning that "when the reality we have created no longer is experienced with joy or value, we can return to skepticism and relativism, deconstruct this reality, and then reconstruct it again" (1996: 255).

Postmodernism is decentered. While religion was the center of the premodern world, rationality and technology became the center of the modernist project. Postmodernists seek to unmask the operations of power that sustain our knowledge/power hierarchies. Instead of the totalizing modernist "grand narrative," postmodernists prefer the individualized "local" account (Lyotard 1984). This may be reflected as a postmodern preference for ethnographic stories over quantified data.

The figure *below* summarizes some of the differences of pedagogies based on premodern, modern, and postmodern assumptions.

Greenback Company Class-Based Organization

Greenback requires students to engage in a not-for-profit activity for a broadly defined concept of community benefit. In the course of the semester, Greenback employee-students are compelled (by various structural mechanisms) to experience for themselves what it is like to be organized according to first premodern, then modern, and finally postmodern concepts (Boje and Dennehy 1994: Appendix A). Students tell stories about their group experiences, and they are also taught to deconstruct these stories. Thus, students go beyond simply creating a business organization to the more complex task of controlling their own evolution from the instructor-defined modernist organization to a group-defined postmodern organization.

The semester begins with the instructor as "Guildmaster" creating a fraternity- or sorority-like "guild" composed of all the students in the class. Students are told that the motto of Greenback Company is "putting green back into mother earth." This "putting back" can be in the form of environmental or social-service-type projects. In the initial premodern or "guild" phase, all students are "greenies" who are initiated with oath, candles, music, and guild secrets. With minimal guidance from the Elders (the instructor and Greenback veterans who have volunteered to be mentors), the guild democratically chooses both a fundraiser (to provide capital) and a "postmodern campaign" project that is ecologically or community-service oriented. A critical requirement is that the project must involve some "sweat equity" and some "hands-on" opportunities for all class members. Simply raising money to be donated to a worthy cause (checkbook charity) is not sufficient. While in the guild phase, the fundraiser and service project are planned. But before conducting the fundraiser, the instructor transforms the entire class into a modernist organization. Students elect a CEO and heads of five well-defined bureaucratic departments. Each student has a job description. After four to six weeks of this traditional bureaucracy, the

	Premodern	Modern	Postmodern
Location	Job-site apprenticeship	Classroom-based tutorial	Multiple locations: internships, community-based projects, distance ed, and classrooms
Instructor	Master crafters, aristocracy, church	Subject expert, depersonalized knowledge conduit, now being replaced by a computer	Expert at deconstruction, presents neglected views
Goals/Values	Respect for elders and tradition	Respect for expert learning	Respect for local learning, question the dominant paradigm
Evaluation of Students	Personalized assessment by master, elder, or guild	Standardized assessment and achievement test banks	Negotiated format involving students, instructor, others

instructor uses assignments (such as rewriting job descriptions and reviewing departmental goals) to guide the students in transforming their very modern organization into something more postmodern. Students are invited to experience the transitions corporations all around them are making in this postmodern world (Boje and Dennehy 1994; Clegg 1990).

At the beginning of the term, students are told that this approach involves much more time and effort than students (or instructors) expect for a typical class. One or two students usually drop the class at this point, citing time constraints.

The Storied Experiences of the Greenback Company

This story comes from one of the authors' Greenback Company classes. As usual, students were required to write about their experiences as stories, and the stories were to have a focus on managerial concepts. After writing their stories, students were required to deconstruct them. Some students claim that the story deconstruction is the hardest part of the class, and some complain they should not have to write so much in a business class. Explaining that stories in organizational theory are mechanisms for organizational change and presenting some examples of previous classes' stories and deconstructions help most students to see the value of this aspect of the course.

The story in question has three parts; the first two parts are actual story assignments written and deconstructed by the students. (See "Story Deconstruction Method" at the end of this chapter for more details on story deconstruction.) The final part of the story is the instructor's own telling of the "end" of the story.

To put the project in context: a Greenback Company had planned to have a "Lip Sync Contest" in which contestants pretended to sing while a popular song was played. Money from this fundraiser would be used to support the class community service project — the refurbishing of a nearby homeless shelter in a small rural town. There was a controversy over how much money should be awarded for first, second, and third prizes, and a lot of tension was apparent among the class members.

The three parts follow:

(1)
Who's the Boss

Author:
Beth Leonard, story used with permission (Rosile and Boje 1996b)

Date:
March 20, 1995

Who:
Tim: *medium build, easy-going CEO who occasionally loses his temper*
Maura: *tall, poised, and professional, outspoken, member of Earth in the Fingernails Department (production)*
Beth: *quiet and soft-spoken department head of Earth in the Fingernails*
Ahmed: *large powerful football player, well-liked head of Friends Department*

Tim (CEO): I feel that the decision has been made for the prize money. The posters have been printed. The amounts are $300 for first, $150 for second, and $50 for third place.

Maura (EFN Dept. member): Tim, you will be taking all this money away from the homeless shelter! The prize money is way too high, and it's going to put us in the hole.

Tim (CEO): I have heard enough from you! The decision has been made and that's final! Beth, you are her department head. Will you take care of her, please?

Beth (EFN Dept. head): Maura, why don't you let this rest for now. We can discuss this at a later time.

Maura (EFN Dept. member): I don't need you to patronize me!! This whole project is ruined. These people in the shelter aren't going to get a damn thing.

A short time later, Maura leaves the room 15 minutes before the end of the class period. During the next class period, the executive committee (the CEO and all department heads) met with Dr. Rosile to discuss the progress of the fundraisers and the class as a whole.

Tim (CEO): Something is going to have to be done about Maura. She's unhappy with the prize money amount, and she told me that I am doing a shit job as CEO. I don't need to put up with this.

Beth (EFN Dept. head): Maura is a very emotional person. She's just really into making this project work.

Dr. Rosile (prof.): What do you all feel you should do about her? You must consider the fact that Maura is very dedicated and hardworking, and has also put in a lot of time working for this company.

Tim (CEO): I know we can't fire her; this is a class.

Ahmed (Friends Dept. head): Why don't we give her some sort of executive position? It may change her attitude and make her feel more involved.

Tim (CEO): Then we would give her exactly what she wants. That is just telling her that if she yells and complains enough, we'll give her an executive position! That won't work.

Dr. Rosile (prof.): Let me suggest something. Beth, you are her department head and her friend. What if you ask her to make a list of goals and strategies to implement that she thinks will make the fundraiser more successful.

Beth (EFN Dept. head): That sounds like a very good idea. Maura likes to have a say in things. It probably will make her feel better.

After class, Beth met with Maura and offered Dr. Rosile's suggestion. Maura liked that idea and agreed to formulate a list of goals and strategies to better the success of the fundraiser. This alleviated the tension, and Maura felt a lot better. In addition, Maura wrote Tim a letter of apology for the things she had said to him.

Moral:
Influencing people in a tactful, positive way can help them to feel better and to work for, not against, the organization.

Deconstruction:

- Premodern: Attitude. Attitude attracted or repelled success or failure. Positive mental attitude (Boje and Dennehy 1994: 170). In the story, Dr. Rosile suggested that giving Maura the task of suggesting goals and strategies would change her attitude and work in a positive way for Maura. If we deny the plot, we would say that Maura shows her bad attitude because she does not like the class.

- Modern: Yielding. Man yields to the pace of the machine and to the layers of authority over her/him (Boje and Dennehy 1994: 162). The executives felt Maura was stepping out of the bounds of her job, even though she wanted to try to help make the company better. State what is between the lines: The executive committee wanted to tell Maura to calm down a little bit without hurting her feelings.

- Postmodern: Unconforming. Self-disciplined rather than other-disciplined; rebel against authority (Boje and Dennehy 1994: 200). Maura was rebelling against Tim and voicing her opposition to the amount of prize money to be awarded. Rebel voices: Tim, being the CEO, did not want to listen to Maura. Maura felt very frustrated.

NOTE: Some time after this episode, after much agonizing, the executive committee decided to abandon the entire Lip Sync fundraiser as too risky. They decided to substitute a last-minute car wash to replace the income required for their homeless shelter project.

(2)
Further Adventures

Author:
Kelly Apple, story used with permission (Rosile and Boje 1996b)

Who:

Tim: *CEO of Greenback*
Maura: *Member of Earth in the Fingernails Dept. (production)*
Ahmed: *Head of Friends Dept. (human resources)*
Kelly: *Member of Friends Dept.*
Jen: *Head of Cultural Survival Dept. (social responsibility)*
The Entire Greenback Company

It was the day after Maura and Tim argued in class over the Lip Sync fundraiser. Maura just discovers that the Friends Department had marked her absent for that previous class, because she was 10 minutes late for class and left 15 minutes early. Maura confronts Ahmed, the head of the Friends Department, as follows:

Maura (EFN Dept. member): I told Beth that I was leaving. I don't think I should be marked absent.

Ahmed (Friends Dept. head): Beth is not in charge of attendance; the Friends Department is. You should have told us.

Maura (EFN Dept. member): I thought that telling Beth was enough, because she is my department head. I had a meeting to go to.

Kelly (Friends Dept. member): How were we to know?

During the next class, Ahmed was given a petition signed by all the members of the Earth in the Fingernails Department. It insisted that Maura be marked present for the class being disputed.

Ahmed (Friends Dept. head): *(to the entire class)* Maura will no longer be marked absent. We did not change our minds because of the petition but because of the misunderstanding regarding the attendance policy.

Maura (EFN Dept. member): I appreciate that, but we have never seen anything in writing regarding these rules. We did not know you were taking attendance.

Kelly (Friends Dept. member): We announced during the proposal presentation that if you missed more that three classes, you would be fined. Obviously, this meant that we were going to monitor attendance.

Ahmed (Friends Dept. head): That's right. If you did not hear it, then you weren't paying attention.

Jen (CSD Dept. head): I have been taking attendance for my department.

Kelly (Friends Dept. member): Nothing was turned in to us.

Maura (EFN Dept. member): Why did we set department goals, then, if we don't get to control them?

Kelly (Friends Dept. member): My understanding was that the goals were for each individual department concerning its meeting time, but overall for the class it was the Friends Department's responsibility.

Tim (CEO): What's the big deal? If their department wants to take attendance, let them.

The arguing continued until class ended, with nothing being resolved.

The next class period was a Company Flex Day, when company executives choose how they wish to use the time, including as "vacation" time for some or all. Apparently a few class members had been rewarded with vacation time, but most of the class was having departmental meetings. In the Friends (human resources) Department, department head Ahmed pulled member Kelly aside and showed her a copy of a memo given to him by EFN Department member Maura stating she felt the rules should be voted on and put in writing.

Kelly (Friends Dept. member): This is the modern phase; we don't need to take a vote. I had Tim's approval to do this.

Ahmed (Friends Dept. head): Well, from now on each department will be responsible for its own attendance.

Kelly (Friends Dept. member): But it is our responsibility.

Ahmed (Friends Dept. head): If they want to do it, let them.

Kelly (Friends Dept. member): We don't get to do anything else. Why should we give that up?

Ahmed (Friends Dept. head): I am tired of fighting. There are more important things to be done.

Kelly (Friends Dept. member): Okay, you're right.

<u>Moral:</u>
Ahmed gave in to the pressure and influence of Maura and the petition, and Kelly gave in to the influence of the decision dictated by the department head.

<u>Deconstruction:</u>

- <u>Premodern:</u> "Journeymen could call a democratic meeting to vote in a fine to enforce shop rules" (Boje and Dennehy 1994: 162). The Friends Department voted to fine whoever missed more than two days of class. Rebel voices: The rest of the company were not given the opportunity to cast their votes and have a say in this policy.

- <u>Modern:</u> "There must be obedience and respect by employees for their firm" (Boje and Dennehy 1994: 162). Ahmed showed respect to the company by complying with the wishes of the CEO, the department heads, and Maura instead of fighting. Other side of the story: Maura was not showing obedience and respect for the firm, and she should have been penalized.

- <u>Postmodern:</u> "Unconforming -- rebel against authority" (Boje and Dennehy 1994: 162). The Earth in the Fingernails Department rebelled by circulating a petition against procedure. Deny the plot: The Earth in the Fingernails Department agreed with Ahmed and thought Maura deserved to be punished.

(3)
A Tale From the Field

Author:
Grace Ann Rosile

The smell of disaster was in the room. It was three weeks before the end of the term, a cold and dark November day in a high-ceilinged old classroom in western Pennsylvania. The class again had opted against the fluorescents in favor of this day's gray light coming from the huge, multipaned windows. Twenty-some business undergraduates were sitting in a circle, in small wood chairs with graffiti-engraved writing platforms attached to one side. Class members had been at odds with one another, confused and floundering for weeks. The class's semester project was barely begun, with little more than three weeks left in the term. I had called an emergency "town meeting."

I explained to this morose group that the purpose of the community service project was to provide an opportunity for the class to work together as an organization. I said that I believed that the conflicts they had over strategy decisions, the fundraising project that was canceled midstream as being too risky, and the subsequent slump in morale were all valuable lessons in management. The class could still earn A's by focusing the final "annual report" on what they had learned from their rocky road. I asked for a discussion and decision on whether they wished to carry on with the refurbishment of the homeless shelter, or whether they wished to use the remaining few weeks to focus their energy on their final paper.

Into the quiet that followed my comments, for the first time all term, Lou spoke. He talked of his carpentry work on the project, and the coordination difficulties he had experienced in attempting to work with his classmates. He concluded by saying how frustrating such organizational problems were, especially when there was so much need at the shelter. Others chimed in with similar complaints about delays, miscommunications, carpooling difficulties, and other problems. Finally Maura asked how many students had actually been to the shelter. Only a handful raised their hands. With deep feeling, she talked of the people she met at the shelter and how much good the project would do. Then another student told of meeting a man who had been all over the world as a cook in the Navy. The man was residing at the shelter and doing volunteer work elsewhere, three afternoons a week, until his next job would begin the following week.

After a few more comments, I reminded the group that time was short, and that they could fulfill class requirements by simply writing up their experiences at this point. I was about to call for a vote. Then one person said, "I can go on Wednesday, and take some people in my car who want to work on masking the rooms to be painted." The atmosphere shifted instantly, and individuals began volunteering to coordinate certain aspects of the project. As each spoke, two or three others would offer to join in their task. Within minutes the entire class were bursting with energy. They had motivation and purpose, and they were happy.

It took some effort to quiet the group for the final five minutes of class. I asked if there were any remaining questions about the requirements for the final "annual report," reminding them that Natasha was the new coordinator of that group writing effort. Natasha was an attractive young woman from Moscow, married with two children. She was bright and well-spoken, and also had missed many classes. She said, "I think you should have done this [the town meeting] sooner. You could have prevented all this floundering and confusion." I said I had thought carefully about when and if I should intervene in the class's process, and believed that they had learned a great deal by grappling with their problems on their own. After class, Natasha said to me, "You know, we tried this in Russia and it didn't work." Interestingly, about a year later Natasha saw me and stopped to talk in a stairwell at school. She said her views of the class had changed over the past year, and she understood better what I had been trying to do.

When the class met the next week and I asked for a progress report, Tim and Maura looked at each other, as if for mutual approval, before answering me. I was puzzled, remembering the semester-long feuding between Greenback CEO Tim and Maura, who had run against him for president and lost. I asked, "What is going on here?" Maura held up a hand with the index and middle fingers twisted together, and said, "We're like this now." And so it was, for the remainder of the term. At the end of the semester, there was another circle of the same students. It was a bright, sunny day, and I was videotaping their comments to be passed on to future Greenback Company classes. The class's mood matched the weather, as they talked and joked about the term. They remembered the teenager who kept insisting that the students must be getting something else for doing all that work. They remembered the former Navy cook, and the mothers and children. There were tears as students told of hugs from grateful residents of the shelter.

I asked if Tim and Maura wanted to tell the story of their overcoming their differences and ending their nearly semester-long feud. They laughed and declined, implying the new partnership might not last if old conflicts were discussed. I am convinced they joined forces when they realized their differences were dwarfed by their mutual commitment to the greater cause. The class had pulled together at the town meeting because of the acknowledgment of, and recommitment to, their service project. Everyone worked together with enthusiasm, and the refurbishing work was completed. The final paper did suffer from the shortage of preparation time; however, this class had greater esprit de corps at the end than their one-hour earlier counterparts.

That other class section's project went smoothly, and their final paper was finished to a polished perfection, with photos, charts, and graphs, exactly on time. When the "problem" class asked me about the other group's progress, I candidly told them how smoothly the other group's project went. I also reminded them how much they had learned from the difficulties they had encountered, and asked permission to use the story of their class to help future classes learn about the Greenback process. Pleased and very flattered to think their experiences might help others, they all proudly agreed to have their story told.

Epilogue:

Now you, the reader, have been invited into this Greenback Company story. You will have your own interpretations and your own tellings. Unlike some cultures, we do not punish inaccurate tellings with death. We do quite the opposite, from a postmodern perspective. We encourage alternative interpretations. Further, we use the process of acknowledging alternative interpretations to highlight the possibilities for people to influence and create their own stories, both individually and in groups. Service projects can highlight alternative and hidden stories, break the stereotypes of the "other" and the "needy," and foster critical reflection on our society and the role of business in society.

The Poststory

The above stories reveal, among other things, a few critical points regarding service-learning pedagogy. First, it is important that students engage in hands-on work that is directly related to the people being served. This encounter with people not usually part of a college business curriculum, and not usually part of the corporate world, is invaluable. Quite frequently students will comment that they discovered that "they [those the students helped] are a lot like me!" Another potential benefit is what John Miller (in a discussion at a 1998 Organizational Behavior Teaching Conference session on service-learning in LaVerne, California) called "empathic mutuality." Miller calls this the feeling among those helped that they also are not much different from the college students helping them; therefore, they might consider taking college courses or making other life choices they might not consider in their usual environment.

This encounter with the "other" relates to a second point — that students adopt an ethnographic model of help, whereby those being helped are the experts and those serving seek to learn from those they wish to help. Using this concept self-reflexively in the class's self-management naturally leads to recommending a servant-leadership style as appropriate for the postmodern phase of the class.

Third, control rests with the students. They must choose their own project and determine how to meet their own objectives. Significant dollar amounts and human lives are affected by their choices. This control must extend to classroom management; for example, students may vote to alter or discontinue quizzes. Students report they are not used to telling another student, or being told by another student, what to do. These are real management issues, as reflected in the above stories. (In the first of these stories, author Beth left out the professor's response to CEO Tim's comment that he could not fire Maura because this was a class. The professor said, "Yes, you can fire someone; it's been done before.")

Fourth, the motivational value of a worthy project, a project of the students' own choosing, cannot be underestimated. Such motivation provides the incentive for students to work through relationship and task difficulties — difficulties that would otherwise likely result in apathy, poor performance, or constant internal conflict.

Fifth and finally, the process of putting students — who typically feel that they are powerless victims of the educational system — in the role of helpers does a great deal to enhance self-esteem and thereby promote learning and development of true managerial skills. This process of putting the "victim" in the role of "helper" is best reflected in the comment made by a student who had worked with a group of grade-school children. She said the children acted as if she and her teammates were some famous national group touring all the elementary schools. Such reactions may be why so very many students involved in these service projects return to offer more service on their own time, beyond a class's requirements.

(For a complete treatment of the Greenback Company pedagogy, see Rosile and Boje 1996b.)

Discussion: Perils, Pitfalls, and Potential Rewards

A story in the Wall Street Journal discusses how the service-learning trend is being incorporated into college classes across the United States (Butler 1994). By sending students out into the community to do service projects, service-learning teaches social responsibility. In the context of a management class, the management of the experience of collective learning becomes a part of such experiential learning projects, since students can work in nonhierarchical and self-managed study and service work teams.

Working in nonhierarchical arrangements may pose serious challenges to the curriculum of a business school. When one of Professor Rosile's Greenback classes decided to do Tarzan yells to charge themselves up for class that day, five faculty complained to her dean, and her department head accused her of not having control of her classroom. The students' response to these developments was to say, "Let's yell louder!" But after a discussion of good citizenship and the values of Greenback, the class chose to accept the challenge of having energizing activities that would not disturb the rest of the building. They also noticed that our educational system is more sympathetic to sleeping than to yelling in the classroom. And when someone in one of Professor Boje's Greenback classes gave a condom to a Jesuit priest, Boje was called to his academic vice president's office. The class was distributing condoms as part of an AIDS awareness campaign associated with their refurbishing of a shelter for mothers and babies with AIDS. The Jesuit administration insisted the students abide by a rule forbidding promotion of birth control methods on campus ("University" 1994: A6).

Giving students more control may entail other problems. Leaving the classroom is risky. Since it is the nature of service projects to reach beyond classroom walls, such projects will be questioned. Academia resists such innovations with, among other things, what has been termed the "tyranny of the disciplines" (Aronowitz and Giroux 1991: 149). But what do we accomplish by the tight control (and ensuing passivity) that we demand in most of our classrooms? If we are to teach empowerment and self-management — currently hot topics in business schools — our teaching methods must reflect these values. Vance observes that "schools will face major problems if they believe they can continue effectively to pour these new potent wines of change into old curricular bottles of instructional content" (1993: xi).

Pedagogy critical of modernism must raise the issue of whose interests are served and whose voices are heard. A presentation at the 1998 Organizational Behavior Teaching Conference suggested that the current literature on service-learning is dominated by an "us and them" approach the presenters call the "charity model." This model reinforces the status quo power differences between helpers and those helped, in contrast to emphasizing the reciprocity of giving and receiving. As service projects become more commonplace, we in business schools run the risk of "MBA-ing" such projects into efficient, predictable, McDonaldized nuggets of learning. Can we prevent ourselves and our students from molding such inherently messy and unpredictable experiences into more standardized mirror images of traditional educational fare? And, more important, can we avoid the colonizing impact of having our students simply import business practices and values into a field setting, rather than entering that setting to experience a different set of values?

Instead, management education must shift its focus from reinforcing the status quo to critically examining today's business agenda (Boje 1995; Fineman and Gabriel 1993; Fox 1989). As Bradford (1993) notes, "We need to make sure that we don't send the wrong meta-message. The U.S. is late on the scene for the call to move outside the confines of modernist education" (x).

Service-learning, combined with a critical postmodern pedagogy, can help students demystify the ideological underpinnings of the managerial narrative that does not see homelessness, women's shelters, and environmental destruction. By seeing and experiencing these hidden side effects of our current social system, our students may be inspired to harness the power of the business corporation to ameliorate such pressing social issues rather than exacerbate them.

A critical postmodern approach does not mean that the class is mired in endless debates about the subtleties of control in modern life. On the contrary. What happens is that we discuss the fact that quizzes are modernist strategies of power that value consistency above almost everything else. What happens is that students decide to eliminate penalties for nonattendance at meetings as they attempt to organize according to postmodern, freedom-enhancing values. Then no one shows up for meetings, and they re-institute the penalties. What happens is that a lot of things happen, students take lots of actions, and lots of learning occurs. One of our favorite stories is the time when one CEO, Rob, said, "Dr. Rosile, I am not sure if we should have asked you about this earlier, but we went ahead and created a company newsletter to keep all the departments informed of what's going on. Is that okay?" Giving up some control involves risks, but our experience has been that the risks are far outweighed by the rewards that follow.

Still another indication of the success of this approach is the fact that each term students from previous semesters come back to work as mentors (consultants, elders, board members), all on their own time. This phenomenon is part of the creation of a learning community. It may also reflect a belief that this course can make a difference. A few years ago, students from one class, after the term had ended, created a "Greenback" student organization of their own to engage in community service projects ("but we will not be writing annual reports!"). This reflects a trend in the business world also, where more and more companies have followed the lead of the Body Shop, Ben & Jerry's, and others "doing well by doing good." Such organizations are creating a "caring capitalism" model of business with supportive relationships with the community and the global environment.

In conclusion, the Greenback Company's class-based organization offers one approach to incorporating service-learning into the management classroom. Service-learning lends itself to a pedagogy rich in opportunities for applying critical and postmodern concepts to management topics. In this regard, the greatest endorsement of this pedagogy may have been the comment of one Greenback veteran who said, "After this class, I don't see anything the same way anymore."

References

Aronowitz, S., and H. Giroux. (1991). *Postmodern Education: Politics, Culture, and Social Criticism*. Minneapolis, MN: University of Minnesota Press.

Binzagr, G., and M. Manning. (1996). "Reconstructions of Choice: Advocating a Constructivist Approach to Postmodern Management Education" In *Postmodern Management and Organizational Theory*, edited by D.M. Boje, R.P. Gephart, and T.J. Thatchenkery, pp. 251-265. Thousand Oaks, CA: Sage.

Boje, D.M. (1995). "Stories of the Storytelling Organization: A Postmodern Analysis of Disney as 'Tamara-land.'" *Academy of Management Journal* 38(4): 997-1035.

———, and R.F. Dennehy. (1994). *Managing in the Postmodern World: America's Revolution Against Exploitation*. 2nd ed. Dubuque, IA: Kendall Hunt.

Bradford, David. (1993). "Foreword." In *Mastering Management Education: Innovations in Teaching Effectiveness*, edited by C. Vance, pp. ix-x. Newbury Park, CA: Sage.

Butler, S. (December 30, 1994). "Service Courses Teach Students Some Lessons in the Real World." *Wall Street Journal*: B1, B4.

Clegg, S. (1990). *Modern Organization: Organization Studies in the Postmodern World*. Newbury Park, CA: Sage.

Derrida, J. (1978). *Writing and Difference,* translated by A. Bass. London, Eng.: Routledge and Kegan Paul.

Fineman, Stephen, and Yiannis Gabriel. (July 1993). "Changing Rhetorics: The Case of the Introductory OB Textbook." Paper presented at the 11th EGOC Colloquium, Paris, France.

Foucault, M. (1980). *Power/Knowledge.* New York, NY: Pantheon.

Fox, S. (1989). "The Panopticon: From Bentham's Obsession to the Revolution in Management Learning." *Human Relations* 42(8): 717-739.

Lyotard, J.-F. (1984, orig. 1979). *The Postmodern Condition: A Report on Knowledge,* translated by G. Bennington and B. Massouri. Minneapolis, MN: University of Minnesota Press.

Rosenau, P.M. (1992). *Post-Modernism and the Social Sciences: Insights, Inroads, and Intrustions.* Princeton, NJ: Princeton University Press.

Rosile, G.A., and D.M. Boje. (1996a). "Pedagogy for the Postmodern Management Classroom: Greenback Company." In *Postmodern Management and Organizational Theory,* edited by D.M. Boje, R.P. Gephart, and T.J. Thatchenkery, pp. 225-250. Thousand Oaks, CA: Sage.

——— . (1996b). *Welcome to the Greenback Company: An Action Learning Organization.* Dubuque, IA: Kendall Hunt.

"University Says No to Condom Distribution." (April 27, 1994). *The Chronicle of Higher Education:* A6.

Vance, C. (1993). "Preface." In *Mastering Management Education: Innovations in Teaching Effectiveness,* edited by C. Vance, pp. xi-xiv. Newbury Park, CA: Sage.

Story Deconstruction Method

1. Duality Search.
Make a list of any bipolar terms, any dichotomies, that are used in the story. Include the term even if only one side is mentioned.

2. Reinterpret.
A story is one interpretation of an event from one point of view. Write out an alternative interpretation using the same story particulars.

3. Rebel Voices.
Deny the authority of the one voice. What voices are not being expressed in this story? Which voices are subordinate or hierarchical to other voices?

4. Other Side of the Story.
Stories always have two sides. What is the other side of the story (usually a marginalized, underrepresented, or even silent story character)?

5. Deny the Plot.
Stories have plots, scripts, scenarios, recipes, and morals. Turn these around.

6. Find the Exception.
What is the exception that breaks the rule, that does not fit the recipe, that escapes the strictures of the principle? State the rule in a way that makes it seem extreme or absurd.

7. State What Is Between the Lines.
What is not said? What is the writing on the wall? Fill in the blanks. Storytellers frequently use "you know that part of the story." What are you filling in? With what alternate way could you fill it in?

Source: Boje and Dennehy 1994: (Appendix A) 340

For more details regarding the Greenback Company, see Rosile and Boje, *Welcome to the Greenback Company: An Action Learning Organization* (Dubuque, IA: Kendall Hunt Publishers, 1996).

Main Features of Postmodern Pedagogy

The following section summarizes the main features of postmodern pedagogy, with examples of how the authors have incorporated the feature into the Greenback Company classroom-based organization.

1. The approach presents many sides to a given story. Students are invited to reflect upon their own experience in and out of the classroom. They are taught how to deconstruct their stories (see "Story Deconstruction Method" above), to reveal the hidden stories and marginalized voices.

2. The material shows several interpretations, including alternatives to dominant interpretations. For example, in the Greenback Company Department called "Balance," the students are told that "balance" means more than "financial profit"; it also is to include "spiritual profit."

3. The approach brings traditionally marginalized persons or groups to the center of attention. Community action projects get students to interact with people not normally included in their protected-university worlds. Projects to date have included working with homeless, gang members, AIDS victims, battered women's shelters, Big Brother/Sister/Littles, and other communities. When they encounter the "other," students oftentimes report "This has been the most valuable part of my university education."

4. The lesson plan encourages instructors and students to discuss the often hidden, formal and informal "rules of the game." We let the students know what parts of this are modernist. The syllabus says, "You will be graded on your value-added performances." We purport to use new pedagogic practices, but we still use the written examination and in the end rank students using numerical grading practices.

5. Students have opportunities to change the "rules of the game." During the guild phase, students use Robert's Rules of Order to make any changes they want in the syllabus, including voting out quizzes, changing deadlines, dropping assignments, changing the final into a non-event, and declaring off-days (company flex days).

6. Instructors encourage students to question the game itself, and self-reflexively examine the tendency to view everything as a game. In the AIDS project, "questioning the game" became "questioning the nature of university education" when the Jesuit university kicked the aids-benefit dance off campus because students intended to distribute condoms and condom-literature at the event.

7. The classroom is treated as the "real world." For example, one of the benefits of the Greenback Company design is real-world environmental turbulence and chaos that students must deal with directly. Robert became the champion of the tree-planting campaign. Before, during, and after some California fire storms he gave daily progress

reports. "We do not have the tree site yet." "No one can talk to me because of the fires." The fire storm finally ended and the students planted fifteen Oak and twenty California Bay trees.

8. Student peer evaluations are not forced into hierarchical patterns. Students (as in other courses) evaluate each other's group work. Some sections have dismissed the whole idea of performance assessment as "performativity." Others, taking a more Enlightened (Jameson calls it "high" modernism) stance, try to reform the empirical scale to capture student performance more equitably. In short, we can only be somewhat postmodern in the context of a modernist university.

9. The material is explicit about underlying values. For example, gender becomes a topic for discussion. Almost identical statements were made by several male students regarding their female CEO in one case, and by males regarding a female department head (of an all-male department) in several other cases. "Who does she think she is, telling us what to do? What is she going to do, sit around and watch us do the work?"

10. The methods encourage student discourse and critique. In one section, requirements in the syllabus about attendance were voted out during a guild meeting. However, during the modernist phase, with fewer and fewer people coming to class, department heads complained that communications were getting "fouled up" and they were having to call missing members to keep them informed. The executive committee responded by reimplementing the attendance requirement. When people still did not come to class, they began to deduct ten points a day from their grade. The point is that when students control parts of their classroom context, they engage in lots of discourse and critique to get things under control. This raises a more fundamental issue: Do postmodern methods really work when we have to resort to modernist controls?

11. The material addresses who stands to gain (or lose) politically and economically from the labels and categories being espoused. Just the label of "CEO" creates interesting classroom dynamics. On the first day in office the female CEO, Michele, was confronted by a male who pulled out a wad of money and offered to buy the stock of the company from the class members for $300. He said: "I think I can do a better job of running this company. I am willing to put my money where my mouth is." The Executive Committee bolted to the front of the room and one by one opposed the takeover attempt. There was a lot of yelling, and David had to step between the takeover artist and several female employees. "You are just upset because you lost the election." He replied, "You are not letting me express myself. I have a voice in this." David had many class discussions about this incident.

12. The approach reveals the essentializing and totalizing effects of labels and categories. The real-world encounters with the "other" (as described above) are the best antidote to stereotypical labels. "I didn't think a homeless person would be like that. He had many different jobs in his lifetime and had traveled all over the world. Even now, he spends part of his day doing volunteer work. Next week he is expecting to start a new job."

Experiencing Strategy at the University of Notre Dame

by James H. Davis and John G. Michel

> *For the free man there should be no element of slavery in learning. Enforced exercise does no harm to the body, but enforced learning will not stay in the mind. So avoid compulsion, and let your children's lessons take the form of play.*
>
> — Plato, *The Republic*, vii, 536

In the College of Business Administration at the University of Notre Dame we teach a course entitled Corporate Strategy. Our goal in this essay is to share our experiences in teaching this course and, most important, to discuss experiential and service-learning features we have introduced into the course.

For those already utilizing either experiential projects or service-learning in their courses, we offer our observations as an opportunity to compare and contrast implementation of these pedagogies. In our own evolution toward an experiential, service-learning course, we have benefited enormously from discussions, advice, and readings offered by colleagues both at Notre Dame and elsewhere; we hope through this paper to contribute to and expand such opportunities. The link between service-learning and experiential education in general is important and will be considered later in this study. For those not currently utilizing any form of experiential education in their courses, this article will identify both advantages and disadvantages of such an approach and provide a template of how it works in the Corporate Strategy course.

The paper is organized into six sections. The first section provides a brief overview of the Corporate Strategy course. The second describes the methodology used to implement the experiential and service-learning features of the course. The third offers guidelines for the management of successful projects. The fourth consists of a brief discussion of experiential projects and service-learning in the context of the Corporate Strategy course. The fifth provides specific examples and descriptions of experiential/service-learning projects sponsored by the course. The sixth presents limitations and challenges of experiential projects. A final section offers concluding comments and personal reflections.

A copy of the course syllabus is reproduced at the end of the paper.

The Corporate Strategy Course

Corporate Strategy is the capstone course in the business curriculum in both undergraduate and MBA programs throughout the country. As a capstone course, Corporate Strategy exposes students to models and literature from strategic management. Students are expected to integrate and apply tools learned in other functional courses such as finance, marketing, and operations to strategic decision making in organizations. The strategy course is designed to explore an organization's vision/mission, examine tools and models of organizational and environmental analysis, discuss the theory and practice of strategy formulation and implementation, and investigate outcome evaluation. The specific objectives of the course are to:

1. develop an awareness of the strategic decisions that organizations make and an ability to engage in strategic planning;

2. provide a conceptual framework for identifying, evaluating, and formulating strategies;

3. integrate material learned in the basic functional courses;

4. convey an understanding of the formal and informal processes involved in formulating and implementing strategies.

In order to meet these objectives, instructors traditionally divide class time between lecture/discussion and business cases. Lecture/discussion ensures coverage of strategy theory, models, and tools, whereas business case analysis is designed to link the classroom to business actualities by employing a problem-solving instructional mode (Barnes, Christensen, and Hansen 1994). Business cases give students an opportunity to apply theory and assume the role of a businessperson through rapid analysis, synthesis, and problem solving. Exposure to a wide variety of business cases helps students to recognize patterns in and solutions for many business situations.

While this traditional approach to Corporate Strategy utilizing lectures and cases has much to recommend it, it nonetheless possesses a major shortcoming in leaving students detached from the organization under study. Students have no contact with decision makers, no ability to influence decisions made or outcomes realized, and no interaction with critical organizational stakeholders.

To help diminish this sense of detachment, we have adopted an experiential learning approach that places students in contact with actual organizations and their corresponding decision makers, products, plants, employees, and communities. Experiential learning can be defined as learning activities that engage the learner directly in the phenomena being studied (Kendall and Associates 1986; Kolb 1984). Through this experience, students are able to see the consequences and human drama of significant business decisions and become more willing to invest in hard-won knowledge that is personally meaningful.

Because the primary purpose of this essay is to understand Notre Dame's experiential education exercise and its service-learning component, the remainder of the paper will be limited to a discussion of that feature of the course.

Experiential and Service-Learning Course Component

Experiential education in Corporate Strategy gives students an opportunity to exercise the skills of strategic analysis and business planning by evaluating an organization and its environment, formulating strategies to achieve organizational objectives, and writing a business plan. Students also have an opportunity to serve a wide variety of organizations throughout the world.

Client Organizations

Obtaining client organizations to participate in the experiential exercise is not difficult; in fact, more organizations seek participation than we can accommodate. The offer of free planning assistance is alluring to a great many organizations, in both the for-profit and the not-for-profit sectors. Furthermore, much of our ability to attract clients is due to an effective partnership with organizations that channel to us groups seeking assistance. These organizations include the Indiana Small Business Development Center, Service Corp of Retired Executives (SCORE), Notre Dame's Center for Social Concerns, and the State of Indiana Business Manufacturing Assistance (BMA). Former client organizations also refer projects, and we encourage our former students to submit projects from their employing organizations. In addition, we make sure that the dean is aware of our need for projects, since alumni and advisory council members are often looking for opportunities to establish more extensive contact with students. Finally, strategic planning projects are often available right on the campus. One very successful project analyzed the question of whether the new campus hotel should be a stand-alone hotel or an integrated hotel and conference center.

To enhance student learning, a pool of small and large, for-profit and not-for-profit, public and private, and domestic and international organizations is identified. Each context provides a different planning experience that enhances class discussion and student exposure. In our experience, students have considerable interest in selecting the projects. As an example, students enjoy contrasting planning in for- and not-for-profit organizations. In this respect, one can think of service-learning as a subset of experiential education.

Project Scope

Through simple questionnaires and interviews with organization leaders, we attempt to develop a profile for the scope of the planning project. For small organizations (fewer than 50), not-for-profits, and business start-ups, students are generally asked to write a full strategic plan. For large organizations, students may write a plan for a division or a product/service line. We have found that some screening is necessary at this stage to ensure a good fit between organizational expectations and student abilities. For example, some projects may have a heavier component of a particular function, such as finance, operations, marketing, etc., and students need to be aware of this prior to choosing projects. Likewise, it is important to screen out would-be clients that are too ambiguous and do not have a clear conceptualization of their business/service.

The scope and nature of planning projects often develop in unpredictable ways, and it is important to emphasize to students that the initial, "presenting" scope of their project may change somewhat. For example, once the students begin meeting with the organization, the scope of the project will evolve as new issues and areas of exploration crystallize. Still, we have found that it is important to encourage organizations to be as clear as possible in defining their business/service and need for planning. As experiential exercises, projects work best when the areas and issues of planning assistance and analysis are well specified.

Project Management

Team ownership of the students' planning project is critical. Rather than having the instructor assign teams to projects, students are permitted to select their own. This greatly enhances their sense of project "ownership." Project ownership is especially critical given the fact that the average student will put in approximately 75 project hours. In selecting their project, students learn to accept the consequences of their decision.

There is a fine line between monitoring and micromanaging. Students tend to take their projects very seriously and do not want to let down their client organization. This seems to be particularly true for students working with not-for-profits, because such students tend to develop a commitment to the values of their organization. If an instructor becomes too involved with a project, it can become his or hers. Therefore, we have learned to allow students to learn from their experience, while we still monitor their team's progress.

At mid term, the student teams present a situation audit that contains internal and external analyses of their client organization. This is an in-class presentation that does not include the client. Instructors invite a panel of retired executives (SCORE) to help facilitate the ensuing discussion. We have found these discussions to be open, honest, and lively, as teams get valuable input from peers, executives, and instructors. Enhancing the projects in this way midway through the semester significantly improves the end product.

Team memos are another way in which team progress is monitored. We ask teams to send biweekly memos to their client to report on their progress, and to copy memos for their instructor, so the instructor stays current with team progress or lack thereof. Finally, teams are asked to maintain a log of activities. Experience suggests that successful teams make frequent contact with their client, and the activity log helps document that contact while serving as a valuable project management tool.

Grading

Students earn grades on their final written strategic plan (application of theory and best practices in planning), management of the planning process, and their oral report to the client organization. Their client organization participates in the grading process by completing an evaluation of the team's professionalism and value added to the organization (see the "Strategy Consultation Assessment" reproduced at the end of the chapter).

To ensure an equitable allocation of grades among team members, each student fills out a peer evaluation form that assesses the relative contribution of each team member to the project (see "Strategy Consultation Project Peer Evaluation"). The activity log is used as a supplement to help substantiate any discrepancies.

Project Costs and Liability

At the beginning of every semester in which Corporate Strategy is taught, all cooperating organizations are invited to campus for an orientation. In this orientation, we describe the means and ends of the exercise. We explain that the teams are made up of students, and that the quality of their strategic recommendations must be appropriately judged by their organizations. While the end result of most plans enhances organizational performance and efficiency, some do fall short. The university itself is not responsible for the outcomes of student reports and recommendations.

All students sign confidentiality agreements with their partnering organization. They must keep all of their analyses, recommendations, and company-specific information confidential. We keep copies of their confidentiality agreements on file and send a copy to the cooperating organization.

Client organizations are requested to cover expenses incurred by teams during the planning process (e.g., long distance phone calls, surveys, faxes, copying costs, etc.) up to a maximum of $200. Given the consultation they will receive, most organizations willingly commit to cover student expenses. Any expenses in excess of $200 must receive additional approval from the participating organization.

Some organizations are willing to pay students for the services they render. This is not permitted. If students are paid, consideration occurs and an employment contract is initiated. With an employment contract come rights and liabilities that hurt the learning and service nature of the projects. Therefore, we do not accept payment for student services rendered. If a firm is insistent, we suggest that it make a contribution to the university, independent of the student project.

Guidelines for Successful Experiential Projects

Below we list some simple, practical guidelines and recommendations, based on our experience, to help increase the probability of realizing successful experiential projects in Corporate Strategy. Some of these items are mentioned above but are also listed here because they have been particularly helpful.

Orientation. Hold an orientation for all potential participating organizations. It is important to communicate the format of the projects, the requirements for client organizations, and appropriate client expectations. It is of great importance that client organizations be open and accessible to student teams. Indeed, projects work best when key organizational decision makers are accessible and even involved. Failure to attend the orientation is often a sign that a client organization will not be sufficiently accessible.

Expense Coverage. Require all participating organizations to commit to cover up to $200 in team expenses. Organizations unwilling to cover such modest expenses may not be seriously interested in receiving planning assistance. In the majority of cases, students' expenses are well below the $200 level.

Choice. Allow teams to choose their project from several alternatives. This increases student interest in and "ownership" of the project.

Memos. Every two weeks, require each team to submit a memo to both the client organization and the instructor describing recent activities. Successful projects require frequent contact between the team and the organization, and memos help ensure this takes place. We have found that memos are particularly important early in the term to ensure that a team has established contact with its organization and that potential problems can be identified quickly.

Midterm Report. Require a written and oral midterm report that addresses internal analysis, external analysis, and proposed deliverables. This important monitoring device offers an opportunity for the instructor to provide constructive feedback to the team while there still is time to take corrective action.

Involve Outside Executives as a Resource. We invite members of SCORE to the midterm presentations. Usually at least one member of SCORE has extensive experience in the specific area in question, and thus possesses contacts and firsthand knowledge. Moreover, we have found that the SCORE representatives ask challenging questions and enliven class discussion.

Client Attendance. Make it clear from the earliest stages that the client organization will be expected to attend the team's final presentation. This increases the commitment of both the team and the cooperating organization to put forth a good-faith effort. Additionally, offer flexibility in choosing the location of the final presentation. Some organizations prefer to have it on-site with their board of directors present. Finally, inform the client organization that if it desires, presentations can be given in a closed session to protect confidentiality.

Size Doesn't Matter. Successful projects are not dependent on organization size. What matters most is the organization's cooperation and the interest and availability of its key decision makers.

Experiential Learning and Service-Learning

Throughout this discussion, we have referred to the class projects as "experiential learning exercises." However, for many of the projects, there is an important service-learning component as well. As mentioned earlier, experiential learning pertains to direct engagement in the phenomena being studied. Service-learning involves active participation in service designed to meet the needs of the community, foster civic responsibility, enhance the academic curriculum, and provide an opportunity for reflection on the service experience (Kendall and Associates 1986). Weigert (1998: 5) argues that key elements of service-learning include meaningful student work that meets a community need, is well integrated with course objectives, and is evaluated accordingly.

Many of the projects used in the Corporate Strategy class come from not-for-profits and community service agencies — examples of which are offered in the following section. The work students engage in at these sites is meaningful both for them and for their clients. It helps to meet a community need in that these organizations benefit greatly from the planning assistance offered and generally do not have the resources to get such assistance elsewhere (Graham 1996). The learning is clearly well integrated with course objectives that center on the development and refinement of strategic planning skills. In addition, there is a strong interest in community service among Notre Dame students, and an opportunity to engage in strategic planning with community organizations contributes to project ownership and enthusiasm.

Reflection on the service-learning experience occurs in a number of ways. Students who work with community service agencies are usually exposed to the values of key decision makers in these organizations. Such organizations are, in fact, "value driven," and in order for students to offer meaningful planning assistance they must understand the values that drive the organization and its key players. Understanding an organization's key values and translating such understanding into practical action require careful reflection. For example, one team discovered the importance of the organization's values as it hotly debated the merits of establishing an endowment or using resources to redress current social ills; the organization was adamantly against an endowment. Opportunities for reflection also occur in the planning analysis phase as students consider the role that service organizations play in society and the social factors that give rise to the overwhelming need for their services. Additional chances for reflection on the experience include meetings between the team and the instructor, and open-ended comments on the peer evaluation form. Finally, whenever possible we attempt to schedule time immediately after the final presentation to allow for debriefing and a reflective exchange among the client, the students, and the instructor.

However, we believe that strategic planning assistance offered to a number of for-profit businesses also meets many of the criteria for service-learning. Many of the for-profits we work with are small, local businesses with meager resources and an absence of formal business training or education. For example, planning assistance for a small machine shop owned by Vietnamese immigrants is closely aligned with service-learning criteria.

Finally, to complete the picture, we must acknowledge that some of our client organizations are large, profitable firms. In such a case, the planning assistance offered, while experiential, does not meet the service-learning criterion of addressing community needs that would otherwise be unmet.

Project Examples

This section offers a description of three service-learning projects undertaken by students in the Corporate Strategy course.[1] Our intention here is to illustrate the types of organizations involved, the issues addressed, and the outcomes delivered.

St. John's Community Association

St. John's is an international, religiously affiliated, charitable organization whose mission is to offer assistance to the needy and suffering. The regional office, confronting a number of challenges, sought planning assistance to help address them. Some of the key challenges included an aging membership who were not being replenished, wide variance in the accomplishments of local chapters, and concerns about the organization's financial health.

A student team toured the facilities, met extensively with all the key players in the organization, and also met with other charitable organizations that could serve as a benchmark. Following this process, the team discovered that the membership was aging because no new members were being recruited at the local church level. The team offered several suggestions for events and activities that could be targeted to attract new and younger members from local area churches. In addition, the team discovered through interviews that potential new members did not come forward because, although they valued the mission of the organization, they were afraid to interact in person with the poor and needy. The team proposed a mentoring program so that new members could interact with the needy under the guidance of more experienced members until the newcomers felt sufficiently comfortable to interact on their own. The students also developed a plan for greater coordination among the organization's local chapters in an attempt to ensure that programs and tactics that were successful in one chapter were adopted elsewhere.

One of St. John's most important activities is its clothing operation, wherein it collects clothing from donors and gives that clothing to needy recipients or sells it in its thrift store. As part of the team's analysis, the team discovered that, in fact, only 55 percent of clothing was being given to the needy or sold in the store; the rest were being sold as rags to an organization that baled them and sold the bales to rag brokers. A detailed financial analysis demonstrated that it would be more profitable for St. John's to bale the rags itself and to sell them directly to a broker. Based on this analysis, St. John's contacted the organization to which it was selling the rags and immediately negotiated a 150-percent price increase. St. John's sells 280,000 pounds of rags a year, and this event had a significant effect on its annual budget.

South Bend, Indiana, Near Northwest Neighborhood Revitalization

The declining condition of neighborhoods in northwest South Bend has resulted in substantial financial and social losses. Declines in both human and financial capital have contributed significantly to the blighted state of the region. While symptoms of the problem are easily identified, the City of South Bend has had difficulty assessing the financial impact on the city of declining neighborhoods. The South Bend Heritage Foundation asked Notre Dame to help it identify the costs associated with urban decay by focusing on a particular U.S. census tract. The team was also asked to develop strategies that would revitalize the neighborhoods.

A team of students developed a framework for estimating the total cost to the community at large of the decay of a given area. This framework, applied to the Near Northwest Neighborhood, was designed as a template the South Bend Heritage Foundation could use for other neighborhoods suffering decay. The team also proposed a number of strategies and tactics that could help to revitalize the neighborhoods and hence reduce the costs of decay.

Homeless Shelter

The local homeless shelter has existed for more than 10 years and provides temporary room and board to indigent individuals and families. The shelter has a national reputation for quality service. It approached Notre Dame for help in developing a plan to establish a business that could provide operating revenue as well as job training for its guests.

A student team developed a comprehensive business plan that outlined the vision and objectives of such a business. The students defined how the business would fit into the center's current operations. Finally, the team described three alternative businesses that would fit into the center's mission and would help it achieve its objectives. The plan included both broad strategies and specific implementation tactics.

Limitations and Challenges of Experiential Projects

Experiential projects have become an important component of the Corporate Strategy course, and they greatly expand opportunities for students to apply, in a meaningful way, the theory and techniques they have learned. While the benefits of such an exercise are substantial, a number of costs must also be acknowledged and taken into consideration. First is instructor responsibilities to line up projects, coordinate an orientation, and act as a liaison among the partnering units. These activities involve a significant commitment of instructor time. Fortunately, most of this commitment occurs early in the semester, and, with sufficient planning, the instructor can comfortably manage responsibilities arising in the later half of the term.

To some degree, no matter what the instructor does, some projects work well and others do not. This is, of course, no different from any other academic or instructional activity. However, the consequences for experiential exercises are somewhat higher because of the involvement of external parties. Thus, an instructor must be willing to risk part of his or her reputation capital and the institution's when projects fail to live up to their promise.

Finally, although it is important that the instructor avoid micromanaging student projects, at times he or she must become more heavily involved. This can occur when a rift develops between a team and a client, when issues of confidentiality arise, or when strife within a team threatens to derail its work. Such circumstances do not occur often, but they do occur, and an instructor should be prepared to intervene when they do.

Conclusion

This essay has described the purpose and method of the experiential, service-learning projects in the Corporate Strategy course at Notre Dame. Over the past several years, the centrality of the experiential exercises in the course has increased as the value of such experiences as effective, complementary learning vehicles has become clearer. Lecture, discussion, and case analysis all play important roles in the course; however, only the strategy project places students in contact with real organizations and real stakeholders.

Contrasting projects focused on not-for-profit organizations with those focused on successful, for-profit businesses provides for a tremendous learning opportunity for students. Students quickly see that there are subtle differences in the way they must apply their analytical tools depending on the planning context. Students working in a service-learning environment typically work with people who have a passion for the values, vision, and mission of their organization but may lack operational and "business" skills. Alternatively, students working in large, for-profit businesses typically work with people who have excellent operational and business skills but at times can lack a broader vision that encompasses multiple stakeholders. It is easy for service-learning students to become "value committed" to their projects while the other students are "continuance committed" to theirs (Mayer and Schoorman 1992). This contrast in experiences, approaches to planning, and final products adds significantly to student learning: Students leave the class with a clearer understanding of how context affects strategic planning.

The experiential exercise described here is the ideal project for the capstone course in a business curriculum. No other learning vehicle offers such potential for students' analyses and recommendations to be studied, evaluated, discussed, and acted upon by key decision makers.

Note

1. Names were changed to protect the privacy and confidentiality of the partnering organizations.

References

Barnes, L.B., C.R. Christensen, and A.J. Hansen. (1994). *Teaching and the Case Method.* Boston, MA: Harvard Business School Press.

Graham, J.W. (1996). "Business Plan Proposals for Inner-City Neighborhoods: A Strategic Management Assignment for MBA Students at Loyola University–Chicago." *Journal of Business Ethics* 15(1): 87-94.

Kendall, J., and Associates. (1986). *Strengthening Experiential Education Within Your Institution.* Raleigh, NC: National Society for Internships and Experiential Education.

Kolb, D.A. (1984). *Experiential Learning: Experience as the Source of Learning and Development.* Englewood Cliffs, NJ: Prentice-Hall.

Mayer, R.C., and R.D. Schoorman. (1992). "Predicting Participation and Production Outcomes Through a Two-Dimensional Model of Organizational Commitment." *Academy of Management Journal* 35: 671-684.

Weigert, K.M. (Spring 1998). "Academic Service-Learning: Its Meaning and Relevance." In *Academic Service-Learning: A Pedagogy of Action and Reflection,* edited by R.A. Rhodes and J.P.F. Howard, pp. 3-10. San Francisco, CA: Jossey-Bass.

Strategy Consultation Assessment

Organization Name: _____

Name: _____ Date:_____

Please help me determine the success of the team of students working with you this semester, providing consulting and planning assistance. Circle the appropriate number to indicate your evaluation of service provided by the student team.

	Strongly Agree	Agree	Undecided	Disagree	Strongly Disagree
1. We thought of the students in the same way we would professional business consultants.					
	1	2	3	4	5
2. The student team correctly identified the problems our business was having at the time.					
	1	2	3	4	5
3. When students met with me or my staff, they were well prepared and asked good questions.					
	1	2	3	4	5
4. Students made an appropriate number of contacts with me and my staff.					
	1	2	3	4	5
5. The student team made useful recommendations for our business.					
	1	2	3	4	5
6. The analysis and recommendations offered by the team were thorough, detailed, and well documented.					
	1	2	3	4	5
7. My overall assessment of the quality of this strategy project is very high.					
	1	2	3	4	5

COMMENTS:

Strategy Consultation Project Peer Evaluation

Name: _____

Project: _____

1. Please evaluate each member of your team (including yourself) on the items listed below. Utilize a scale from 1 to 5 where:

    5=excellent   4=good   3=satisfactory   2=needs improvement   1=unacceptable.

	Team Member				
Preparation for group meetings					
Cooperativeness, enthusiasm, willingness to work					
Leadership and initiative					
Creativity and inventiveness of ideas					
Quality of analysis					
Performance of assigned responsibilities					

2. Assume the team has been awarded a $10,000 bonus. Allocate this bonus among the team members based on their relative contribution to the project.

Team Member Name	**Bonus**
_____	_____
_____	_____
_____	_____
_____	_____

Additional Comments:

CORPORATE STRATEGY AND PLANNING
MGT 519
Spring 1998

Dr. Jim Davis
229 College of Business
631-8614

Office Hours: T, Th   4:00-5:00
          By Appointment

TEXTS: Package of Readings and Cases at Lafortune Copy Shop

Objectives

This course is intended to provide a view of managerial strategy that integrates the knowledge of the functional areas of business taught in MBA curriculum. The objectives of the course are to:

1. To develop an awareness of the strategic decisions that organizations make and an ability to engage in strategic planning.
2. To provide a conceptual framework for identifying, evaluating, and formulating strategies.
3. To integrate material learned in the basic functional courses.
4. To convey an understanding of the formal and informal processes involved in formulating and implementing strategies.

Approximate Grade Breakdown

Situational Analysis	15%
Business Plan	25%
Examination I	15%
Examination II	15%
Case Analysis	10%
Internal Case Competition	10%
Participation	10%

Description of Class Components

Participation

The following format is used to award points for class participation. Positive points are given not for restatement of facts in the case nor for statements of the obvious. They are presented for significant statements that lend significant insight to the situation. The assignment of these points is obviously subjective on the part of the instructor. No more than three points will be assigned on any one day to any one person. Since attendance is so critical to learning in a discussion class such as this, negative participation points will be assigned for class absence *in excess of two times*. The two times are a "free day" meant to accommodate illness, interviewing trips, etc. All business students are expected to be able to freely discuss business situations, especially in a strategic environment where there is often no one "correct" answer. This is a skill that most business occupations have as an understood expectation.

Finally, every team is required to send a memo at least every two weeks to the firm in the community it is working with. A duplicate of the memo must also be turned in to me. I will read the memos and keep them on file as a measure of your continuing contact with your organization.

Case Competition: Analysis and Presentation

The class will be divided into groups of four students for case analysis and presentation. Each group will participate in the Notre Dame Case competition. During this week long event, each team will be assigned to prepare a thorough analysis of one business case. You will be required to submit a five page written report (described below) and a hard copy of presentation slides. Six teams will be selected as finalists and present their analysis on Friday, February 28. Of these six teams one will be selected to represent Notre Dame at its annual case competition. The winning team will receive a $400 cash award. Other finalists will receive $200 cash rewards..

The oral presentation must demonstrate the depth of your analysis and professionalism of your team. The presentation should last a maximum of 30 minutes. Feel free to bring any information you believe applies to the case into the discussion (from sources outside the text and this class if necessary). Use overheads, PowerPoint, Harvard Graphics, videos, or any other medium which may support your claims, contentions, and conclusions.

Your analysis should not be a book report of the written case from the text! Assume that the reader is familiar with the case. Much of your grade comes from the depth of your analysis and your ability to professionally defend your decisions. This is easiest done where the presentation and analysis has depth and quality.

Format for Executive Summary

The executive summary typically consists of four parts. The four parts are described in some detail below. The summary must be typewritten (dot matrix word processing is acceptable, double spaced on standard 8 1/2 by 11 white paper with 1 inch margins all around each page). The executive summary should not exceed 5 pages exclusive of exhibits. The written case analysis is due the day your group presentation. NO EXECUTIVE SUMMARY WILL BE ACCEPTED LATE. Following the introduction (which includes the problem statement/central issues), the four major parts that must be covered in the analysis include:

1. Industry Analysis: Sets the firms in the context of its industrial environment, Customer segments are identified, competitive rivalry is discussed and potential sources of competitive advantage are explored. Major trends analysis should be done to identify opportunities and constraints presented by the social and political environment of the firm. This includes analysis of social attitudes and regulatory trends that may impinge on the firm. Socio-Political Analysis should identify the dynamics of the industry to anticipate the industry structure, threats and opportunities that the firm will face over the planning horizon. Uncertainties are explicitly addressed so that the need for market research can be assessed and strategies for flexibility or hedging can be evaluated.

2. Firm Analysis: Establishes an overview of the firm from the points of view of the major functional areas of business: operations, marketing, accounting, finance and human resource management.

3. Central Issue(s) Identification and Strategy Formulation: presents to the client firm a range of strategic options for consideration. Each option's advantages and disadvantages are discussed, and the ease or difficulty of implementation is evaluated in broad strokes. One particular strategy is recommended, though this strategy may identify contingencies that call for its modification or abandonment as uncertainties in the industry are resolved over time.

4. Tactics and Implementation: describes the policies and programs by which the recommended strategy can be put in place. A timeline of more detailed activities is given for the first year and in broad strokes for the second to fifth years. Where possible, budgets are developed and staffing recommendations are offered.

Because you are required to limit your summary to **5 (five)** pages, you must decide how much emphasis each of the four components should receive. While all four must receive some consideration, special attention should be given to the components that are critical to the case! Special consideration should always be given to strategy formulation and implementation. Specific guidelines for each of the of the parts can be found at the conclusion of the discussion of course requirements.

Planning Practicum

The purpose of the strategic analysis is to exercise the skills of strategic analysis and business planning by evaluating a firm and its environment, formulating strategies and writing a business plan. There are three uses of this skill.

1. As a management consultant, one would have to formulate a strategic plan and construct a schedule for implementing and controlling it. Most of the firms that we will be working with are asking for this type of assistance. Your team may write a business plan from the corporate level (product/service portfolio and vision), the business level (planning for a single product or service) or functional level (writing a marketing, management information system, human resources financial unit plan). The rhetoric of the plan must match the context. A successful consultation team will be very organized and immerse itself in the business.

2. A second type of planning occurs from the perspective of an analyst. As a fundamental analyst at an investment banking firm or on the "corporate development" staff of a large firm, one would have to use publicly available information to identify the best strategy and then use that information to predict the financial performance of the firm under study and evaluate the firm as a candidate for investment (or acquisition). In this second use, the strategist carries the analysis into a rigorous financial evaluation of the firm rather than into an implementation plan.

3. A third type of planning that a team may perform is for an entrepreneur. The entrepreneur may be a member of the team (i.e., the project may come from your group) or you may be asked to work with an entrepreneur who has asked for planning assistance. Typically, your team will write a plan so that the entrepreneur can get funding from venture capitalists, banks, the state or some other source. Thus, the plan must accurately describe the product/service, markets, growth potential, anticipated cash flow (cash flow proforma), etc. This type of planning is often the most difficult due to the difficulty in obtaining meaningful market data. The rhetoric of the plan must match the requirements of the funding target(s).

Experience suggests that successful teams make frequent contact with their cooperating company. Managing your project is critical. You should start early and constantly monitor your progress. Last minute planning usually ends in disastrous outcomes! Your final project MUST INCLUDE A LOG OF ACTIVITY. You should design a table that has the following information:

Date	Time	Activity	Team Member(s)

You must determine how your team's tasks are assigned. Because of the work load it is unwise to expect to do everything together. You MUST work as a team and delegate tasks. You must view the team projects as a portfolio of tasks to be accomplished. While these tasks are overwhelming for an individual, they can be accomplished if your team is appropriately managed! Still, the possibility exists that a team member may shirk his/her responsibilities. To ensure that each team member gets the recognition they earn for your team's performance you will be asked to assess each team members contribution at the end of the semester. This is done by dividing a "bonus" of $10,000 among the other team members. The sum of the assignments to each participant, as a fraction of $10,000, will be multiplied by your group's score to yield the individual's score for this 40% of one' grade. (The log will be used to substantiate any indescrepicies).

Roughly speaking, the Practicum project should include the same sections as the written case report described above. These include:
   1. Industry Analysis
   2. Firm Analysis
   3. Central Issue Identification and Strategy Formulation
   4. Tactics/Implementation or Financial Evaluation

The format of the final report must be typed using double spacing on standard 8 1/2 by 11 inch white paper. Appendices may be located at the end of each section but number them 1-1, 1-2, 2-1,

2-2, 2-3, etc. according to the section location. Your references may also appear at the end of each section if you do not want to sort them all and place them at the end of the report.

It is recommended that you organize the final report under section headings and subheadings as needed.

The final written report will be graded primarily on its **content**. Grading will also consider the report's **organization** (sequence of ideas), **balance** (evidence of comparable degree of analysis in sections of comparable importance), and **style** (English usage, grammar and punctuation). You will be required to provide a copy of the report to the company.

In addition to the written report each consultation team will prepare and present a 20 minute presentation to the class and company representatives at the end of the course. This presentation will be followed by 10 minutes of discussion and questions.

Situation Analysis

As part of the strategic analysis above each group will present a fifteen minute situation analysis to the class which will include internal and external analyses of their cooperating firm. The report occurs around mid-term and should demonstrate the **depth and breadth of the team's understanding of the firm, its industry and environment and the issues that will be addressed in the plan.** The analysis may include, but is not limited to, an examination of the firm's strengths and weaknesses and opportunities and threats, competitor analysis, exploration of major environmental trends, firm workforce analysis, cultural analysis, market analysis, financial analysis, etc. A report must be written as part of this assignment. There is no page requirement or limitation for this part of the analysis.

Time Table

Jan. 13	Strategy Introduction	Henderson, B.D. 1989. "The Origin of Strategy." Harvard Business Review. November-December. 139-143.
Jan. 15	Strategy Introduction	Hamel, G. and Prahalad, C.K. 1989. Strategic Intent. Harvard Business Review. May-June. 63-76.
		Hamel, G. and Prahalad, C.K. 1994. Competing for the Future. Harvard Business Review. July-August. 122-128.
Jan. 20	CASE:	Dakotah, Inc. Case Analysis
Jan. 22	Strategic Thinking	Bartlett, C.A. and Ghoshal, S. 1994. Changing the Role of Top Management: Beyond Strategy to Purpose. Harvard Business Review. November-December. 79-88.

Jan. 27	CASE:	Frito-Lay, Inc.: A Strategic Transition--1980-1986 (Harvard Business Case: 9-194-107)
Jan. 29	Industry Analysis	Hambrick, D.C. Environmental Scanning and Organizational Strategy. Strategic Management Journal. 3. 159-174.
		Barney, J.B. Types of Competition and the Thoery of Strategy: Toward an Integrative Framework. Academy of Management Review. 11(4). 791-800.
Feb. 3	Industry Analysis	Collis, D. and Ghemawat, P. Industry Analysis: Understanding Industry Structure and Dynamics. in Fahey and Randall (eds). The Portable MBA in Strategy. New York: John Wiley & Sons, Inc.
Feb. 5	CASE:	Paper Machinery Industry (Harvard Business Case: 383-185
Feb. 10	Situational Analysis	Rumelt, R.P. 1991. How Much does Industry Matter? Strategic Management Journal. 12. 167-185.
		Hitt, M.A., Ireland, R.D. and Hoskisson, R.E. 1995. The Internal Environment: Resources, Capabilities, and Core Competencies. Strategic Management. Chapter 3. New York: West Publishing Company. 64-96.
Feb 12	Situational Analysis	Prahalad, C.K. and Hamel, G. 1990. The Core Competence of the Corporation. Harvard Business Review. May-June. 79-87.
	Strategy Formulation	Mintzberg, H (1991) "Strategy Formation: Schools of Thought," in J W Fredrickson, (ed.) Perspectives on Strategic Management, New York: Harper Business, 105-235
		Barney, J. 1991. Firm Resources and Sustained Competitive Advantage. Journal of Management. 17(1). 99-120.
Feb. 17	CASE:	Dominion Engineering Works (Harvard Business Case: 383-184)
Feb. 19	CASE:	Circus Enterprises, Inc. 1994

Feb. 20-23 Internal Case Competition
• Feb 20, 9:00a.m. case pick-up, MBA offices
• Feb 23, executive summary and slides by 12:00, MBA offices

Feb. 24 Internal Case Competition

Feb. 26	Implementation	Bourgeois, III.L.J., Brodwin, D.R. 1984. Strategic Implementation: Five Approaches to an Elusive Phenomenon. Strategic Management Journal. 5. 241-264. Thompson A., and Strickland, A. Implementing Strategy: Commitment, Culture, and Leadership. Strategic Management. Chapter 10. Boston, Irwin.

Feb. 27   Finalist Presentations 9:00 - 1:00
  • Required to attend two presentations

Mar. 3	CASE:	Cleveland Twist Drill A and B Abridged (Harvard Business Case 9-391-024)

Mar. 5   Midterm Examination

Mar. 10-12   Spring Break

Mar. 17   Situation Analysis
           Presentation
  • ASSIGNMENT: Industry/Situational Analyses Due

Mar. 19   Situation Analysis
           Presentation
  • ASSIGNMENT: Industry/Situational Analyses Due

Mar. 24   Situation Analysis
           Presentation
  • ASSIGNMENT:
  • Industry/Situational Analyses Due

Mar. 26	The learning organization	CEO FROM LEAP ADVERTISING Senge, P. 1990. The Fifth Discipline. Chapter 1-4. New York: Double Day. Nonaka, I. The Knowledge-Creating Company. Harvard Business Review. November-December. 96-104.
Mar. 31	The learning organization	Bartlett, C.A. and Ghoshal, S. 1995. Changing the Role of Top management: Beyond Systems to People. Harvard Business Review. May-June. 132-142 Quinn, J. B. Large-Scale Innovation: Managing Chaos. in McCarthy, Minichiello, and Curran (eds). Business Policy and Strategy. Homewood, Ill: Irwin. 96-104.
Apr. 2	CASE:	CEO from BRITE HORIZONS

General Motors' Asian Alliances (Harvard Business Case 9-388-094)

Apr. 7 GROUP DAY>>>> CHICAGO PRESENTATION

Diversification & Acquisition Hitt, M.A., Ireland, R.D. and Hoskisson, R.E. 1995. Corporate-Level Strategy. Strategic Management. Chapter 6. New York: West Publishing Company. 160-191.

Ramanujam, V. and Varadarajan, P. 1989. Research on Corporate Diversification: A Synthesis. Strategic Management Journal. 10. 523-551.

Apr. 9 CASE: Walt Disney Co. 1994 (Harvard Business Case 9-395-109)

Walt Disney Co. 1995 (Harvard Business Case 9-796-149)

Apr. 14 General Motors' Asian Alliances (Harvard Business Case 9-388-094)

Strategic Alliances Hamel, G. Doz, Y. and Prahalad, C.K. 1995. Collaborate with Your Competitors - and Win. In Bartlett, C.A. and Ghoshal, S. (eds). Transnational Management. Chicago: Irwin. 459-467.

Contractor, F.J. and Lorange, P. 1988. Why Should Firms Cooperate? The Strategy and Economics Basis for Cooperative Ventures. in Contractor and Lorange (eds) Cooperative Strategies in International Business. New York: Lexington Books. 1-28.

Apr. 16 CASE: Guardian Glass (Harvard Business Case 9-292-083)

Apr. 21 CASE: Giddings & Lewis: In Search of the Cutting Edge (Harvard Business Case 9-495-018)

Apr. 23 Practicum Report

Apr. 28 Practicum Report

Apr. 30 Practicum Report

Exam II (Final)

Teaching Leadership and Management Through Service-Learning

by Gaylen N. Chandler

Starting in 1994, the Management Department at Utah State University began to integrate service-learning into its entry-level management course. This course, Managing Organizations and People, is specifically designed to integrate conceptual knowledge with real experience and opportunity to lead and manage a project. It is required for all College of Business majors at the university and for several other majors and minors in other departments. Most students take the course in their junior year, with eight or nine sections being offered during a typical academic year. The class meets twice a week in two-hour time blocks for the duration of a 10-week quarter with an average class size of about 80 students. For about half of these students, the course represents their only exposure to management concepts.

Because of the broad mix of backgrounds students bring to the class, it focuses on the knowledge and skills required of individuals who find themselves in any kind of managerial or leadership position. It then seeks to provide students with opportunities to participate in a service-learning experience that allows them to practice key course concepts. One of the course texts, *The Leadership Challenge* (Kouzes and Posner 1995), identifies five key leadership imperatives: (1) challenge the process, (2) inspire a shared vision, (3) enable others to act, (4) model the way, and (5) encourage the heart.

This framework allows us to teach and practice key leadership skills. Students have opportunities to develop and communicate vision, recruit others, use motivational techniques and reward systems, provide feedback on performance, administer discipline, and celebrate accomplishments as they work in conjunction with community nonprofit or public service agencies such as Kiwanis, community food pantries, schools, the Make-A-Wish Foundation, chambers of commerce, the Forest Service, and local city governments. These real and meaningful projects seem to capture student interest and lead to increased levels of participation while at the same time producing positive service outcomes for client organizations and the community.

Course Structure

As mentioned above, the course is structured around the five basic leadership principles postulated by Kouzes and Posner (1995). Students have an opportunity to learn about the principles through reading the text, reading a variety of additional materials from the popular and business press, and engaging in classroom discussion. However, they learn to develop leadership skills by participating in a leadership project.

Challenging the Process

As instructors, we ourselves "challenged the process" by completely changing the way we teach Managing Organizations and People. The major component of our redesign involved inclusion of leadership projects as a part of the curriculum. Over time, these leadership projects have evolved to become substantial undertakings in which students have an opportunity to work in teams and practice leadership skills while rendering community service. We expect our students to "challenge the process" by contacting a variety of potential client organizations and identifying a pressing unmet need. The best projects result when students identify a clear need in the local community. Roughly half the projects have been oriented toward fundraising for a cause. For example, student teams have organized golf tournaments, 5K runs, benefit concerts, and other fundraising activities to benefit local schools, libraries, and nonprofit organizations. The other half have involved a variety of community service projects in which students have organized groups of volunteers to participate in activities such as park and National Forest cleanups and city and neighborhood improvement projects.

Students are told to remember the following guidelines as they select service opportunities. Their projects must:
- meet a real and pressing community need
- have a meaningful impact on the university, local community, and team members
- increase experience and effectiveness in working with groups
- improve skills related to organizing and managing people
- contribute to credentials for the job market, for graduate school, or for promotion
- enhance the reputation of Utah State University, its business school, and its students
- avoid potential liability problems
- go beyond community service–related responsibilities; i.e., if a student currently holds a leadership position in a fraternity, sorority, informal student group, or at work, the leadership project must go beyond his or her normal activities
- use course concepts such as motivation, teamwork, and communication.

A minimum of six and a maximum of 12 students are involved in each project. A day is scheduled early in the quarter when students discuss their ideas with the instructor, and a leadership project proposal is due at the end of the second week of class. The proposal must state whom the project will benefit, explain why the project is worthwhile, describe its objectives and goals as well as its short-term and long-term benefits, and provide a detailed time line for its accomplishment.

Great care is taken to ensure that academic learning results from the service. In conjunction with the project, students are responsible for a substantial amount of more traditional academic coursework. During the first two weeks of the quarter, they read the first two chapters of Kouzes and Posner (1995), which deal with challenging the process. They also read recent articles from the popular press (Kiechel 1994; Kotter 1992; O'Reilly 1994) that discuss the challenges students will face in the new workplace and strongly reinforce the importance of learning leadership and self-reliance. Weekly quizzes and discussions help ensure that students are current in the reading and academic exercises.

Inspiring a Shared Vision

Students are then given an opportunity to share their visions. Not only is it important for them to have a shared commitment within their groups; they must also reach beyond their groups to involve nongroup members. Many groups recruit dozens of additional individuals to help them in accomplishing their leadership projects. The importance of vision is emphasized. Students work in class in their groups to prepare vision statements for their projects that can be used to unify their groups as well as to recruit additional, outside support. Students also interact closely with client organizations to ensure that their project visions align closely with the visions and missions of their partner organizations. Thus, the importance of establishing and communicating a vision is established as far more than just an academic exercise; students gain real experience in establishing and sharing their visions as they strive to make things happen in the community.

Student groups must also share their visions with students who are not members of their groups. Groups prepare five-minute presentations designed to do this. After each presentation, the class spends five to 10 minutes discussing the presentation. It discusses those parts that most helped communicate the vision clearly and also reviews the statements, behaviors, or actions that did not communicate effectively. Thus, even before the groups go out to recruit community support, they have had an opportunity to polish their vision presentations.

Enabling Others to Act

This portion of the course deals with two major issues: first, group empowerment, and second, enabling and encouraging individuals who are not class members to act. Topics for discussion include group dynamics and delegation. The students read chapters from Kouzes and Posner (1995) about enlisting the support of others, fostering collaboration, and strengthening others by sharing power and information. The class discusses motivational theories (goal setting, expectancy theory, and equity theory) and how these theories can be applied to getting things done. Frequently, students bring to class examples of problems they are confronting with their projects. In such cases, the class has real-time applications for the theories it is discussing. Often, other students have confronted similar problems and have useful insights about how theory can be applied to a specific situation.

The students' need to seek to enlist support from individuals in the community provides a good springboard for discussing basic recruitment and selection principles. Students read several articles about preemployment testing and interviewing. In-class exercises include a discussion of interviewing techniques. Students are taught how to identify key work competencies and use behavioral-based interviewing practices. Role plays or short case scenarios are also used to teach important concepts. This section of the course is not as tightly linked to the community-based projects, since in most cases groups are, in fact, disposed to include whoever is willing to participate. However, the exercises reiterate the importance of recruiting able and reliable people.

The process of working in a group to accomplish a meaningful objective also provides opportunities to discuss mechanisms for defining acceptable group behaviors. Group members are instructed in how to design a performance management process that will enable them to provide clear feedback to other group members. They read about 360-degree feedback and performance management models, and are taught how to develop behaviorally anchored rating scales that capture the most important dimensions of group member performance. In this exercise, students work together in their groups to develop a behaviorally anchored rating scale. The completed scales are then handed in as a homework assignment. When students write their final project reports, they include a summary of their ratings of all other group members. Thus, the class not only reads about 360-degree feedback but also practices it. This exercise, along with the vision-building exercise completed earlier in the term, helps students to define clearly expected behaviors for all group members. Client organizations are also asked to provide feedback about team accomplishments and behavior.

By this point, students are well into their projects. Since most groups encounter some difficulties, the class reads an article about bouncing back after failure (Sellers 1995). Students discuss specific failures they have encountered on their projects and jobs, as well as strategies for "bouncing back." Some very interesting projects have emerged after an initial plan has failed and contingency plans have had to be devised and put into effect. For example, one group set out to raise funds to benefit the Disability Resource Center on campus. After an initial fundraising plan failed to produce intended results, the group revisited and redefined the problem. The DRC had been paying individuals to accompany disabled students to class and assist them in taking notes. The group was able to develop a system that allowed the DRC to recruit students who were already attending relevant classes to provide notes to DRC clients as an unpaid service. Thus, although the initial plan produced minimal results, the "bouncing back" plan allowed the DRC to save about $2,000 each quarter since the plan's implementation more than two years ago.

Several class periods are spent discussing how to handle problem behavior. Students are taught specific techniques for giving feedback. The class develops a performance analysis model in which students are taught to diagnose and respond to the *causes* of dysfunctional behavior and not the *symptoms*. Positive and punitive discipline procedures are compared and contrasted. Students are taught techniques for using positive discipline procedures to eliminate negative group behaviors. They also discuss a variety of short performance cases, analyze problem behaviors, and propose positive solutions. Of special importance is the problem of dealing with free riders in work groups.

Not all groups get hands-on practice with disciplinary procedures, but in some groups there are students who do not shoulder their share of the workload. Thus, students are empowered to dismiss group members who do not perform and who fail to respond to the group's positive disciplinary procedures. Dismissed students receive no score for the project unless they make specific arrangements to complete an alternative project that is acceptable to the instructor. For example, one student going through divorce proceedings was unable to meet group expectations. The group used positive procedures to uncover the real causes of the student's inadequate performance. The group worked out some alternative ways the individual could contribute to the group with more flexible scheduling. In a few cases, students have not responded to positive procedures and have failed the course as a result of their failure to contribute positively to a group effort.

Modeling the Way

Students read the chapters in Kouzes and Posner (1995) about setting an example by keeping commitments and achieving small wins to build commitment to action. By this point in the quarter, they are well into their projects, and these strongly reinforce the importance of setting a good example and following through. For example, one group was raising money for a Children's Justice Center by selling car-wash tokens. Sales were going slowly until one group member sold 500 tokens to one organization to be used to signal appreciation for a job well done. Other group members, encouraged by this success, contacted several other organizations, some of which also bought substantial numbers of tokens. Individual example and small wins allowed the group to surpass its own initial fundraising objectives.

Encouraging the Heart

Students are taught that celebrations are a good way to help gain and maintain momentum. They are encouraged to celebrate significant achievements as they seek to complete their projects. The final project report is also intended as a celebration. The last week of class is reserved for individual groups to talk about what they have done. Refreshments are provided in class during this last week, and students are encouraged to invite representatives from client organizations to be part of the celebration. Videotapes, Power Point presentations, and testimonials from clients are often part of these final reports.

Results

During the past two years, students in Managing Organizations and People classes have raised in excess of $120,000 for a variety of clients. In addition, they have provided thousands of service hours to local schools, communities, and service agencies. As two key measures of project success, we look at the amount of money raised and the number of service hours generated by nongroup members. Many group projects raise in excess of $2,000. Many service-oriented projects generate more than 150 hours of service by nongroup members. The table *opposite* lists some sample results.

Assessment and Grading

Both project-oriented and classroom-oriented activities are assessed and graded. The course is currently taught in a 10-week quarter system. During the quarter, a 10- or 15-question quiz is given each week. Quizzes focus on the reading materials and key concepts we have discussed in class. In addition, there are three graded writing assignments. The first assignment is the project proposal. This is a group assignment with only one proposal submitted per group. The second assignment is the group vision statement exercise discussed above. The third is a final version of the behaviorally anchored rating scales developed by each group to clarify expected behaviors and rate individual group member performance. Quizzes and writing assignments constitute 200 of the total 300 points available. The remaining 100 points

Sample projects from my Managing Organizations and People

Project	Client	Outcome
Golf Tournament to raise funds for a community library	Providence/River Heights Library	$9,000
Taste-test contest sponsored by Nabisco for "newton" flavors in competition for a $2,500 prize from Nabisco	City of Newton	$2,500
Book drive and fundraising to better supply a middle school library	Adele C. Young Middle School, Brigham City	2,000 books and $2,000
Organize volunteers for the campus disability center	Utah State University Disability Resource Center	an estimated $2,000 saved each quarter
Organize volunteers to inspect and document sidewalk damage in the City of Logan	City of Logan	140 service hours
Gathering paper towels, diapers and other goods for the food pantry	Cache Community Food Pantry	$1,600 worth of nonfood items
Complete 20 "bird houses" to be auctioned as a fund-raiser	Make a Wish Foundation	$6,000 auction value
Acquire computers for Headstart program	Head Start	10 computers, several books
Organize 5k fun run	Cache Community Health Clinic	$859
Clean up park and paint 50 picnic tables at Willow Park	City of Logan	210 service hours
Raise seed money for a skate park in Brigham City	Brigham City	$6,000
Acquire a piano for the Hyde Park civic center	City of Hyde Park	$15,000 commitment
Organize volunteers to document street light failures in the City of Logan	City of Logan	138 service hours
Acquire a defibrilator for the City of Mendon first response unit	City of Mendon fire department	$2,250
Develop a basketball area in a community park	City of Nibley	180 service hours

come from the group projects, project reports, and in-class presentations. Part of the group evaluation is based on measurable components such as nongroup service hours generated and money raised. The professionalism of the project report and the in-class project presentation is also taken into account. As part of the final project report, each student writes an essay that describes what he or she has learned with respect to the management and leadership principles discussed in the course. Students are required to provide critical incidents from their project experience to demonstrate how each leadership principle has been applied in their respective groups.

Student Reactions

Historically, student teaching evaluations for Managing Organizations and People were significantly below departmental averages. However, since changing the course to a service-learning format, ratings have gradually improved. This past year's evaluations for service-learning sections are now above departmental averages. However, it is important to note that this change did not occur immediately. The evaluations for the first sections taught with a service-learning component were no better than those for their predecessors. In fact, during the first few iterations of the new format, there was a good deal of student complaining. They complained about the workload's being too high, about subjectivity in grading projects, and about the difficulty of working beyond the confines of comfort. However, as the course's reputation grew, students began coming to the instructor to discuss project ideas even before the quarter started. Indeed, several organizations in the community began inviting students to come and talk to them about potential projects. Now that the course's expectation of a leadership project has been established, complaints have greatly diminished. The following comments come from teaching evaluations for Spring 1998:

- "The leadership project made this class very challenging, but also a lot of fun. Practical learning helped with the theoretical topics discussed."
- "I felt that the projects done in this course were excellent learning opportunities."
- "I felt that the content of this course is relevant to many situations I've encountered in leadership positions. This is a worthwhile class, and I have learned a lot."
- "I liked the leadership project. It gave us a chance to actually lead."
- "The use of class discussion and group projects to learn ideas was great."
- "Good chance to learn and challenge yourself."
- "Although I don't like group projects, I did learn a lot this quarter by doing a meaningful project."

- "The opportunity to put in action what we learned was excellent."
- "I thought the overall content of the class was excellent. I had a lot of fun in the class and doing the project."
- "I thought the group project was a great way to implement what we learned in class."

Of course, negative comments also occasionally appear. For example, one student remarked, "I completed an Eagle project [Boy Scouts of America] 10 years ago, and this wasn't that much different."

Client and Community Reactions

Campus and local newspapers frequently report on the leadership projects. Some stories have been published in Salt Lake City and Provo/Orem newspapers. Thus, the projects have provided positive publicity for the students and the university. With almost every project completed, students receive letters thanking them for their efforts. The following two notes written to the same project group help to illustrate its impact on the community. One group acquired kitchen appliances for a single mother with a handicapped child. She wrote: "I wanted to write you guys a little note to tell you how much I appreciate you and for all your help. I can't believe anyone would be so kind to someone they didn't know." The same group also raised money for the Cache Community Food Pantry. The food pantry manager wrote:

> As Shakespeare said, "Thanks, thanks, and a thousand thanks." What a wonderfully successful project! I was thinking in the neighborhood of two or three hundred dollars and here this group of shining-faced people come into my office bearing tidings of GREAT JOY to me! I am overwhelmed and more than a little humbled by your gift.
>
> I ask that you tell everyone involved how very much we appreciate your donation of $1,140.00. I promise I will send each of the donors a thank you and a copy of our tax-exemption number so they can claim it as a tax write-off. Again, I can't thank you all enough. May God bless you and MERRY CHRISTMAS.

Advice to Instructors

Advice to instructors revolves around two major themes: how to manage the dynamics of projects within the classroom and how to smooth the way for students outside the classroom.

Managing Projects in the Classroom

Helping students have successful learning experiences begins with setting clear expectations for desired project outcomes. This should be accomplished early in the quarter with a discussion of guidelines and successful examples. The most successful projects occur when students are empowered to make contacts, select projects, establish a vision, recruit additional help, resolve interpersonal conflict within the group, carry out their project, and celebrate successes. The instructor's role is to provide encouragement and support, become a coach and mentor, and become a "cheerleader" for student success.

However, it is important not to expect great success from all projects. Indeed, some of the early projects were not in the least "awe inspiring." For example, one group envisioned being able to raise a substantial sum of money by selling sledge hammer blows to an old car. After considerable planning and working through bundles of red tape, the event was held and raised only $75.00. Eventually, positive projects and positive reactions start to increase as the course establishes new levels of expectations. However, these expectations do not become firmly established until after several iterations.

It is important to link classroom discussions back to the project process on a regular basis. For example, motivation becomes more tangible as students strive to understand the dynamics of motivation and apply motivational techniques in the context of their projects.

Smoothing the Way for Students

Frequently, there are university or client organization guidelines that students must follow. At Utah State, it has been very beneficial to establish strong links with campus service organizations. For example, VOICE is a student organization that supports service activities across campus. As a part of student government, VOICE can gain free access to resources, such as auditoriums and other facilities that could not be otherwise accessed. Each quarter, we ask a representative from VOICE to come to class during the first week and explain to the students the resources that it can make available.

If fundraising is involved, it is usually preferable to use the guidelines, procedures, and bank accounts of the client organization. Initially, a special student projects account was established through the Department of Management and Human Resources, but potential conflicts with university development activities necessitated a change in strategy. Unless the university is itself the client, it is preferable not to funnel money through university accounts.

Although initially some felt it would be advantageous to provide "seed" money for student projects, this has not proved to be necessary. Student groups have been very creative in acquiring the resources required to carry out exceptional projects.

Conclusion

Service-learning has provided a very powerful method to teach basic management concepts and leadership principles. Service-learning projects meet a real and pressing need in the community. They have a meaningful impact on students, the university, and the local community itself. They help students gain experience and develop effectiveness in working with groups, and improve their organizational and managerial skills. Finally, they help enhance the reputation of the business school and the students who attend it.

References

Kiechel, W. (April 4, 1994). "A Manager's Career in the New Economy." *Fortune*: 68-72.

Kotter, J.P. (1992). "What Managers Really Do." In *Managing People and Organizations*, edited by J.J. Gabarro, pp. 102-114. Boston, MA: Harvard Business School Publications.

Kouzes, J.M., and B.Z. Posner. (1995). *The Leadership Challenge*. San Francisco, CA: Jossey-Bass.

O'Reilly, B. (June 13, 1994). "The New Deal: What Companies and Employees Owe Each Other." *Fortune*: 44-52.

Sellers, P. (May 1, 1995). "So You Fail. Now Bounce Back." *Fortune*: 48-57.

MANAGEMENT AND ORGANIZATIONS

MHR 311: 7:30 to 9:20 A.M. Monday and Wednesday
B319
Spring 1998

Gaylen N. Chandler
Associate Professor
Management and Human Resources
Utah State University

Formal office Hours: 10:00 to 11:20 AM Monday and Wednesday
(You can stop by my office or call any time)

Office Number: B404
Telephone: (Office) 797-2365   (Home) 752-2247
(E-mail) Chandler@B202.USU.EDU

Required Text and Readings: **The Leadership Challenge.** Kouzes and Posner. Jossey-Bass. 1995.
Readings Packet: on reserve in the Merrill Library.

COURSE OBJECTIVES:

I have designed this course to introduce you to leadership, regardless of where you find yourself in an organization. The course is intensive and requires substantial self-directed learning. As you successfully complete the course, you will feel a real sense of achievement.

Management is the integrative discipline that is required to develop effective organizations. This course is designed to emphasize the importance of management as a discipline and to help you appreciate that management is not just "common sense" but rather the development of specific competencies. These competencies will allow you to chart the course of an organization, lead or motivate, communicate with employees, and provide useful feedback as you guide an organization towards its objectives.

MY ROLE:

It is my role to create an environment that stimulates learning. The best learning occurs when students are active participants in the process.   I will assume that you can read; therefore, very little time will be spent regurgitating text materials. Time in class will be spent in discussions, group problem solving sessions, experiential exercises, and work on your leadership projects. I can not learn for you, but I can help you direct and focus your learning.

I believe that your preparation and participation in class are good indicators of how valuable the class will be for you. The book and readings we will use in this class are written in such a fashion that allow you to participate largely in self-directed learning. A conceptual grasp of the major course concepts is important, but it is of no value unless you learn to apply and use them.

I recognize that you are adults and should be responsible for your own learning. At the same time, reward systems theorists tell us that behaviors not recognized and rewarded will not be repeated. I have devised some mechanisms that will help motivate you to prepare and learn. Instead of having large tests, each week there will be a 10-question multiple choice quiz. These will focus on key course concepts. There will be some short writing exercises. These will help you develop your thinking skills, but will also help you begin to assimilate the skills and abilities you will need to be a leader throughout your career. The quizzes and writing assignments have the effect of not only encouraging you to prepare before class and to listen and participate actively in class, but also to develop competencies you can take away from class.

I will help you learn to study and organize information. I will provide opportunities for you to apply the information to meaningful projects and situations. I will also provide feedback about your performance. I also will provide a sounding board outside of class. If you want to talk to me about ideas for leadership projects, specific issues with respect to the course, or even your career plans and goals, I will be happy to listen. Office hours are posted at the beginning of the syllabus. I spend a lot of time in my office, so feel free to drop by at other times, or call and make an appointment.

YOUR ROLE:

It is your job to learn and do. Traditionally, professors come to class with a lecture from the textbook and spew forth carefully planned and canned knowledge with interspersed witticisms. Students take notes, read the book, and regurgitate the already chewed but only partially digested knowledge for an exam. In this system students frequently ask, "Is this on the exam?" somehow assuming that professors are all-knowing and that only the material on the exam is worth knowing. This approach assumes that knowledge is valuable only for a short time period until the exam is over and the student can perform the perfunctory mind flush.

I will expect you to understand the key points in all of the reading assignments. The text is straightforward and uses examples from a variety of different settings (not just corporate America) that most of you are familiar with. The readings have been gathered from popular magazines and practitioner journals. They are readable and current. I expect that most of you will understand most of what is written in the text and the readings. If you have specific questions, it is your responsibility to ask clarifying questions. It is not my responsibility to anticipate where something may not be clear to you and rehash that material in class unless you specifically request me to do so.

Leadership and management are applied activities. You can learn about them by reading books. You learn to lead and manage by applying what you have read. The quizzes and writing assignments will require you to engage in critical thinking, synthesize material, and develop your own insights. These assignments can not be completed successfully without some significant thinking and analysis. The assignments will give you an opportunity to develop and exercise critical thinking skills and written communication skills. You will be expected to be an active participant in learning exercises. Experiential exercises and small group discussions will allow you to contribute more fully to your own learning.

To give you an opportunity to practice what you learn, you will become part a **leadership project.** The following list is representative of the accomplishments of previous leadership projects:

- Raising over $1000.00 in goods (diapers, toilet paper, etc.) for the food bank.
- Designing scheduling, accounting, and bidding systems, etc., for local businesses.
- Collecting over 900 pairs of used eyeglasses to distribute to needy individuals.
- Raising over $9000.00 for the Providence/River Heights library.
- Winning a "Newton" contest and donating $2500.00 to the city of Newton to purchase a defibrillator for the EMT unit.

- Collecting 2000 books and $2000 for the Adele C. Young middle school in Brigham City.
- Being involved in numerous community clean-up projects.
- Donating almost $5000.00 worth of "bird-houses" to the Make a Wish Foundation.
- Painting hundreds of fire hydrants and picnic tables in Logan.

By becoming actively involved in a leadership project you will (1) begin to learn the importance of leadership skills, (2) find some areas where your skills need to be improved, (3) become a valuable asset to the community, and (4) develop material to put in your portfolio of experience to make you more employable. We have some students who have received job offers because of their involvement with a significant leadership project.

Your leadership project can make a difference. You can tackle projects that will benefit the university, community, or local business. I will try to accommodate a wide variety of ideas that you might generate for a leadership project.

COURSE ORGANIZATION:

The course will be organized to help you develop leadership and management skills that can help you regardless of your future work or position in an organization. Preparation materials include readings from the text and reserve material. Much of what we learn is geared towards helping you complete a successful leadership project.

GRADING:

I have structured the grading system in such a way that it rewards personal and team initiative, honest effort to learn, and accomplishment.

Components of Grading:

Quizzes: There are 11 short multiple choice quizzes valued at 20 points each (you may drop one). Only ten are counted in the final grade. Questions from the quizzes will come from the text, readings and class discussions. Although some of the issues from the text will be discussed in class, I will not attempt to rehash the text for you. It is not hard to read. If we do not discuss something in class that you do not understand, it is your responsibility to ask clarifying questions. The quizzes are scheduled in the syllabus. You may not take the quiz at other than the regularly scheduled time unless you arrange it with me **before** the quiz is given in class

Home Work: During the quarter you will write a mission statement, a leadership project proposal, and a behaviorally anchored rating scale. These assignments are designed to cause you to do reflective and synthetic critical thinking. I will accept late assignments, but they will be given one half credit. A late assignment is anything turned in after the class period is over.

The combined quizzes and homework will allow me to assess your daily preparation.

Leadership Projects: You will have the opportunity to participate actively in a leadership project. I do not want to restrict your thinking in terms of the types of projects you propose, but I urge you to consider the following criteria as you generate your ideas. You should engage in projects that

- increase your experience and effectiveness in working with groups.
- improve your skills at organizing and managing people

- contribute to your attractiveness on the job market, for graduate school, or for promotion.
- enhance the reputation of the business school, university, and USU students.
- have a meaningful impact on the business school, university, local community, or local businesses, and your team members.
- avoid potential liability to you, me, and the university.
- extend beyond your normal responsibilities. If you currently hold a leadership position in a fraternity, sorority, informal student group, or at work, you leadership projects must extend beyond your normal activities.
- use class concepts, such as motivation, teamwork, and communication.

Leadership projects will be spearheaded by teams of students from the class. A minimum of six and a maximum of twelve students should be involved in each team. A day is scheduled early in the semester when you can discuss your ideas with me. Subsequently you will submit a proposal with objectives and a timetable. I will ask you to prepare a brief presentation to explain your project to the class to solicit advice and participation from other students, or to stimulate their thinking about possible projects — some students may have difficulty generating ideas. In-class presentations of your ideas are to enlist support from your peers. This is not a competitive exercise. Each of us should be able to take real enjoyment from the individual and cumulative accomplishments of peers. Because of the shortness of the quarter, all proposals for leadership projects are due no later than April 1st.

When you complete your project (no later than May 25th), you will submit a formal summary of your accomplishments, the processes you used, and what you learned from the experience. These should include letters from individuals or organizations you have assisted. They might also include photographs of the activity or newspaper articles written about your projects, or any other validating source. You will also prepare a formal presentation for other class members and client organizations to see.

Grading for the course:

7 quizzes (20 points each)	140 points
3 writing assignments (20 points each)	60 points
Leadership Project	100 points
Total	360 points

A	Requires a minimum of 280 points
A–	Requires a minimum of 270 points
B+	Requires a minimum of 260 points
B	Requires a minimum of 250 points
B–	Requires a minimum of 240 points
C+	Requires a minimum of 230 points
C	Requires a minimum of 220 points
C–	Requires a minimum of 210 points
D	Requires a minimum of 180 points
F	Below 180 points

Course Schedule:

---

25 March
Introduction to class

Pass out and discuss syllabus.

Learning Exercises:
A. Icebreaker
B. Expectations for the course
C. What you need to know as a manager.
D. Leadership projects/proposals/Gantt charts

---

30 March
Historical Perspectives on Management

The purpose of this chapter is to give students the opportunity to become aware of the major movements in management history.

To prepare for class: Read "The Historical Roots of Current Management Practice" (readings packet)

In-class learning exercises: Class members will break into small groups: Each group will be assigned a specific topic (i.e., scientific management, bureaucratic organizations, administrative principles, human relations, behavioral sciences, systems theory, contingency view, kaizen, etc.) You may caucus for 20 minutes. At that time, each group will have the opportunity to present its findings.

At the end of class you will have the opportunity to discuss the kind of project you want to do. By the end of class you will have organized into groups and started to focus on your leadership project.

---

1 April

Quiz #1 will be given at the beginning of class, focusing on the historical perspectives discussed on Tuesday.

Be prepared to spend time with your project groups. Before you leave class I want to discuss project ideas with each group.

---

6 April
First writing assignment: Leadership project proposal is due.

The first writing assignment will be due. This will be done as a group. Write a two page proposal that discusses each of the following issues:

A. Who will your project benefit?
B. Why is this a worthwhile project?
C. What are your goals and objectives?
D. What will the long-term benefits be?
E. What is your time-line for accomplishment?

Environmental changes that make leadership important at all levels of organizations.

To prepare for class: Read the preface of Kouzes and Posner, "The Leadership Challenge". Read: "The New Deal," "A Manager's Career in the New Economy"

A. Be prepared to discuss major environmental changes that are impacting the way work must be done. With this background we will discuss how your career aspirations "fit" the new world of work.
B. We will use a variation of the nominal group technique to identify a list of core skills needed for success in the changing business environment. This will help you to identify the skills you should try to develop with your leadership project.

---

8 April
Quiz 2 at the beginning of class.

To prepare for class: Read Chapters 1 and 2 of Kouzes and Posner. Also read "What Leaders Really Do" (readings packet on reserve).

A. Discussion of important leadership attributes.
B. Presentation of the Kouzes and Posner Leadership model. Be prepared to do some self-assessment of your leadership skills and abilities.
C. Class time to organize and coordinate leadership projects.

---

13 April
How Leaders Add Value and Motivate Employees/Followers

Preparation for class: Read Chapter 3 of Kouzes and Posner. Read "One More Time: How Do You Motivate Employees?" Herzberg: readings packet on reserve.

A. Discussion of what it means to challenge the process and how we—as leaders—search for opportunities to add value.
B. Discussion of basic motivation theories: What really motivates people?
      1. Expectancy theory
      2. Equity Theory
      3. Goal Theories

---

15 April
Quiz 3 at the beginning of class.

Read Chapter 5 of Kouzes and Posner. Also review "Samples of Corporate Vision/Mission

Statements" (on reserve)

In class: Developing a group vision statement:

A. Discussion of the components of a group vision statement for your project.
B. Each team will work on the preparation of a mission or vision statement for the team.
C. Work on a presentation that will communicate your vision to the class. Each group will present its "vision" in class next time.

Individual writing assignment: "Lifeline, What You Want, and Vision Statement"
The overall objective of this assignment entails writing a vision statement for yourself: something that reflects you, and what you try to accomplish in your interactions with others. This is to be handed in 4 November. When I grade the assignments I will pay close attention to the inclusion of all three parts listed below.

1. The first step in this assignment involves creating a "lifeline" that reflects major events in your life, as described by Kouzes and Posner on p. 112. Draw your lifeline and include a summary paragraph analyzing the common threads you see across most of your "high points," strengths or key characteristics you've displayed in each of the high points, or what made each a "peak experience."

2. The second step entails generating ideas of what you want to include in your vision statement. Kouzes and Posner describe this part of the exercise as the need to "Determine What You Want" (pp. 112-113). Think about the questions they raise (e.g., what do I want to accomplish in my career and in my life? Or what do I feel passionate or genuinely excited about? Also incorporate the ideas from their notion of writing an article on how you made a difference by asking "Ten, 15, or 20 years from now, when I look back on my life, what do I want to have accomplished?" or "What would I want to be remembered for at the end of my life?" This second step involves generating ideas, so you may want to simply list your answers or ideas. You may then want to share them with a friend you trust to help you visualize and communicate the things you really want.

3. Now you are ready to write your personal vision statement. There are several more examples of corporate vision and mission statements in the reading packet. More examples can be found by perusing the corporate reports on the second floor of the library. The examples do not represent the *only* way to write a vision statement, but they seem to truly reflect what each organization wants to accomplish. Good mission statements have a few things in common. First, they identify the major constituencies the organization is seeking to work with. Second, they express values and objectives with respect to each of the constituencies. The vision statement should truly reflect what you want to accomplish when interacting with others, but also be concise enough to remember easily.

---

20 April
Enlisting the Support of Other People

Preparation for class: Read Chapters 6, 7, 8 of Kouzes and Posner

In class:

A. Discussion of communication behaviors designed to help enlist the support of other people.
B. Each team will prepare a presentation for class designed to communicate their mission and vision and enlist support.

---

22 April
Quiz 4 at the beginning of class.

Experimentation, Creative Problem Solving, and Learning from Failure and Success

Preparation for class: Read Chapter 4 of Kouzes and Posner. From the readings packet read "So You Fail. Now Bounce Back."

Assignment: Come to class prepared (you do not have to write about it) to discuss a "failure" you've experienced. What were the circumstances surrounding the incident? What happened? What did you learn from the experience? How did you feel about it?

In class: We will continue our discussion of how leaders succeed by taking risks, experimenting, and learning from failure. Enhance your own understanding of your own willingness to take risks and fail by trying the exercises in the commitment section at the end of chapter 4 in Kouzes and Posner.

---

27 April
Establishing group norms. Measuring behavior.

Read: "Ten Reasons You Should Be Using 360-Degree Feedback" (Readings Packet)
Read: "Making Your Training Stick" and "Performance Management Analysis Model"

In class we will learn how to design a performance appraisal instrument that will help you to provide clear feedback to other group members.

A. Agree on the major dimensions of group values and norms.
B. Identify behaviors that exemplify the agreed upon dimensions.
C. Develop a Behaviorally Anchored Rating scale for each key dimension.

---

29 April
Quiz 5 at the beginning of class.

1. Chapter 9 Kouzes and Posner
2. "Making Performance Appraisal Work" (readings packet)
3. "Evaluating the Evaluators" (readings packet)

A. In class we will focus on the performance appraisal process. How does it work? What can managers and leaders do to provide good performance feedback?

B. Find a copy of a recent performance appraisal you received on a job, or find someone who has received a performance appraisal on the job and find out how it went. Was there a structured form? Does the appraisal impact future salary allocations? What kinds of behavior were discussed? How did you, or the person being interviewed, feel about the appraisal? Was it motivational? Describe the performance appraisal and its implications and discuss what should have been done to make it better.

C. Be prepared to practice your skills in giving feedback by participating in role-played interviews in class.

---

4 May
Selecting Employees and Followers

The objective is to learn how to interview applicants for a position, so as to improve your chances of hiring followers/employees who will do the job, perform well, and add value to the organization.

To prepare for class read the following all from the readings packet on reserve:
1. "Bizarre questions aren't the answer"
2. "Guide to Pre-Employment Inquiries. Interview Questions: What You Can and Cannot Ask"
3. "ABCs of Job Interviewing"
4. "Group Assessments Produce Better Hires"

In class:

A. After reading the assigned material, come to class with four good questions that could be asked in an employment interview.

B. Discussion of recruitment and selection techniques.

---

6 May
Quiz 6 at the beginning of class.
Using positive discipline for problem behaviors.

To prepare for class: Read Chapter 10, Kouzes and Posner. Read "Punitive and Nonpunitive Discipline: A comparison" (in readings packet on reserve).

A. Discussion of punitive and nonpunitive discipline techniques.
B. We will break into groups and practice providing nonpunitive discipline in a number of different disciplinary cases.
C. How can you use nonpunitive discipline for group members who are not meeting expectations in your project group.

---

11 May
Rewarding Desired Behaviors
Quiz 7 at the beginning of class.

To prepare for class: Read Chapter 11 of Kouzes and Posner. "On the Folly of Rewarding A, While Hoping for B." (readings packet)

In class: People often become frustrated because they do not get the desired behaviors from others in organizations. As your reading for today points out, people's behavior usually reflects what's rewarded in the organization. Leaders need to have a wide variety of rewards from which they can choose, and link them to desired behaviors. Be prepared to discuss the use of rewards in organizations to encourage desired behaviors. You may also want to consider how you might use reward systems to get desired behaviors from people working on your leadership project.

---

13 May
Celebrations and Rewards as Symbols and Motivational Tools

To prepare for class: Chapters 12 and 13 of Kouzes and Posner.

We will watch the movie *Flight of the Phoenix* in class. In the movie a number of different leadership behaviors are displayed. Be prepared to use Kouzes and Posner's model to determine which of the main characters display the best leadership behaviors.

---

18 and 20 May
Quiz 8 will be offered at 8:00 A.M.

You should essentially be done with your leadership project. You may use the time slot to work with your groups to compile project reports. I will be in class to answer questions. Feel free to discuss with me any resources you might need to do your work on the 18th and 20th.

---

27 May

Your final project report will be due at the time you present. This is your opportunity to present your accomplishments to the class and your clients. Each group will have 10 minutes to describe and display what they accomplished. We will also celebrate the accomplishments.

Congratulations on the successful completion of the course.

The More We Serve, the More We Learn:
Service-Learning in a Human Resource Management Course

by Sue Campbell Clark

One of the primary objectives of the upper-division Human Resource Management course I teach at the University of Idaho is to have students learn to carry out human resource management functions as professionals in real-life contexts. While this objective is primarily academic and student-centered, I have found that the best way to meet this objective is by having students focus on serving and helping organizations in the community. Students are required to work in groups as consultants for local organizations in order to analyze a human resource problem and suggest workable solutions. Service is stressed in two ways: (1) Students must work to solve a problem the organization has identified, and (2) the assistance students provide to a local organization must outweigh the time and effort expended by the organization to inform and help them.

When I first began to require students to carry out these consulting projects, I thought of them as just another form of experiential learning. The benefits of experiential learning are many. Because such projects require greater learner involvement, students are more likely to retain what they have learned than when listening to lectures (Bowen 1987; VanEynde and Spencer 1988). Experiential learning also gives students the opportunity to reach a deeper understanding of why issues are important, and about cause-effect relationships (Miner, Das, and Gale 1984). In addition, Mintzberg's (1975) famous arguments for out-of-class learning remain convincing:

> No doubt much important cognitive material must be assimilated by the manger-to-be. But cognitive learning no more makes a manager than it does a swimmer. The latter will drown the first time he jumps into the water if his coach never takes him out of the lecture hall, gets him wet, and gives him feedback on his performance. (60)

The consulting project addressed all these needs. It forced students to learn about people and organizations, and about the effect of human resource practices. However, some of my first attempts at this type of learning were awkward, and I found that many students no more appreciated "getting wet" than a cat does. Many disliked the messy, unpredictable nature of the out-of-class experience. Though I refined elements of the project to make it smoother, I also realized that students' attitudes about learning needed to change.

During the time I spent rethinking the consulting project, I became connected with others who were doing something called "service-learning." There were many similarities between my consulting project and the service-learning activities my colleagues sponsored: Both were action oriented and involved out-of-class work with local organizations. One conspicuous difference, however, was students' and teachers' attitudes toward their projects. In service-learning, students and teachers are required to think more about helping, serving, and giving and to accept some personal sacrifice as part of the learning process — attitudes that make both students and teachers more tolerant and teachable. Students and teachers focus on a higher purpose as they learn, so that they go beyond caring only about the subject matter and begin to also care about the people, organizations, and communities they serve. These attitudes seemed to be the missing element in the consulting projects I had designed.

Gradually, I made the transition from experiential learning to service-learning. According to Kolb (1984), a complete learning process involves four kinds of activity: concrete, abstract, active, and reflective. The original consulting projects had concrete, abstract, and active elements. The service-learning perspective added the missing element: reflection. While I had previously relied on traditional, deductive teaching (i.e., giving ready-made conclusions to be applied in practice), I began to add an inductive element (i.e., drawing conclusions from experience) to help students learn from their projects, thus giving them a more complete learning experience (Whetten and Clark 1996). To add more reflection and inductive learning, I spoke about the needs organizations had, talked more of learning lessons beyond simply carrying out a human resource function in an organization, and had students reflect more on what they were learning about themselves, their organization, and their communities.

The remainder of this essay explores in greater detail how service-learning can enhance students' education. I describe (1) how service-learning is used in my course, (2) how service-learning benefits students, and (3) how service-learning has affected me as an instructor. Finally, I conclude with some observations on how service-learning benefits all involved: students, faculty, and community organizations.

Service-Learning and the Course

The service-learning component is a major part of the course. I emphasize its importance by making it a sizable percentage of students' course grades, and by giving significant time and attention to the students as they work on their projects throughout the semester. A description of the service-learning project follows. (A course syllabus is included at the end of the chapter.)

Forming Student Groups

Students in this course are academically diverse. Most are juniors and seniors majoring in business, and some students are pursuing a master's degree in public administration. Only about one-fourth of the total students are majoring in human resource management. The remaining students take the course as an elective in order to develop their capacities as future managers who may hire, fire, promote, train, and evaluate or simply to learn about human resource services they may use as future employees.

Because students report that the biggest challenge of the service-learning project is working in a group, they observe the following steps to ensure that the groups they form have the best chance of being successful. First, they fill out an information sheet indicating their interest in various projects, and specifying when they have time for group meetings. Based on this information, I form groups with four to six students who have compatible schedules and overlapping interests. Finally, grading procedures ensure that full participation is rewarded and poor participation is discouraged. Group members grade each member's contribution to the project, and this becomes part of each student's final grade. If groups report repeated incidents of nonparticipation, I personally talk with the nonparticipating member to assess the problem, provide help, and clarify expectations. In severe cases, I reserve the right to drop an individual's service-learning project grade by as much as two levels (i.e., A to C, B to D) for repeatedly poor participation.

Identifying Organizations to Serve

The organizations we work with are primarily identified by my contacts in the local community, and occasionally by student contacts. Projects have also been solicited by placing a notice in the local chamber of commerce newsletter. When I contact an organization, I explain that our objective is to learn through service. After explaining what kinds of human resource problems the students can work on, I ask whether the organization has need of assistance in any of these areas. Nearly every organization contacted has wanted to participate. Furthermore, despite the fact that the University of Idaho is located in a small town with a population of fewer than 20,000, there are always enough organizations with human resource concerns to meet our needs.

Many students have identified organizations to serve through their current or past employment or volunteer work. Organizations located in this way can be excellent, since at least one student in the group already has access to information about the organization and an inside understanding of its challenges. An occasional problem with student-identified organizations is that they are more hesitant to share employee problems and information out of a concern for keeping information on other employees confidential or, occasionally, for exposing the organization's own weaknesses. For example, one student was a former employee of a long-term-care facility, and this facility requested her and her group to do a turnover analysis. This student's experience as an employee who quit her job with the organization aided the group in uncovering the reasons for its high turnover rate. However, because the contact student personally knew current and former employees, the employer was hesitant to show the group all the records and statistics related to employees who quit. In cases like this one, students are told to talk frankly with the organization in question and to clarify what information is appropriate for them to examine and what is not.

Approximately half of the organizations served are not-for-profit organizations, including health-care centers, environmental groups, the university Human Resources Services division and other university divisions, and governmental agencies. For-profit organizations are typically small restaurants or new businesses. Most of the organizations served do not have human resource staff and are not especially adept at dealing with human resource issues. As a result, students often find a strong need for their services, though there are few resources within the organization to mentor and direct them.

Project Proposals

After students have been formed into groups and partner organizations have been identified, students take two weeks to meet a representative from their organization and write a project proposal. In this proposal, they are required to explain the nature of the human resource problem, list information sources they need to understand the problem, list tasks they need to do to undertake to complete the project, and set deadlines for these tasks. A common problem with the proposals is that the students define problems that are too large in scope to be solved in a single semester. Typically, I encourage groups to narrow the human resource problem they are examining. I have observed that when students define a single problem, their recommendations are more likely to be adopted and have a ripple effect throughout the organization, positively impacting it in multiple ways. On the other hand, when students attempt to solve multiple, ill-defined problems, their recommendations are less likely to be clear and less likely to be adopted by the partner organization. After receiving feedback, the students are asked to rewrite their proposal (if necessary), show it to the organization, and make sure that they are meeting the organization's expectations. A sample of student projects would include:

• Revising a performance evaluation form for caretakers of severely disabled persons, and giving general suggestions about performance appraisals that the employing organization could use to improve this process for other jobs as well.

- Making suggestions for improving communication between the new managing owners and employees of a recently acquired trucking firm.
- Creating a "realistic job preview" video to be shown to job candidates at a nursing home (which has had very high turnover, in part because applicants do not understand the nature of the job).
- Developing a training program (including demonstration video and illustrated handbook) for new student employees in the university media center (which has a very high, unpreventable turnover and must bring new employees up to speed quickly).
- Improving the interview process to select better-performing wait staff at a local restaurant.
- Creating job descriptions for volunteer positions in a nonprofit environmental organization.
- Surveying local businesses about awareness of the Americans With Disabilities Act (ADA), and their policies and practices to accommodate disabled applicants and employees.

Because every student group's proposal and project requirements differs, it is important to make sure that the students know what they must do and how they will be evaluated. Once their proposal has been approved, students begin working on their project.

Students and Organizations

Setbacks and frustrations are typical when students work with organizations. In comparison with case studies and other assignments done in and out of class, service-learning is messy and unpredictable. These characteristics, however, add to its learning value for students, who soon find that working with people requires patience, persistence, and careful planning. One student group, for example, which had carefully scheduled a day to film a realistic job preview video at a long-term-care facility and had obtained the necessary consent forms from a patient who agreed to be filmed, arrived only to find that the patient had died the night before. This group learned that the unexpected does happen when working with people and that persistence is required. Another group prepared questionnaires for all the employees of an organization to fill out but then received only one or two responses. This group learned that face-to-face interaction can be much more effective, although more time-consuming, than an impersonal questionnaire. Another group was assigned by management to interview employees to find out what kinds of low-cost benefits (e.g., candy machine vouchers, award ceremonies) would motivate them. In the interviews, employees clearly informed the students that nickel-and-dime benefits were an insult and that regular, personal interaction with management as well as additional job training would better motivate them. The students faced a dilemma: Should they make recommendations about low-cost benefits and please the manager, or should they make recommendations about managerial communication and meet the needs of the employees? They chose to focus their report on managerial communication because it would benefit the organization the most, and as a result the students learned powerful lessons about how often managers misunderstand what motivates employees.

Because students' interaction with organizations is so crucial to the success of their projects and to future partnerships (e.g., internships, future learning projects), it is essential to explain to them what professionalism entails and to communicate standards. Students are asked to dress a few steps up from their normal going-to-class attire when meeting with organization representatives and members. Students also need in their reports to correctly spell relevant organization members' names and titles. When interfacing with employees, volunteers, and customers of the organization, students must be able to explain their project in a clear and accurate way, especially if their project is sensitive in nature. Students are also encouraged to check in regularly with the organization to see whether their project still meets the organization's expectations. Gundry and Buchko's *Field Casework: Methods for Consulting to Small and Start-up Businesses* (Sage, 1996) is an excellent source of additional tips for teachers and students who are doing consulting projects with organizations and wish to approach the projects more professionally.

I have observed that even small lapses in students' professionalism can lessen a group's ability to make an impact. For example, a manager who had just received one group's final report related that the students had misspelled the name of nearly every organizational contact mentioned in the report, and this lessened the report's impact, even though the report's recommendations were technically sound. On the other hand, when students act professionally, organizations are more likely to provide needed information and to take students' recommendations seriously.

Mentoring Students

Mentoring students throughout their service-learning projects is essential and must be done in several ways. First, because many groups find they must change some aspect of their project in the middle of the semester, students must be assisted as they further define *what* they want to accomplish for their partner organization and *how* they want to accomplish it. Second, midsemester meetings between me and each group are necessary if I am to check students' progress and answer questions. Third, I keep a small library of human resource magazines and how-to books on various human resource practices that I make readily available. Students should also be encouraged to ask for help whenever they need it.

Project Reports

Typically, groups submit a report that (1) defines a problem, (2) describes the effect of this problem on the organization, (3) offers a solution or several solutions, (4) explains the costs and benefits of these solutions, and (5) explains how the solutions will solve the problem identified. If the project results in a product other than an actual report (e.g., a training manual or "realistic job preview" video), they simply submit the product itself and a sample cover letter to their organization. Cover letters are typically about two pages long and concisely explain (1) why the project product was developed, (2) the rationale for developing it in its present form, (3) how it was developed, and (4) what positive effects the product may bring about for the organization.

At this point, the reports are critiqued and frequently returned for revision. Typical report problems include a lack of emphasis on the benefits and costs of the proposed solutions to the organization, and lack of candor about the limitations of the project, especially when recommendations must be in compliance with employment laws. In these situations, students are asked to be sure to include a statement explaining that they have made recommendations to the best of their knowledge but that professional legal counsel should be sought before implementing a particular solution.

Oral Reports and Reflection

Students present oral reports to the class about two weeks after turning in their initial project reports. They present as groups and treat the class as a board of directors (or other relevant managers) in the organization they are serving. The class, in turn, asks relevant, role-appropriate questions at the conclusion of each presentation. The oral reports give students a chance to rehearse presenting their projects, allow them to get additional feedback from class members, and show others the products of their efforts. Students also turn in their rewritten reports at this time, if revisions were required.

Oral reports also provide an opportunity for students to present their reflections on their experience and what they learned beyond the technical focus of their written report. Many students report learning about their own strengths and abilities, some report feeling more connected to the community, and some report that they feel more connected to the organizations they served. In cases where students have worked with not-for-profit organizations, they also come to understand the causes those organizations work for (e.g., issues surrounding long-term care for the elderly or disabled, the need for environmental awareness in the community). In cases where they have worked with businesses, they come to see just how much managers and human resource practices can influence employees' quality of life.

The final exam (described in the syllabus) also provides students with a chance to reflect on lessons learned. They are asked to comment on what they have learned about human resource management, about themselves, and about the impact of human resource policies and practices on employees, organizations, and communities.

Reporting to the Organization

Students are required to give a copy of their report, or project product and cover letter, to their organization. Oral presentations to the organization are generally not as formal as those given in class. Typically, group members assign only one or two members to deliver the report, explain its features, and answer questions. On these occasions, group members are encouraged to be as professional as possible — checking to be sure that they have met their organization's expectations, clarifying the limitations and benefits of their project, and thanking their organization for letting them learn by serving. Organizations are then free to implement the suggestions, use them as the basis for a new set of solutions, or disregard them altogether. Most organizations use the students' recommendations, at least in part.

To ensure that the class has adequately served each organization, I check to see whether its expectations have, in fact, been met and to get suggestions for improving the service-learning project process. I also send a note thanking participating organizations for giving my students an opportunity to learn. Many of these organizations are eager to have student groups do additional projects with them.

Grading

Following their oral presentation, students are given a grade for the entire project. Because the projects often vary in scope and content, reports are not graded competitively but are evaluated in terms of how well they satisfy the objectives listed in the project proposal. Students also receive a participation grade from their fellow group members.

Service-Learning and the Students

Service-learning in this course meets several important student needs. First, students appreciate an opportunity to gain additional career-relevant experience. They are encouraged to put their involvement in this project on their resumes, and to show their reports or products to potential employers. Several students who have done this have said that recruiters who interviewed them were amazed at the quality of the experience and the responsibility this opportunity gave the students. One student who found employment said that she was able to use her project report at work and present some of the project findings to several departments in her division.

Second, the project makes the course material more relevant. Because students are carrying out human resource management techniques in an actual organization, the relevancy of the material covered in class and in the text is clearer. Students report better understanding of class material relevant to their project topic, and better performance on exams that test items relevant to their project. Students' interest is also heightened when lectures cover topics relevant to their project and when classmates share their experiences in class discussion.

Third, students want to try out their developing skills and make an impact, and the service-learning project allows them to do this. Several students who felt their project was very successful have said how satisfying it was to see changes occur because of their recommendations. They were happy that they could make a difference in employees' quality of life and in the effectiveness of an organization. One student reported that, if nothing else, she and her group members had a better understanding of an important issue and what community organizations need in order to improve.

On the negative side, students describe two common frustrations. First, groups that have one or more members who do not fully participate find that dealing with such group members makes the project more difficult. Though peer participation grades and instructor intervention are helpful sanctions, noncooperating group members still create problems. Second, students sometimes find that organizations are not cooperative (e.g., do not give them full information, miss scheduled appointments, do not fully define expectations). Some of these problems stem from a lack of student professionalism and initiative; for example, students can ask more directly for what they need to know, can call to confirm appointments, and can ask for clarification of expectations. However, many times, problems stem from the fact that organizations are struggling or ineffective or their managers themselves lack professionalism. In these cases, I encourage students to be patient and persistent, and to realize that their services are genuinely needed if the organization in question is to become more effective.

Service-Learning and the Instructor

The service-learning component in this course helps me more effectively convey the importance of its subject matter. I am very concerned that my students understand the serious impact for good and ill that human resource practices can have on organizations and organization members. Learning through lectures, textbooks, and even in-class simulations and role plays (while all valuable) does not adequately communicate the significance of the course material. Sensitivity to people and organizations is best gained through actual experience. Students learn from the service-learning project that the human resource practices they recommend can affect the well-being of organizations and the quality of life for organization members.

The service-learning project motivates me to convey the course material in a way that is demonstrably relevant. Theories need to be explained so they allow my students to conceptualize better real problems in real organizations. They need examples of concrete solutions. This focus on relevance, I believe, has also changed my research efforts, as I have become more conscious of the effect of my own work on organizations and people.

As a result of these outreach efforts, I have been able to develop more relationships with local businesses and not-for-profit organizations. These relationships have, in turn, resulted in internships and subsequent opportunities for students to carry out additional service-learning projects.

I have found that the single drawback of using service-learning is the increased time it requires. Contacting organizations, working with students, keeping up with the latest developments in a wide variety of human resource practices, and grading — all take more time than they would if I were to teach the class without a service-learning component. I believe this is simply part of the service-learning package: Service, by definition, is not service unless there is sacrifice by the giver. Furthermore, while there are rewards for using service-learning, they are mainly intrinsic. Although my department and my college appreciate the extra effort I put into effective teaching, it is not likely that my utilization of service-learning will be rewarded in the form of a pay raise or promotion. The primary reward remains that I feel more effective as a teacher and more relevant to the people and organizations my profession is designed to serve.

The More We Serve, the More We Learn

As I made the transition from experiential learning to service-learning, I learned that there is a spiritual side to education: The more I can help my students concentrate on serving, the more they personally gain in terms of learning. I noted several synergies emerging here. First there was the synergy between service and learning, such that when they are combined, the results are greater than the sum of the parts. Another synergy is that among the organizations served, the students, and the instructor — a synergy such that when the students and I focused on serving organizations, everyone's needs were simultaneously fulfilled (see the figure *opposite*). Students gained career-relevant experience, an understanding of the relevancy of the

Organization, Teacher, and Student Needs Filled by Service-learning

Organization Needs:

Improve efficiency and effectiveness of organization

Improve the quality of organization life for organization members

Teacher Needs:

-- effectively convey course material

-- increase relevancy of course

-- be involved in outreach

Student Needs:

-- gain career-relevant experience

-- understand relevancy of course material to "real world"

-- make an impact with their skill

course material to the "real world," and an opportunity to make an impact with their skills. I became more effective in conveying course material, increased the relevance of the course, and became involved in outreach. Organizations learned of ways to improve their efficiency, effectiveness, and the quality of organizational life for their members. Service-learning not only effectively encourages learning, it also simultaneously benefits all stakeholders.

Syllabus

The syllabus that appears at the end of this chapter is an abbreviated version for this essay designed to show how service-learning is used and explained to students, and how service-learning fits with other course objectives.

References

Bowen, D.D. (1987). "Developing a Personal Theory of Experiential Learning." *Simulation and Games* 18: 192-206.

Kolb, D.A. (1984). *Experiential Learning*. Englewood Cliffs, NJ: Prentice-Hall.

Miner, F.C., Jr., H. Das, and J. Gales. (1984). "An Investigation of the Relative Effectiveness of Three Diverse Teaching Methodologies." *Organizational Behavior Teaching Review* 9(2): 49-59.

Mintzberg, H. (1975). "The Manager's Job: Folklore and Fact." *Harvard Business Review* 53(4): 49-61.

VanEynde, D.F., and R.W. Spencer. (1988). "Lecture Versus Experiential Learning: Their Differential Effects on Long-Term Memory." *Organizational Behavior Teaching Review* 12(4): 52-58.

Whetten, D.A., and S.C. Clark. (1996). "An Integrated Model for Teaching Management Skills." *Journal of Management Education* 20(2): 152-181.

HUMAN RESOURCE MANAGEMENT

SYLLABUS

Course Overview
[mention something about service-learning]

The purpose of this course is to help you understand important issues and topics in human resource management. The course is designed for anyone who works (or would like to work) in an organization, and especially for those who will either become part of an HR division within an organization or who will eventually take supervisory roles where they will make decisions about strategic planning, hiring, training, compensation, promotion, etc.

This course has five specific objectives. The assignments, text, and classroom activities will be focused on the following:

1. Learning to value people as an organization's greatest resource
2. Learning laws and regulations that organizations must abide by
3. Learning to increase your awareness of current issues in HR
4. Developing managerial communication skills, especially as they relate to HR issues
5. Learning how to apply HR techniques to improve work situations

Requirements

3 Exams (100 pts. each) 300
HR Manager CD-ROM Simulation 100
Participation (Peer- and Instructor-assessed) 100
Service-learning Project & Oral Report 200
Final.. 50

Total Points Possible 750

A=90% or above, Exceeds expectations   B=80's, Meets high expectations
C=70's, Meets basic requirements   D=60's, Does not meet basic requirements
F= below 60%.

Schedule

Week	Topic	Assignment/Exam
1	Introduction to Course & HRM	
2	Equal Employment Opportunity	
3		Service-learning Project Proposal due
4	Job Requirements	Exam #1
5	Planning & Recruiting	

6	Selection	CD-ROM HR Manager Simulation Due
7		
8	Training & Development	Mandatory meeting with professor Re: Service-learning Project
9		Exam #2
10	Compensation & Benefits	
11		
12	Safety & Health	
13		
14	Employee Rights & Discipline	Service-learning Project Due
15		Exam #3
16	Service-learning Project Oral Reports	Oral Report
Finals Week	Final Exam	Final

Description Of Course Assignments

Exams

There will be three exams covering the chapter material, readings, lectures, and current issue reports. A list of topics covered on the exam will be given the class period prior to each test.

HR Manager CD-ROM Simulation

What it is. The HR Manager simulation on CD-ROM allows you to make decisions about hiring, firing, promotion, training, and balancing the demands of worker satisfaction, performance, and company profits. This is an excellent opportunity to experiment, to get some feedback on your decision-making, and get a sense of the financial impact of HR on a business. The simulation will carry you through four years. The CD is on reserve in the library.

Writing your paper. Address the following in a five to ten page paper. What were your objectives? What decisions did you make and why? Was there a difference between your objectives and what actually happened? Why? What went well, what was difficult? What did you learn? Did some strategies work in the long run, but not the short run (or vice versa)? What effect do you think HR has on company profits? Based on your experience, what does it take to succeed as an HR Manager?

Service-Learning Project and Presentation

The Project. One of the objectives of the course is to give you some hands-on experience with common human resource professional duties. You will be assigned to a group with whom you will complete your project. You and your group will be assigned to work with an organization that has requested help with a human resource problem. Professionalism and an attitude of service are expected and will greatly benefit your ability to work with the organization and complete your project.

Project Proposal. After receiving your assignment, you will have two weeks to meet with an organizational representative (e.g., a manager) and write a project proposal. In the proposal you and your group must a) explain the nature of the HR problem, b) list information sources needed, c) list tasks that you must do to complete the project, d) and set deadlines for these tasks.

Project Report. Typically, your project will result in a report in which you must a) define the problem, b) tell the effect of this problem on the organization, c) offer a solution or solutions and the costs and benefits of these solutions, and d) tell how the solutions will solve the identified problem. Sometimes your project will result in a product. If so, you will only be required to turn in the product and a cover letter explaining a) why the product was developed, b) the rational for developing the product as it appears, c) how this was done, and d) what positive effects the product may have on the organization.

Oral Reports. All groups will give a brief presentation (twenty minutes) to the class at the end of the semester. The class and teacher will act as the board of directors of an organization to evaluate the quality of the project.

Present Report to Organization. After reporting to the class and receiving feedback, you will be expected to give your project to the organization you were assigned. You may wish to give a presentation of your findings, or just meet with an organization representative informally. This is a good time to thank the organization for allowing you to learn through serving, and to see whether their expectations of the project have been met.

Grading Criteria. Group projects will be given a grade based on rigorous professional standards (i.e., acceptability as an HR report conducted within an organization).

Participation

Your participation grade will consist of two parts: a grade from your service-learning group members and a grade based on participation in class. Group members will evaluate your participation on the basis of your contribution and ability to follow through in a timely manner. The teacher reserves the right to lower your grade by as much as two grades (i.e., A to C, B to D) for repeated poor participation. Participation in class will be based on the teacher's assessment of your participation in discussion, volunteering to help in role plays and simulations and special reports, being prepared for class (i.e., doing the reading, preparing cases or other short assignments), being on time, not continually leaving early, and giving thoughtful feedback to others.

Final Exam

The final exam will be an essay exam which you will take home and return during the final exam period. These essays must be printed. You will be asked to write about what you learned in the course, and how you plan to continue to learn after the course is over. This is a good opportunity to reflect on what you learned about HR, your own abilities, and about the impact of human resource policies on employees, organizations, and communities.

The Oklahoma Integrated Business Core:
Using a Service-Learning Experience as a Foundation for Undergraduate Business Education

by Larry K. Michaelsen, James M. Kenderdine, John Hobbs, and Forest L. Frueh

Citing the results of a comprehensive national study, Porter and McKibbin (1988) concluded that business school programs were doing a good job of developing students' technical skills, but were not adequately preparing them for their future jobs in three important areas. Business school graduates frequently (1) have a difficult time viewing business organizations from an interdisciplinary perspective, (2) are limited in their ability to work and communicate effectively with others, and (3) are unable to solve unstructured problems.

In large measure, all three of these deficiencies result from students' lack of meaningful work experience combined with the prevailing practices in business education. For example, business majors typically encounter two problems in developing an integrated view of business organizations. First, few have worked in anything but low-level, part-time jobs that contribute little to their understanding of the workings of business organizations. Second, coursework through the discipline-based structure of business schools does little to alleviate the problem. In most programs, students first complete a series of core courses, each of which focuses exclusively on the concepts and terminology of a single business discipline. They then complete a series of specialized courses that are both increasingly narrow in scope and primarily concentrated within their major field of study. In fact, students' *only* cross-disciplinary exposure to the business world typically occurs in their final term when they enroll in a policy/strategy course.

Similarly, although typical student jobs involve working with others, they seldom provide any significant responsibility for organizing work activities, dealing with human resource issues, or solving unstructured problems. Further, traditional lecture/discussion courses, even those that use supplementary group assignments, seldom provide opportunities to learn any of these critical skills. In fact, many common group assignments (e.g., group term papers) are often counterproductive because they leave students with a bad feeling about group projects. This occurs because students typically work independently on their own piece of the total project and (particularly the better students) end up feeling like they were forced to "carry" their less-able or less-motivated peers (e.g., see Michaelsen, Black, and Fink 1996).

The Integrated Business Core: A Service-Learning–Based Solution

At the University of Oklahoma, undergraduate students have the opportunity to enroll in a comprehensive service-learning–based program called the Integrated Business Core (IBC), which addresses directly all three problems cited by Porter and McKibbin. IBC was inspired by the MG 101 course at Bucknell University, which, for more than 20 years, has been used to introduce second-semester freshman and first-semester sophomore students to business concepts while the students are in the process of completing their general-education requirements (see Miller 1991). Students both in the Oklahoma Integrated Business Core and in MG 101 at Bucknell create and manage simultaneously two significant enterprises: an actual start-up company and a hands-on community service project. Thus, both Oklahoma and Bucknell use a service-learning experience to provide (1) the opportunity for students to develop interpersonal communication and group-interaction skills in a work-like setting, and (2) the opportunity for students to practice using analytical tools and business concepts to solve a wide range of unstructured problems.

However, despite basic similarities, the Oklahoma Integrated Business Core differs from MG 101 in several significant ways. Indeed, many of the distinctive features of IBC have been *specifically designed* to provide students with an integrated exposure to business concepts. First, students enroll in IBC approximately a year later than do the students at Bucknell: Most participate in IBC during the first semester of their junior year. Second, IBC is an integral part of the business school core curriculum (see Figure 1). Students in IBC are required to concurrently enroll in three linked core business classes along with a three-semester-hour Entrepreneurship and Community Service Practicum. Third, much of the course content and many of the class activities and assignments in each of the core courses are specifically timed to help students resolve the issues they face as they attempt to organize and manage their business and service ventures.

Key IBC Program Elements

The primary motivation for the initial design of IBC was a desire to enable students to develop a cross-disciplinary view of business organizations. A faculty group working to address this issue felt that such a cross-disciplinary view could best be achieved by creating a setting in which students were simultaneously exposed to related concepts from multiple courses and required to apply the concepts in a work-like setting. Further, the faculty design team felt that the impact of the program would be greatest if the

Fig. 1

Business degree requirement summary

Lower-Division Requirements
    Communications
    Behavioral and Social Science
    Humanities
    Science and Mathematics
    Basic Business (Accounting, Economics, Information Systems)

Upper-Division Core Requirements (All Business Majors)
    Business Finance
    Legal Environment of Business *
    Principles of Marketing *
    Principles of Organization and Management *
    Business Strategy and Policy**

Upper-Division Requirements in Addition to the Core
    Major Requirements (18-24 semester hours depending on major)
    Upper-Division Electives (11-20 semester hours) ***
    Free Electives (6-7 semester hours)

 * IBC students must simultaneously enroll in these three courses.
** Capstone; must be taken during students' final semester as a senior.
*** The IBC Practicum course counts in this category.

experience occurred during students' first full semester in the business school so that it could provide a foundation for the remainder of their coursework. The way IBC fits into students' overall business program is shown in Figure 1.

Coursework Linked to Service-Learning

All students in IBC:

1. Simultaneously enroll in three of the four junior-level core business courses — Principles of Organization and Management, Principles of Marketing, and business law — plus a three-hour Entrepreneurship/ Community Service Practicum. The classes are scheduled in a Monday/ Wednesday/ Friday four-hour time period, and on most class days, companies meet in separate rooms during the final hour of the block.

2. Work in six- to eight-member teams that remain constant across the core courses for the entire semester.

3. Complete a number of individual and team projects and exams while being held responsible for mastering the concepts and terminology of each of the functional area core courses.

4. Work as an "employee" of a five- or six-member team (i.e., 30- to 40-member company) that becomes a "laboratory" in which students have the opportunity to apply the concepts from the core business disciplines as they organize and carry out two major projects during the semester — a start-up business venture and a hands-on service project on behalf of a nonprofit campus or community organization.

5. Develop a company business plan in which the business venture is required to make a profit that will then be used to provide the resources needed for the service project. The plan is then presented to a loan review committee, which grants, denies, or defers the loan application (real money up to $5,000 provided by First Fidelity Bank).

6. After obtaining a loan, implement their business plan and generate enough income to pay back their loan and business expenses (plus a 3% "tax" on gross profit to cover future bankruptcies) and to finance their service project.

7. Prepare and present a report on their business and service activities just prior to the final exams in the core content courses.

The Uses of Team Learning

It was clear from the beginning that the traditional lecture/discussion approach to teaching would work against the achievement of the learning objectives described above. As a result, the majority of faculty members who have taught in IBC have used team learning (e.g., see Michaelsen and Black 1994) to ensure that:

1. students have ample opportunity to develop interpersonal/group

interaction skills;

2. the groups in the core courses developed into effective teams;

3. the content in each of the core courses can be covered while reserving the majority of class time for group activities and assignments through which students can develop content-application and problem-solving skills.

Student Autonomy in the Operation of Service-Learning Ventures

Overall, IBC students are very much on their own with respect to organizing themselves, creating a business venture, and developing and implementing a significant community service activity. Faculty guidance is limited to two areas. One is the faculty role in establishing the grading criteria in the Entrepreneurship and Community Service Practicum. The faculty make it clear that students' grade in the practicum will be, in part, determined by how effectively they meet the needs and respond to the concerns of their stakeholders. These stakeholders include fellow students, university faculty and staff (including the janitorial staff who clean the rooms the students work in), customers and suppliers of their business, and recipients of their community service efforts. The other way faculty members provide guidance is by establishing specific deadlines for many of the key business and service activities and decisions. These key milestones are summarized in Figure 2.

Assignments Linked to Multiple Courses and Service-Learning Ventures

Over time, faculty members have developed a number of assignments that help students gain an integrated view of business organizations by requiring the students to use concepts from (and often receive a grade in) more than one of the core courses. In addition, many assignments (both within individual courses and across courses) are also timed so that they provide input on issues facing the IBC companies. Several examples of the linked assignments are shown in Figure 3.

Grades Based on a Broad Range of Conceptual and Interpersonal Skills

Grading in the core courses. Students receive a separate grade for each of the three core courses involved in IBC, based on the grading criteria established by each instructor. Further, even though many of the linked assignments are included as part of the grade for more than one course, each instructor independently decides on how much the assignments "count" and evaluates them using criteria relevant to his or her content area.

There are, however, a number of common features in the grading structures of the three courses. First, faculty members maintain the overall grade point average for each course at approximately the same level as the stand-alone sections of the same core courses. Second, the grading system in all three courses includes three common components: individual performance,

Fig. 2

Schedule of key business and service project milestones

Week	Milestone	Nature of Assignment and/or Required Deliverable	Link to Company Activities/Decisions
2	Team "Planning to Plan" memo	1-page memo from each TEAM that outlines a PROCESS that companies might use to: 1) decide on business and service projects, and 2) pick someone to be in charge until project decisions are made and permanent leaders are chosen.	Ensures broad-based input on decisions about leadership and direction of IBC companies.
2	Company "Planning to Plan" memo	1-page memo from each COMPANY that outlines a PROCESS that companies might use to: 1) decide on business and service projects, and 2) pick someone to be in charge until project decisions are made and permanent leaders are chosen.	Provides push to quit talking and get started doing something
4	Team SWOT analysis	Assignment (independently graded assignment in management and in marketing) requiring each team to conduct a SWOT analysis of one potential business venture and one potential service project organization/site.	When properly managed, provides data on five or six potential business and service ventures.
4	Company SWOT analysis	SWOT analysis (by each company) to the two most promising ideas for a business venture and the two most promising ideas for a service project organization/site.	Ensures systematic evaluation of favored business/service ventures.
5	Choice of business and service ventures	Public commitment on what they are going to do.	Guides all subsequent activity.
5	Organizational charts	Two organizational charts – one for service and one for business. All members must appear on both charts; supervisors in one CANNOT be supervisors in the other.	Forces company members to get organized to complete their work.
5	Mission statements	Companies must articulate what they want to accomplish in business and service.	Gives direction to company activity.
5	Operational web pages	Companies must establish web pages that are linked to a college IBC web page and that support: 1) internal company communication and, 2) product advertising and sales.	Facilitates company operations and expands potential company markets.

Week	Deliverable	Description	Purpose
5	Draft of accounting and control systems	Statement of plans to account for money and product inventory.	First try at nuts 'n bolts procedures for accounting and control activities.
6	Dry run and draft of loan proposal	Oral and written presentation of financial need and why the bank should view them as an investment opportunity (critiqued by class).	Allows companies to strengthen their case as a good loan risk.
7	Loan Presentation	Oral and written presentation of financial need and why the bank should view them as an investment opportunity (evaluated by bank loan committee).	Provides financial resources to implement business and service plans.
8	Final accounting and control system plan	Oral and written presentation – evaluated by university financial services and IBC faculty	Establishes nuts 'n bolts procedures for accounting and control activities.
9-15	Weekly activities report	Report – due each Monday morning – that tracks financial status of and hours worked in business and service organizations	Ensures that companies have data to provide feedback on company decisions and individual contributions.
12	interim report to stakeholders	First detailed financial and overall activity report	Allows companies to learn how to prepare financial statements.
16	Draft final report	Summary statement of results of business and service ventures.	Written report of business and service activities and accomplishments.
16	Final presentation	Oral presentation of information that appears in final report.	Oral report of business and service activities and accomplishments.
16	Company peer evaluations due	Assessment to individual contribution to business and service ventures. Input from supervisors in business and service organizations and from company at large.	Provides feedback on individual contributions to company success.

Fig. 3

Examples of content integration related to company activities

---

During Project "Narrowing" Phase *
- ▶ Management
- ▶ Marketing

- ▶ Organizational Decision Processes
- ▶ SWOT Analysis
- ▶ Market segmentation (i.e., who are the potential customers?)

* Students use segmentation concepts to aid in completing Management SWOT analysis.

After Project Decisions/Before Loan *
- ▶ Marketing
- ▶ Legal Studies

- ▶ Targeting Advertisements
- ▶ Liability from Advertising

* Students create potential company ads in Marketing that are evaluated in Legal Studies.

During Organization/Staffing Process *
- ▶ Management
- ▶ Legal Studies

- ▶ Selection/Placement
- ▶ Employment Law

* Students make hiring decisions from resumes in management and develop case for litigation (for candidates not hired) in Legal Studies.

During Development of Accounting Procedures *
- ▶ Management
- ▶ Accounting

- ▶ Organizational Control Processes
- ▶ Establishing Financial Information Systems and Controls *

* Accounting honorary society evaluates proposed processes in week 6 and audits compliance in week 15.

---

group performance, and a peer evaluation. Third, most of the group assignments and many of the individual assignments involve *applying* concepts rather than simply learning about them. Finally, all three instructors involve students in establishing the grading structure for their courses, using a grade-weight-setting exercise described in Michaelsen, Cragin, and Watson (1981).

Grading in the Entrepreneurship and Community Service Practicum. The grading in the Entrepreneurship and Community Service Practicum is handled quite differently. Students are informed that they start out with a B and can move up or down according to two factors. One is a *company* evaluation based on how effectively they meet the needs and respond to the concerns of their stakeholders. The other is each student's individual contribution to the success of his or her business and community service ventures.

As a practical matter, there are seldom more than minor differences in the company part of the evaluation. For the most part, this is because IBC students conscientiously respond to feedback on their mistakes in dealing with constituencies. For example, a group of overexuberant students unknowingly broke a university regulation by putting flyers under the wiper blades of cars in a university parking lot. This prompted a letter of reprimand to the faculty sponsor from the campus office that oversees the activities of student organizations. The faculty sponsor then met with the company, gave the students the letter, and asked them to take care of the problem. Within a few days, the students reported back on the actions they had taken to make amends for this mistake and to avoid similar problems in the future.

Each student's personal contribution component of the Entrepreneurship and Community Service Practicum grade is based primarily on peer evaluations. Furthermore, two important aspects of the process are used to ensure that the grade represents an accurate assessment of each student's overall contribution to the success of the business and service ventures. One is that the instructors require companies to develop a system for maintaining an ongoing record of each individual's involvement in the business and service activities. Second, each student's grade is based on at least three, and usually four, different sources of data. These are evaluations from his or her supervisor in both the business and service organizations, and at least one, and usually two, at-large evaluations of his or her overall contribution to the business and service ventures.

As a result, student grades in the Entrepreneurship and Community Service Practicum represent a combination of two very different factors: (1) how much "work" students have done on behalf of their company, and (2) how well they have handled their interpersonal relationships with company members. Students who score high on both dimensions or who are outstanding on one dimension and at least average on the other typically get A's. Students whose scores are near average in both dimensions or whose scores are high on one dimension and low on the other typically get B's.

Students who get a C or lower in the practicum tend to fall in one of three groups. Some have held a key position but failed to take the responsibility seriously. Some are so abrasive in working with others that they are unable to offset their negative interpersonal contribution, and a third group simply fails to get involved in company activities.

IBC Business/Service Program Summary (Spring 1995–Spring 1998)

A total of 483 students participated in IBC between the first pilot in the spring semester of 1995 and the spring semester of 1998. These students formed and managed 14 remarkably successful companies.

• IBC student businesses received $32,090 in loans and generated a total revenue of $200,128 and a total net profit of $92,374.

• Twenty-four community service or voluntary nonprofit organizations received: $98,779 in direct financial support from the efforts of IBC student businesses; 3,685 hours of community service as part of IBC-organized activities and projects.

A company-by-company summary of the first 12 business and service activities is shown in Figure 4.

Impact on Students

According to data from questionnaires that were used as part of a systematic evaluation of our core undergraduate curriculum, IBC has had a profound positive impact on the vast majority of students who have participated in the program. For example, when asked to identify the single most positive aspect of their undergraduate business education, more than 80 percent of all IBC students specifically cited some aspect of their experience in the IBC program. By contrast, less than 1 percent of a matched sample of non-IBC students even mentioned anything related to any of their junior-level core courses.

Immediate Positive Outcomes

Given the comprehensive nature of IBC, it is not surprising that students report a wide variety of positive outcomes from their participation in the program. When asked to identify the single most valuable aspect of IBC, student responses typically fall in one of three areas:

Fig. 4

Integrated Business Core (IBC) project summaries

Spring 1995

Rosco's Coffee
- Established & operated a coffee, bagel and pastry cart for students and faculty
- $2,300 loan * - $7,900 revenue - $2,800 profit **
- Children's Hospital learning center

Run For an A
- Organized the "April Fools Classic" (5-K Run & 2K walk)
- $1,300 loan * - $2,400 revenue - $800 profit **
- Battered women's shelter

Fall 1995

IBC Enterprises
- Organized the "Sooner Charity Scramble" (golf tournament)
- Self-financed - $6,300 revenue - $2,400 profit **
- J. D. McCarty Center (treatment center for children with developmental disabilities)

Sooner Magic
- Created & sold "100 Years of Sooner Magic" (calendar celebrating OU football centennial)
- $4,300 loan * - $11,200 revenue - $5,800 profit **
- East Main Place (homeless shelter for families)

Spring 1996

Sooner Entertainment
- Organized a rock concert
- $2,500 loan * - $5,200 revenue - $2,100 profit **
- Jesus House (homeless shelter)

Sooner Sandlot
- Organized a benefit dinner & silent auction
- $2000 loan * - $5,900 revenue - $1,900 profit **
- Big Brothers/Big Sisters of Cleveland County

Fall 1996

Original Basket Case
- Created & sold a "care" basket for freshman students in dorms -- marketed to parents.
- $1,000 loan * - $3,900 revenue - $1,300 profit **
- Second Chance Pet Sanctuary

I B Cookin
- Created & sold "Building Oklahoma from the Inside" (cookbook with recipes from famous Oklahomans)
- $2,000 loan * - $8,500 revenue - $4,600 profit **
- Habitat for Humanity

Spring 1997

Social Tees
- Created & sold "Big 12 of Norman" T-shirt featuring logos of 12 popular entertainment establishments
- $2,400 loan * - $24, 400 revenue - $11,800 profit **
- J. D. McCarty Center (treatment center for children with developmental disabilities)

Disco IBC
- Created & sold "Sooner Express" (discount card for OU students and Norman community)
- $2,000 loan * - $41,000 revenue - $15,400 profit **
- Leland Wolf School (residential facility for abused children)

Fall 1997

I B Muggin'
- Created & sold "The Mug" (a 32 oz. mug that entitled the owner to discounts at local merchants)
- $1,000 loan * - $18,540 revenue - $15,239 profit**
- Cleveland County Youth & Family Services and Central Oklahoma Special Olympics

Crimson Classics
- Created & sold "A Shot in the Dark" (a lithograph made from an aerial photo of the first night game played under permanent lights in Owen Stadium.)
- $4,000 loan * - $37,752 revenue - $17,681 profit **
- Action Inc. (umbrella social service agency serving disadvantaged families in Cleveland County)

* Loans are funded by a grant from First Fidelity Bank.
** All IBC company profits are used to benefit nonprofit community organizations either by financing student service projects or through cash donations. Profit is the balance remaining after paying off the loan and all business expenses.

(Note: Products from Disco IBC and IB Muggin' also generated $6,405 in revenue for 12 additional community organizations including sports teams, church youth groups and the Pride of Oklahoma Band.)

1. IBC students report having a better understanding of foundational business concepts, and identify at least three specific reasons for these learning gains. First, the integrated exposure to the material in the core courses provides a "big picture" so they are able to see how the concepts from different disciplines fit together. Second, students frequently report that the hands-on experience helps them gain both a greater understanding of and increased ability to retain the concepts over time. Third, having to solve real problems not only teaches students how the concepts apply to the IBC companies but, more important, enhances their ability to see applications of the new ideas and approaches they encounter in later courses.

2. Unlike most small-group-based class projects, IBC business and service projects require students to coordinate the efforts of 30 to 40 people and, in most cases, serve in both supervisory and nonsupervisory positions. As a result, managing the people side of IBC companies provides some of the students' most valued learning opportunities. Furthermore, many of the lessons they learn come from experiencing the natural consequences of mistakes. Often, the important lesson is that building positive working relationships with others is an essential aspect of running a successful business. For some, the experience serves as a "wake-up call" when they receive low peer evaluations and, for the first time, are confronted with the fact that the way they interact with others is ineffective.

3. IBC profoundly changes the social aspect of the rest of the students' undergraduate experience. One of IBC's many positive by-products is that it creates a very strong sense of community among its participants. In contrast to typical core courses that have a drop-out rate of 10 percent to 15 percent, only one of the 597 students enrolled in the first eight offerings of IBC dropped out after attending more than two classes. Nor does the difference end there. When asked about how things are going in later courses, IBC students invariably speak in terms of *we* — they and one or more IBC peers with whom they have voluntarily chosen to work and study. In fact, many instructors in higher-level courses find that they cannot allow self-formed project groups because other students are simply unable to compete with groups composed of former IBC students.

Future Positive Outcomes

IBC also provides students with an opportunity to learn about their reactions to different roles they might play in the business world. Some learn that they will never want to be in a sales position, while others thrive there. Some learn what managers do and, for the first time, realize they can also do these things. Others, who thought they would be excellent managers, realize they have a lot to learn about working with people.

One especially valuable by-product of the peer evaluation process in the

Entrepreneurship and Community Service Practicum is that the data provide students with both quantitative and qualitative feedback on their interpersonal skills. Students who have done well have learned that prospective employers regard their peer evaluation scores and comments as concrete evidence of their ability to work with others. When students receive low peer evaluations, they benefit by having a way to learn about how they can improve their ability to work effectively with others. In many cases, IBC instructors are able to use verbatim comments to provide substantive examples of three important factors that students will face in their future jobs. First, working with others is like maintaining a bank account: Some kinds of interactions put money in the bank, while others take it out. Second, the only way to change the outcome is to change the way one interacts. Third, one is free to choose how one interacts with others, but if one chooses to be abrasive, one burdens oneself with the need to do more just to come out even in comparison with those who do a better job of working with others.

IBC's greatest contribution, however, may be that it allows an entrepreneurial experience to occur in core courses that must be taken by anyone seeking to earn a business degree. As a result, many students who have been aiming for a job with a large national firm learn that they really enjoy an entrepreneurial business environment. IBC also helps students concretely prepare for entrepreneurial careers in three quite different ways. First, students experience directly the entire process of generating an idea and building a business around it. Second, they learn that, in spite of their mistakes, they can compete. Finally, IBC actually helps some students get a real start in a business of their own. In fact, several of the IBC businesses are still in operation, either as personal ventures for IBC students, or for customers or even competitors who have seen the value in what the students have created.

Service-Learning–Related Positive Outcomes

The IBC program provides community service opportunities in two ways, both of which provide significant benefits for students. First, in recent semesters, students have averaged about 15 community service hours each in activities that were organized by IBC companies. These events provide students with the opportunity to organize and carry out a wide variety of activities that require planning and coordination. While preparing for and participating in such activities, students develop a wide range of interpersonal and problem-solving skills. For example, several hundred IBC students have completed professionally supervised tutor-training programs so that they would be prepared to work with various types of elementary and secondary students and handicapped youth and adults. Others have learned construction skills, ranging from hanging wallboard to finishing cement, and still others have learned to work effectively with individuals and groups with whom, without IBC, they would probably have never come into contact. These include youth and adults who are homeless and/or who have a wide range of physical and mental handicaps.

The IBC program also provides community service through the financial resources that result from the profits of the start-up business ventures. IBC students have experienced a great deal of personal satisfaction in being able to provide needed material and financial resources to community service organizations. These resources have included such things as laundry equipment for a homeless shelter for families, outdoor play/recreation equipment for several elementary schools and for a residential school for children awaiting foster home placement, and checks for up to $15,000 of discretionary funds. Between the initial offering of the program in the spring semester of 1995 and the spring semester of 1998, IBC companies and their products generated a total of $98,779 in direct financial support for 24 public service agencies. Further, the fundraising capacity of the IBC companies seems to be increasing. During the fall semester of 1998 (the semester during which this chapter was being written), the three IBC companies were on a pace that would result in a total profit of more than $50,000. To put that amount in perspective, during 1998, the entire United Way drive in Norman, Oklahoma, raised approximately $1 million. In other words, in approximately two months and through the operation of student-created business ventures, 107 college juniors will have raised approximately 5 percent of that total for public service organizations in the same community.

Another important aspect of the students' service-learning experience is that it leads in two important ways to further involvement in the community. Throughout their stay in Norman, many students simply continue with the work they began with their IBC service organization assignment. Some have even taken on additional responsibilities. For example, a former IBC service organization vice-president is currently serving on the executive board of Juvenile Services Incorporated as director of volunteer activities. It may be, however, that the most important public service contribution of IBC is that every program alumnus has helped conceive and manage a community service fundraising effort that is based on providing a useful product or service instead of simply asking for contributions from potential donors. In fact, two recent IBC graduates are now serving as chairs of other community fundraising efforts. One is on behalf of a Greek fraternity on the OU campus. The other is for a local chapter of the American Red Cross.

Business and Community Response

The response of the business community to IBC has been overwhelmingly positive. The OU career center reports that employers are increasingly focusing their recruiting efforts on OU because they believe IBC teaches many of the most important realities of the business world. Students now find that most interviewers are so interested in IBC that they quickly abandon their "canned" questions in favor of a discussion of what the students learned from their IBC experience. This gives IBC graduates a clear competitive advantage over peers who have little to talk about beyond group projects, part-time jobs, and club activities. As a result, many students credit IBC with having made a significant difference in their securing both internships and jobs — especially in growth-oriented companies.

The response of the nonprofit and community organizations has been equally enthusiastic. For example, their interest in having IBC students work with and for their organizations had at a time grown to the point that simply giving them all a chance to describe their needs was making it difficult for the companies to get started. As a result, in the spring of 1998, the IBC faculty were forced to organize a "service fair" so students could explore their potential service opportunities more efficiently. Even on short notice, representatives of 11 different community organizations participated in the initial service fair. In the fall of 1998, the number of organizations participating increased to 14, and to judge from inquiries received to date, interest is still growing.

Implications for IBC Faculty

From a faculty standpoint, one of the greatest assets of IBC is practicality. Many schools that have attempted to integrate their curricula or introduce a significant service-leaning experience have done so by creating a new set of course offerings. As a result, some of these efforts have involved substantial costs in both dollars and faculty time. In IBC, the integration occurs by linking the content of otherwise freestanding junior-level core courses to the activities of the IBC business and service organizations. The key is that faculty members have adopted "just-in-time" (JIT) coverage of the concepts in each of the courses (i.e., the concepts are presented in a sequence that allows students to attempt to apply them in making decisions in their IBC companies). As a result, IBC was implemented with *no* catalogue changes and only a minimum of program development time and expense. Further, because the service-learning activities are related to three existing courses, the three instructors can share the additional work associated with the Entrepreneurship and Community Service Practicum.

From our experience, we have learned that successful implementation of a pilot offering of an IBC-like program requires only six things:

1. Faculty members from at least three disciplines who are willing to work together to develop a JIT sequence for delivering the content of their individual courses and a philosophy for deciding on grades in the lab course. (The OU program actually started with two tenure-track and one adjunct faculty member; for two of the most successful semesters, it operated with one tenure-track faculty, one adjunct instructor, and one PhD student.)

2. At least one faculty member who understands the team-development process and is both comfortable with and experienced in designing and managing in-class group activities.

3. A faculty member who is willing to monitor and provide ongoing feedback on documents that reflect the progress and financial status of the IBC companies.

4. A faculty member who is willing to oversee grading in the Entrepreneurship and Community Service Practicum. (By far the most time-consuming and challenging part of this responsibility is collecting and compiling the peer evaluation data, and counseling and coaching students who need help in learning how to work more effectively with others.)

5. The cooperation of the staff member who is responsible for making sure that students are enrolled in the specifically linked sections of the core courses.

6. Seed money to cover the loans to the IBC companies. (The Oklahoma experience suggests that this is the least difficult of the six requirements. The IBC idea is so intuitively appealing that numerous organizations and individuals have volunteered to underwrite the loans.)

Institutional Costs and Benefits

The cost of development and implementation has been minimal. The initial start-up cost was limited to a modest stipend for the two adjunct faculty members involved in the IBC pilot. After the benefits of IBC became clear, the college incurred some additional costs in preparing to expand the program to a larger number of students. (During the initial semesters, enrollment was limited to two companies — i.e., 70 to 75 students per semester. In the fall of 1998, the enrollment was expanded to three companies — i.e., 107 students — and was expected to be six companies — i.e., 210 students — in the fall of 1999.) These additional costs include dedicating a room as an office for IBC companies and hiring an upper-division undergraduate student (a former IBC student) as an adviser for each of the IBC companies.

From a business college and university standpoint, the greatest benefit of IBC has probably been the tremendous media coverage the program has received. To take one example, in just eight months, IBC was the focus of eight front page and 22 other articles or photo stories in the major Oklahoma newspapers. In addition, IBC has received a number of regional and national honors. The national honors include being featured in a November 1997 *BusinessWeek* article and receiving a 1998 Leavey Award from the Freedom Foundation of Valley Forge, Pennsylvania. Regional honors include being named a 1998 Program Innovation Award recipient by the Southwest Business Deans' Association, and having the faculty member who took the lead in developing IBC (Larry Michaelsen) named as a finalist in the Ernst & Young "1998 Entrepreneur of the Year" competition.

This kind of recognition and publicity has helped create a positive impression in the community at large and with potential students, employers, and donors. For example, IBC has been featured in the fall 1998 University of Oklahoma parents' newsletter and in a new brochure to be given to students who ask for information on the university's academic programs. In addition, the barrage of favorable publicity about IBC has clearly aided in developing a positive climate for both business college and university fundraising efforts.

Impact on IBC Faculty

The road leading to IBC's becoming a mainstream business college program at the University of Oklahoma has been a rocky one. Many of the faculty frustrations associated with developing IBC have grown out of the fact that it has been very much a bottom-up effort. During the first few semesters, the extra work involved in coordinating across courses, supporting students in managing their business and service ventures, and overcoming obstacles inherent in dealing with the university bureaucracy was neither rewarded nor supported. Furthermore, a significant proportion of the faculty was skeptical about whether the coursework associated with IBC would adequately prepare students for their upper-division courses. As a result, IBC faculty members were forced simply to persevere, relying on their conviction that the positive outcomes of the program would justify both its existence and the effort in getting it up and running.

Fortunately, the positive outcomes now speak for themselves. Students no longer wonder about whether to enroll in a program that requires a considerably greater commitment than do normal stand-alone classes; instead, student demand has grown much faster than the capacity of the program. IBC student performance in subsequent courses has silenced faculty concerns; and instead of worrying about student mistakes causing some sort of a public relations disaster, the administration is now looking for ways to expand IBC and make it even more visible.

From a faculty standpoint, the best part of IBC is its effect on students' willingness to take responsibility for their own learning. The contrast between IBC students and students in the stand-alone core courses is remarkable. Although IBC students still worry about grades, their *primary* focus is on understanding how the ideas from their courses might help them do a better job of dealing with issues they face in their business and service activities. Because of their high level of enthusiasm, teaching in the IBC program is a genuine pleasure.

In conclusion, IBC faculty members strongly believe that the positive outcomes achieved at the University of Oklahoma can be easily duplicated elsewhere. They further recommend two steps to lessen faculty frustration and accelerate the program development process. One is to involve administrators in assessing the need for and the outcomes desired by introducing such a program. The other is to create mechanisms, in advance, for assessing whether or not each of the desired outcomes is being achieved.

References

Michaelsen, L.K., and R.H. Black. (1994). "Building Learning Teams: The Key to Harnessing the Power of Small Groups in Higher Education." In *Collaborative Learning: A Sourcebook for Higher Education, Volume 2*, edited by S. Kadel and J. Keehner, pp. 65-81. State College, PA: National Center for Teaching, Learning, and Assessment.

————, and L.D. Fink. (1996). "What Every Faculty Developer Needs to Know About Learning Groups." In *To Improve the Academy: Resources for Faculty, Instructional, and Organizational Development*, edited by L. Richlin, pp. 31-58. Stillwater, OK: New Forums Press.

Michaelsen, L.K., J.P. Cragin, and W.E. Watson. (1981). "Grading and Anxiety: A Strategy for Coping." *Exchange: The Organizational Behavior Teaching Journal* 6(1): 8-14.

Miller, J.A. (1991). "Experiencing Management: A Comprehensive, 'Hands-On' Model for the Introductory Management Course." *Journal of Management Education* 15(2): 151-173.

Porter, L.W., and L.E. McKibbin. (1988). *Management Education and Development: Drift or Thrust Into the 21st Century?* New York, NY: McGraw-Hill.

Learning Well by Doing Good:
Service-Learning in Management Education

by Christine H. Lamb, James B. Lee, Robert L. Swinth, and Karen L. Vinton

The American Association for Higher Education (AAHE) defines service-learning as "an intellectual and civic engagement of students by linking the work students do in the classroom to real-world problems and world needs" <http://www.aahe.org/service/srv-lrn.htm>. The College of Business at Montana State University-Bozeman (MSU) has integrated this concept of service-learning into its curriculum to provide students with opportunities to put theory into practice in the not-for-profit sector and to encourage students to be productive stakeholders in their education, as well as in their college, university, and community.

Design of Service-Learning

Integration of service-learning experiences into higher education has been occurring for decades (Kraft and Krug 1994). More recently, service-learning has been integrated into business courses (Kohls 1996; Kolenko et al. 1996; Zlotkowski 1996). Overall, engaging students in service-learning has successfully combined the pedagogical principles of experiential learning (Dewey 1938) with a variety of goals: personal development, career development, moral development, academic achievement (Williams 1990), and "reflective civic participation" (Newmann 1990). Recently, the systematic integration of a developmental service-learning agenda into the business curriculum has been attempted (Lamb et al. 1998).

However, the systematic integration of a developmental service-learning agenda into a specific curriculum can be problematic. A recent critique of service-learning projects in business school curricula cites the following major barriers to making service-learning a viable part of a student's educational experience: faculty/organizational resistance, development of an institutional infrastructure for supporting service-learning, and demonstration of the relevance of service-learning to management education (Kolenko 1996: 137-138).

In addressing issues of faculty and organizational resistance, the faculty of the College of Business have been able to rely heavily on the mission of Montana State University to reinforce an organizational culture in which service is viewed as a "value-added" component of teaching and learning. As the state land-grant institution, MSU has a long-standing tradition of service to the state and region. Faculty are expected to contribute to the institution's mission in the areas of teaching, research, *and* service, and the formal performance appraisal system monitors each area in making decisions related to compensation, promotion, and tenure. The university has also integrated service and citizenship into many dimensions of student life. Several MSU documents reflect service expectations for students. An orientation document includes the following student expectations: Students will be "positive contributors to the university and Bozeman community" and "will embrace the value of volunteerism" (MSU 1995: 15). Community awareness is also one of the goals of the university general-education core: Students will be able to "make discriminating moral and ethical choices with an awareness of the immediate and long-term effects on our world" (MSU 1996: 34).

Grounding the expectations of service and citizenship in the organizational culture of the institution has helped to break down both student and faculty resistance to service-learning. Over the past few years, a number of student- and faculty-initiated projects have been developed, ranging from a student-researched seismic awareness symposium to a student chapter of Habitat for Humanity (advised, incidentally, by a College of Business professor).

A second barrier to successful integration of service-learning into the organization is the development of an infrastructure for sustaining service efforts. Much of the resistance to integrating service-learning is related to the routine operation of identifying potential agencies, assisting students with making contacts, maintaining and nurturing good relationships with agencies, and assisting faculty with their design of service-learning activities. Batchelder and Root (1994: 353) also cite promotion of high-quality on-site reflection as one of the major factors related to effective service-learning.

At Montana State University, the operational functions of service-learning efforts are the charge of the Office for Community Involvement (OCI). This office is the institution's permanent and visible liaison with the service-providing agencies of the community and the region. Largely supported by grant funding, the OCI not only serves as a clearinghouse for a multitude of service opportunities but also plays an integral role in promoting service-learning in the organizational culture. One of its first projects was to develop an event aptly named "Into the Streets." Each semester, a wide variety of agencies come to campus for a two-day sign-up opportunity. Literally hundreds of students take advantage of the opportunity to sign up for agency projects. The first Into the Streets event was designed and implemented by College of Business students whose commitment to service had been reinforced through a number of service-learning experiences in their management courses.

The third barrier to integrating service-learning as an effective component of management education — its disciplinary relevance — was addressed by making a conscious pedagogical and philosophical commitment to implementing a series of developmental service-learning experiences within the overall curriculum. Batchelder and Root (1994) cite high-quality, on-campus instruction as their second significant factor in promoting effective service-learning. Curricular integration of service-learning also provides an opportunity to introduce some elements of the content of undergraduate management education in order to make learning relevant to students' personal and professional development. The College of Business's major service-learning goals are as follows:

- *To enhance student learning through a systematic application of business competencies in the context of service to the community.*
- *To introduce students to examples of businesses committed to "doing well by doing good and doing good by doing well."*
- *To promote reflection on the choices businesses make in fulfilling their social responsibilities.*
- *To promote effective teams that not only engage student team members with one another but that also engage students with the community and service to others.*
- *To familiarize students with the goals and organization of not-for-profit businesses and to enrich the content of management education with "lessons of social, intercultural understanding, and ethical reasoning." (Kupic 1993: 8)*

In order to actualize these goals and to promote systematic internalization of a sense of social responsibility, several service-learning experiences were designed and implemented throughout the curriculum. The design of these experiences was developmental in nature and can be best understood using the model of service-learning postulated by Delve, Mintz, and Stewart (1990). This model connects types of service-learning experiences to a continuum of stages in students' moral development as conceived in the work of Gilligan (1982), Kohlberg (1975), and Perry (1970). The model identifies a number of variables to be addressed in each service-learning exercise, as well as developmental phases that engage learners at continuously more reflective and independent levels of learning.

The remainder of this chapter will discuss two of the key service-learning opportunities in MSU's business curriculum: (1) the first course taken by first-year business students, the Freshman Seminar; and (2) the last course taken by undergraduate business students, the Senior Seminar, which also constitutes the capstone course. Outcomes of MSU's service-learning initiatives will be discussed at the end of the paper.

Implementation

Freshman Seminar

Because details of the design of this course are available elsewhere (Lamb et al. 1997; MSU 1997), only those aspects of the course that relate to service-learning will be discussed here. The major objectives of the course are to enhance students' connection and commitment to the college and university, and to introduce them to the profession in the context of a diverse and extremely dynamic global environment, one that calls for broadly educated and professionally knowledgeable stakeholders.

Service-learning in the Freshman Seminar consists of a series of discussions, written reflections, and a direct service project in the community. Service-learning is introduced in the context of the stakeholder model that emphasizes the interconnectedness of businesses and legal, regulatory, sociological, and competitive environments. Students are asked to personalize the stakeholder model by identifying their primary and secondary stakeholders. Discussion focuses on students' roles as stakeholders in the college, university, and community. They examine businesses that have been recognized as doing well by doing good, and discuss the role of business in promoting healthy communities.

Subsequent to this stakeholder analysis, students have an opportunity to hear firsthand about the personal and professional merits of service. A panel of several prominent businesspersons describe their commitment to community service and the impact of their efforts on their personal lives and professional success. Students submit written reflections on the relationship among service, success in business, and social responsibility, and they identify contributions they aspire to make in their personal and professional lives.

The last phase of this sequence involves students directly in a service experience. Students are formed into teams of four, based on their career interests, and in these teams work together all semester on a variety of assignments. Each team's first responsibility is to complete a service-learning project in the community. This experience provides an opportunity for the team to develop cohesion while directing its efforts toward an external goal (in contrast to traditional team-building exercises and activities). In order to mitigate the impact of nearly 450 students a year on community agencies, selection of a service experience is coordinated through the Into the Streets event discussed above. Teams select activities that interest them and agree to three to four hours of service over the semester.

Keeping in mind that the goals of the freshman service-learning experience are positive team building and introductory exposure to the not-for-profit sector, one should not be surprised that student teams engage in traditional community service activities. They build and repair trails, stock shelves at the local food bank, chaperone junior high dances, visit shut-ins, and participate in a variety of programs in the local schools. As has been mentioned, their required commitment is only three to four hours; however, many volunteer for additional time and projects.

After their service work, teams share their experiences in their seminar sections as well as submit a memo detailing the activities and contributions of each member of the team. Each student also submits an individual memo that includes personal reflections on the service experience as well as a response to the question "Why should businesses participate in community service activities?" (See the assignment "BUS 101: Service-Learning Project" reproduced at the end of this chapter for details.)

The impact of this assignment is evident in two subsequent class activities. About mid term, students prepare a Personal Strategic Plan (PSP) that includes an academic course plan as well as strategies for personal and professional development. They begin by preparing responses to 10 typical job interview questions, which they answer as if they were graduating seniors. The intention here is to have students confront the expectations of the employment market and ask themselves, "How will I choose courses, jobs, and other activities that build the knowledge and skills needed for a successful career?" Students prepare a plan of courses (major/minor/electives) and extracurricular activities that support their career intentions. In these plans, they frequently identify sustained involvement in service activities as mechanisms to build interpersonal and leadership skills.

Second, in the team's final assignment, which is to develop a business plan, teams frequently include formal community service agendas in their plans — how their new business will contribute to the community. This service dimension is not specified in either assignment but arises naturally from the students' very positive service-learning activities and from their growing awareness of their roles as stakeholders in their education and community. For example, one team identified an agency to which the team's business would donate a percentage of its profits. Another team indicated it would encourage its employees to participate regularly in service activities, including sponsoring a city league softball team.

In summary, integration of service-learning at the first-year level focuses primarily on the development of student awareness and appreciation of social responsibility and the role of business in sustaining healthy communities. Service-learning activities serve both as the context for effective team formation and as a vehicle to introduce students to the not-for-profit dimensions of business. The overall goal of the freshman experience is to introduce students to service and to prepare them for more extensive and strategic service-learning involvement later.

Senior Seminar

This course is the business capstone course in which students are required to apply concepts, skills, and values mastered in the business core courses (management, marketing, finance, and accounting) to strategic analyses of a variety of firms, including not-for-profits. The structure of the course is similar to that of the Freshman Seminar; however, as a capstone course it requires that students engage in activities at a strategic and integrative level.

While the course has a number of objectives, the service-learning objective of the course is as follows: Students will become sensitive to the value of an organizational philosophy founded on principles of ethical integrity and social responsibility. Like the first-year course, the Senior Seminar embeds service-learning in the context of intellectual discussion, strategic application, and personal/professional reflection.

The concept of service-learning is first introduced into the course by means of a case study. Students analyze the case of a not-for-profit firm and identify those issues and concerns both that are similar to those of for-profits and that are unique to the not-for-profit arena. An experienced manager with expertise in not-for-profit organizations as well as in the specific topic of the case supervises the analysis. Students present their case analyses to this external expert and are provided with feedback. This interactive approach gives them an opportunity to focus on the not-for-profit firm and to practice making strategic recommendations.

The actual service-learning activity is introduced in the second week of the semester. Each team initiates a semester-long project with a local not-for-profit organization. Occasionally, students select agencies with which they have worked in their freshman assignment. Using discipline-specific skills, students conduct a strategic analysis of their client organization and make strategic recommendations. At the end of the semester, they present their findings and recommendations to the whole class. Each team's final report and recommendations are forwarded to its partner agency (see the BUS 474 assignment reproduced at the end of the chapter).

Thus, while freshmen engage in a short-term, awareness-building experience, seniors engage in a long-term, strategic application. Senior teams employ a variety of strategic analysis techniques, such as SWOT assessment and the development of strategic group maps. The following examples of senior projects illustrate the application of competencies and the internalization of values of social responsibility promoted in the senior experience:

• *Big Brothers and Sisters:* This organization matches children ages 5 to 15 with carefully screened volunteers. At the time of this project, BB&S was exploring the best way to position itself in the community. It wished to identify events it could sponsor that would uniquely position it relative to other community service agencies. In this way, it hoped to attract volunteers who were particularly suited to its goals and needs, but not to duplicate events other organizations were sponsoring. This service-learning experience required that students apply concepts of marketing, market segmentation, promotion, and strategic planning in order to make strategic recommendations.

• *Lions Club and Its Mountain Youth Camp:* The Lions Club was reviewing its mission and assessing the function of the youth camp it sponsors each year. A student team interviewed members of the Lions Club's board of directors, evaluated the camp's performance, and helped to develop a vision and mission for the organization. In this project, students conducted primary market research as well as gained a better understanding of how a professional volunteer organization such as the Lions operates, its problems, and its issues. At the same time, they actively engaged in strategic planning for the organization.

• *Gallatin Valley Food Bank:* When the Gallatin Valley Food Bank was notified that it would be one of the designated agencies for a local program called Blue Jean Friday, it contacted a student team from the Senior Seminar. Blue Jean Friday, the first Friday of each month, is a day when employees in local businesses donate $2.00 to wear blue jeans to work. Each month the organizers select a different agency to receive the proceeds for the month. The students worked on marketing and promotional measures to increase participation in the Food Bank. They conducted several analyses and worked with its board of directors to develop a strategy and the steps necessary to implement that strategy. Students benefited from seeing the consequences of their efforts. The Food Bank benefited from a larger than ever turnout for Blue Jean Friday and a chance to introduce a new set of people to its mission.

In addition to their involvement in actual business solutions, students engage in reflection on the fundamental value questions related to business's social responsibility. Students prepare a senior version of the Personal Strategic Plan in which they conduct a strategic analysis of their desired career path. Frequently, they identify continued commitment to service as integral to their personal and professional lives. However, unlike the freshmen, seniors have a broader awareness of the ways in which they can serve. Their work with not-for-profit agencies has made them aware that many are made up of business professionals (e.g., Rotary), are governed by business professionals (through their boards of directors), or need people with business skills. The students' internalization of the values of service and social responsibility is evident not only in their commitment to continue to serve their communities but also in their aspirations to serve on boards and as business consultants to not-for-profit organizations.

Service-Learning Outcomes

Systematic integration of service-learning in the freshman and senior years has been effective in enhancing student learning. Through service-learning, freshmen develop productive team skills, an appreciation of the role they play as socially responsible stakeholders as well as the role businesses play in the health of communities, and an awareness of the not-for-profit sector. In the senior year, student learning is enhanced by the application of professional competencies in strategic problem solving for the not-for-profit sector. In summary, the benefits of integrating service-learning into the College of Business curriculum have been as follows:

- enhanced relationship and collaboration with the community;
- broader definition of self as stakeholder in the community as well as of the community as a stakeholder in the College of Business;
- enhanced appreciation of not-for-profit businesses and organizations;
- systematic learning experiences that challenge students to think critically, apply their learning in the context of service, and analyze firms' organizational culture and service commitment.

The overall impact of this integration of service-learning into the curriculum has been evident in the way in which "service" has become an important element of the culture of the College of Business and of Montana State University. A large proportion of the College's faculty appreciate the value of service-learning, and these faculty members have integrated service-learning into their courses where appropriate. Students in accounting provide volunteer tax preparation assistance to the large number of foreign students on campus (who are unable to afford professional help) and to low-income persons in the community (VITA program). Students in information technology classes design and implement information systems for social service organizations as class projects. One researcher in the College of Nursing, who is attempting to provide outreach assistance to rural women suffering from chronic illnesses, has asked for help in establishing a computer chat line to allow the women to support one another in facing their illnesses and enable them to seek information about their conditions from national associations. Students in the College's information systems course not only have provided the help but also have assisted with the preparation of a grant proposal seeking funding for the project.

This commitment to service has also generated a substantive increase in the number of students who seek to assist local community service organizations outside the context of courses or curricular requirements. Having experienced the personal rewards of service, students reach out on their own (or in coordinated ways through fraternities and sororities) to become a

Big Sister or Big Brother, to become a CAP volunteer or a Peanut Butter Pal at a local elementary school, or to work on a regular basis with the Red Cross.

Conclusion

Although the systematic integration of service-learning into the curriculum of MSU's College of Business represents an attempt to provide an undergraduate management education that promotes the development of well-educated, reflective professionals prepared to serve as productive, contributing members of society, this paper has focused on only two specific College of Business initiatives. However, engaging students in service-learning in any venue demonstrates how community and university collaborations can reinforce mutually beneficial relationships among a variety of stakeholders. Service-learning benefits more than just the classroom community. Through it students get an opportunity to learn about social responsibility firsthand, while honing their team and critical-thinking skills. The community has an opportunity to see the university and its students as something other than consumers of tax resources and beer. Most important, students are given an opportunity to engage in service in ways that will ultimately promote internalization of and commitment to social responsibility and effective citizenship.

References

Batchelder, T., and S. Root. (1994). "Effects of an Undergraduate Program to Integrate Academic Learning and Service: Cognitive, Prosocial Cognitive, and Identity Outcomes." *Journal of Adolescence* 17: 341-355.

Delve, C.I., S.D. Mintz, and G.M. Stewart, eds. (1990). *Promoting Values Development Through Community Service: A Design.* New Directions for Student Services, no. 50. San Francisco, CA: Jossey-Bass.

Dewey, J. (1938). *Experience and Education.* New York, NY: Macmillan.

Gilligan, C. (1982). *In a Different Voice: Psychological Theory and Women's Development.* Cambridge, MA: Harvard University Press.

Kohlberg, L. (1975). "The Cognitive-Developmental Approach to Moral Education." *Phi Delta Kappan* 56: 670-677.

Kohls, J. (1996). "Student Experiences With Service-Learning in a Business Ethics Course." *Journal of Business Ethics* 15: 45-57.

Kolenko, T., G. Porter, W. Wheatley, and M. Colby. (1996). "A Critique of Service-Learning Projects in Management Education: Pedagogical Foundations, Barriers, and Guidelines." *Journal of Business Ethics* 15(1): 133-142.

Kraft, R.J., and J. Krug. (1994). "Review of Research and Evaluation on Service-Learning in Public and Higher Education." In *Building Community: Service-Learning in the Academic Disciplines,* edited by R. Kraft and M. Swadener, pp. 199-213. Denver, CO: Campus Compact.

Kupic, T., ed. (1993). *Rethinking Tradition: Integrating Service With Academic Study on College Campuses.* Washington, DC: Education Commission of the States.

Lamb, C.H., J.B. Lee, and K.L. Vinton. (1997). "Developing a Freshman Seminar: Challenges and Opportunities." *Journal of Management Education* 21(1): 27-43.

Lamb, C.H., J.B. Lee, R.L. Swinth, and K.L. Vinton. (1998). "Integrating Service-Learning Into a Business School Curriculum." *Journal of Management Education* 22(5): 637-654.

Montana State University-Bozeman, College of Business. (1995). *MSU 1995-96 Source Book.* Bozeman, MT: Montana State University.

————. (1996). *Undergraduate Bulletin.* Available at the MSU-Bozeman website at <http://www.montana.edu/wwwcat/>.

————. (1997). "College of Business, MSU-Bozeman" homepage: <http://www.montana.edu/wwwdb/>.

Newmann, F.M. (1990). "Reflective Civic Participation." In *Combining Service and Learning, Volume 1,* edited by J. Kendall and Associates, pp. 76-83. Raleigh, NC: National Society for Internships and Experiential Education.

Patterson, Thomas. (1994). *Montana Land Reliance.* Case No. 9-784-050. Cambridge, MA: Harvard Business School.

Perry, W., Jr. (1970). *Forms of Intellectual and Ethical Development in the College Years: A Scheme.* New York, NY: Holt, Rinehart & Winston.

Porter, L., and L. McKibbin. (1988). *Management Education and Development: Drift or Thrust Into the 21st Century?* New York, NY: McGraw-Hill.

Williams, R., ed. (1990). "The Impact of Field Education on Student Development: Research Findings." In *Combining Service and Learning, Volume 1,* edited by J. Kendall and Associates, pp. 130-147. Raleigh, NC: National Society for Internships and Experiential Education.

Zlotkowski, E. (1996). "Opportunity for All: Linking Service-Learning and Business Education." *Journal of Business Ethics* 15: 5-19.

BUS 101: Service-Learning Project

- **Service-learning Project:** As prospective business professionals it is important that you have experience with many types of businesses. The Service-Learning Project has several very special goals. First, it provides you with an opportunity to be a "service provider" rather than a "service consumer" in the community. We hope that your service to the community of Bozeman will be as rewarding to you as it is useful and meaningful for those with whom you work. Second, it provides you with an opportunity to be involved with the nonprofit sector of business and to gain a broader perspective of "being in business" especially since businesses frequently encourage their employees to engage in community service activities. In order to complete this project, please read the following guidelines carefully.

- **Choosing your experience:** With your business team members, attend INTO THE STREETS to find an interesting project or consult the Community Involvement Calendar either by ASK-US in the SUB or by the Office of Community Involvement, 247 Reid Hall. If you are already involved in service-learning or know of a project not listed on the calendar, you may use that agency or activity.

- **Setting up your experience:** Each team needs to choose a project. The primary criterion to use to determine the most appropriate way to complete the project is to determine how the group can make the greatest contribution to the community. Convenience should not be the major criterion. Once you have decided which option you prefer, contact the person at the agency you have chosen and set up the details of your service.

- **Following through:** Be sure you arrive at your agency on time and locate your contact person. Although each agency has different needs, we prefer that you commit to about three to four hours of service, so plan ahead!

- **Summarizing:** Your report will be in two parts:

  Cover Memo: Each team must submit a work report detailing the process the team used to complete the project, the contributions of each member, the overall success of the team, and recommendations to future teams on strategies for having a successful and enjoyable service-learning experience

  Individual Memo: Each member of team will identify and describe his or her service-learning experience. Then, each will reflect on the following questions: What did you enjoy most about your service-learning experience? Why? What did you enjoy least about your service-learning experience? Why? Finally, make a case for why businesses should or should not participate in service-learning activities.

- **Due Dates:** Please consult your weekly planner for due dates.
- **Performance Evaluation:** Graded

BUS 474: Service-Learning (CS) Strategic Plan

This assignment will demonstrate how ethics and strategy can tie together. Many of us will serve on nonprofit boards of directors at some time during our career. One of the major tasks of any board is to help formulate the strategic plan of that organization. So find a nonprofit organization (preferably one in town); meet with staff and board members; read newsletters, annual reports, etc. Perform a strategic analysis of the organization using the theories and principles learned in class. Develop strategic recommendations to the organization. Your report will be turned into the organization. This is a team project.

PART I: ONE PAGE

1. Brief description of organization.

2. Names of team members.

3. Name and phone number of contact person at organization.

4. Plan of action for doing the strategic analysis. (How will you gather data? What data will you gather? When will tasks be accomplished? Who will accomplish what tasks? Whom will you interview and when?)

PART II: FINAL REPORT AND PRESENTATION

Written Report
(Three to five pages, single spaced, plus attachments; this report will be presented to the organization.)

1. Brief description of the organization.

2. Strategic analysis of the organization. Apply strategic concepts to the client organization and develop strategic recommendations to strengthen the organization's effectiveness.

3. Attachments (documentation, data, materials from organization, etc.)

Oral Report
(About fifteen to twenty minutes)

1. Basically talk about the above issues; assume you are making a presentation to the board of the organization you analyzed.

2. Briefly assess your team's ability to work together (i.e., your strengths and weaknesses, how you could improve working together).

3. Presentation should be professional (i.e., audiovisual aids, handouts, professional dress, etc.)

4. Be prepared to ask and answer questions.

The ICIC Program: An Executive MBA Business School Service-Learning Program Model

by Marilyn L. Taylor

Among the national resources the United States possesses for addressing social issues are institutions of learning. The primary purpose of academic educational institutions is to transmit knowledge, encourage learning, and provide developmental opportunities for tomorrow's leaders or, more recently, "nontraditional students" undertaking lifelong learning or career retooling. Educational institutions can enhance human resource capabilities while focusing student efforts on national and international issues. These experiences can provide superb opportunities for higher-order learning (Bloom 1956). Furthermore, postsecondary schools, unlike lower-level educational institutions, include significant research and outreach components in their missions. These aspects of postsecondary institutions can also be harnessed to address important social issues. However, this chapter focuses on the social potential of the teaching mission of business schools.

To provide insight into service-related — or service-learning — experiences in business schools, this chapter focuses on a national program — the Initiative for a Competitive Inner City (ICIC, or the Initiative) Business School Network. The Initiative is a recently established program that is funded at both local and national levels. However, it is not the first national business school service program. A significant precursor existed in the (now unfunded) Small Business Institute (SBI), which had been funded for almost 30 years by Congress through the Small Business Administration (SBA). Another synergistic SBA program is Small Business Development Centers (SBDCs), which are comparable to the ICIC Advisors program. Both SBA programs were established in the 1970s.

The ICIC Business School Network program has additional precursors in efforts undertaken by individual postsecondary institutions as well as individual professors within their own courses. This chapter draws on the experience of ICIC's current model program in Kansas City for which the author's home institution, the Bloch School of Business and Public Administration at the University of Missouri at Kansas City (UMKC), was the initiating partner. The author was the first director of the Kansas City program and currently directs the ICIC research and Business School Network initiatives in the Kansas City region.

The ICIC programs are focused on economic development in the urban cores of U.S. cities, primarily through private-sector initiatives. Currently marking its four-year anniversary, the ICIC has a multiprong set of programs in four cities (Boston, Baltimore, Kansas City, and Oakland) and alliances with a number of universities throughout the country.

ICIC Origins, Mission, and Programs

The Initiative for a Competitive Inner City was founded in 1994 by Harvard Business School professor Michael E. Porter.[1] Porter's work is well known, especially in the field of strategic management, where he has been credited with the first major paradigm shift since the field's beginnings in the 1950s. Porter became involved in the Field Studies Program (FSP) at the Harvard Business School (HBS) in the early 1990s. HBS established its FSP to provide opportunities for MBA students to undertake consultation projects with a wide variety of companies and, in some instances, nonprofit organizations, such as, for example, the Social Enterprise: People & Practice program funded by the John C. Whitehead Fund for Not-for-Profit Management at the Harvard Business School. Simultaneously, Porter's wife was involved in service activities within the inner-city school system. The interests of these two individuals came together when Porter asked his early MBA teams to undertake consultation projects with companies located in Boston's urban core.

Porter was challenged to bring his considerable theory-development, consulting practice, and government advisory experiences to bear on urban-core issues. With original academic training in organizational economics, he stressed private-sector responses to urban-core challenges. His 1980s work involved identification of the competitive advantage of nations (Porter 1990). The ICIC focuses on identifying and exploiting the competitive advantages of the urban core. Porter argues that inner-city difficulties result as much from economic as from social problems. Indeed, he identifies strong actual and potential competitive advantages accruing from urban-core business locations. According to Porter, there is genuine economic promise in inner cities that arises from four primary existing and potential competitive advantages: (1) underserved market segments with substantial purchasing power prospects; (2) strategic proximity, especially to business customers and major transportation nodes; (3) availability of a stable and underutilized workforce with entrepreneurial possibilities; and (4) opportunities that can emanate from interaction with regional business clusters (Porter 1995, 1997). The Initiative's mission is to "transform thinking, reinvigorate market forces, and engage the private sector in fostering healthy economies in America's inner cities that create jobs, income, wealth, and economic opportunities for local residents" (Dean 1997: 2).

ICIC's program focus involves research, intervention through the Advisors and Business School Network programs, and development of funding sources for business clients. The multiprong groupings of ICIC programs are responses to the well-recognized problem of economic decline in many of America's urban cores. The national Business School Network program is ICIC's business school service program. It harnesses private-sector forces along with the considerable talents of business school students and faculty to provide consultation services to urban-core businesses,[2] area developments, and business cluster efforts while providing learning opportunities for the students involved in its projects. A *business cluster* is a set of related businesses, including suppliers, competitors, and customer companies. Research has identified 10 clusters in Kansas City. The Kansas City Initiative has selected three — health care, business services, and manufacturing — to focus on.

ICIC's Programs

In its first four years, the Initiative's accomplishments have been impressive. It garnered more than $4 million to invest in four ICIC programs, three of which support multiple-city efforts. The four programs are (1) research, (2) ICIC (Inner City) Advisors and Corporate Partners, (3) Venture Capital/Financing Alternatives, and (4) University Alliance Network. A description of each follows.

The **ICIC research program** has targeted issues relating to the economics of urban cores. Its early research, which philosophically and conceptually undergirded the founding of the Initiative, was reported in the *Harvard Business Review*'s May-June 1995 issue (Porter 1995). Subsequent work has included a baseline study of Boston by the Boston Consulting Group, one of ICIC's Corporate Partners; a study of urban-core retail economics in 12 cities; and a HUD-sponsored study of the government resources and programs available to urban-core businesses. In addition, the national ICIC office has been deeply involved in a two-year Kansas City baseline study undertaken in partnership with the Kauffman Foundation and the Bloch School of Business and Public Administration at UMKC. This study was released as "Business Strategies for Kansas City's Urban Core: Executive Summary" (1998). (For copies, contact this author.)

ICIC's Advisor program has offices in four cities — Baltimore, Boston, Kansas City, and Oakland. Each office is staffed with experienced professionals who undertake a variety of consultation engagements with companies currently located in the urban core. The Advisors also engage local Corporate Partners, which are private companies willing to share their expertise with smaller urban-core-located enterprises that appear poised for growth. For example, a national or regional CPA firm might undertake reduced-cost services for a company that has potential to offer stock to the public but is strapped for cash flow. In other instances, the Advisors serve as matchmakers to introduce smaller urban-core enterprises to larger entities. A representative effort in Kansas City was the introduction of a product prototype to Wal-Mart's new product evaluation process. As of this writing, it is unknown whether Wal-Mart will initiate an order. However, the initial evaluation was favorable, which not only gave the company encouragement but also provided impetus in encouraging orders from other potential outlets.

Advisors also identify ICIC clients whose needs might be served by area schools involved in the ICIC University Alliance Network. Generally, the Advisors remain active with the client and business school teams throughout the duration of a project, although the actual extent of Advisors' involvement varies by city, school, and project. The synergies derivable from the carefully orchestrated relationships between the Advisors and the University Alliance Network in their area potentially represent one of the featured attributes of the ICIC program. Indeed, it was this potential that led the author to initiate a partnership between the ICIC and the newly established Executive MBA (EMBA) program at the University of Missouri's Bloch School of Business and Public Administration. The author had been (founding) director of the Small Business Development Center and director of the Small Business Institute at the University of Kansas. As simultaneous director of both SBA programs, she was well aware of the potential synergy between them.

ICIC's **Inner-City Ventures** is a venture capital fund[3] effort that is still in the formative stage. Inner-City Ventures recently formed an alliance with American Securities Capital Partners. American Securities is a well-established investment management and venture capital firm that began by managing the investments of the Sears Company's owners. The ICIC venture capital fund will focus on meeting the capital needs of promising ventures targeting urban-core locations. This effort is in keeping, for example, with the efforts of Jesse Jackson and other prominent spokespeople who argue for the opportunities potentially present in urban cores and who decry practices such as "redlining" that deter investment in urban-core locations ("Jesse Jackson" 1998).

The **University Alliance Network** involves schools that have volunteer or class-related student projects that focus on companies located in the urban core. The Network also involves students in various research projects that focus on urban-core-located companies or economic development. The Harvard Graduate School of Business Administration hosted a national first meeting in April 1995, with some 35 schools and other independent organizations represented among the nearly 70 attendees. An April 1998 conference involved nearly 100 attendees from 50 schools and other organizations. Expectations for future annual meetings are for 70 schools and 150 attendees or more. The purpose of these meetings is to provide opportunity for sharing best practices among service-related programs in university and college business schools. Through Spring 1998, the national University Alliance Network had completed 62 projects involving more than 230 students in the four cities where the ICIC is currently active. (See Exhibit 1 at the end of this chapter for the schools participating in the Network in the four cities that have ICIC Advisors offices.)

The Kansas City ICIC Programs

To date, the ICIC in Kansas City has activated three of the ICIC's programs: research, Advisors, and University Alliance teams. Explorations have begun on establishing a fourth program to focus on funding alternatives for urban-core businesses. The University of Missouri at Kansas City and ICIC's Kansas City Advisors partnered with the Kauffman Foundation to complete a major research project, a two-year baseline study identifying the business clusters and competitive advantages of the Kansas City urban core. That baseline research is now being augmented with a follow-up study of the research participants to determine whether satisfaction with doing business in the urban core has changed, and what factors are associated with varying levels of satisfaction. In addition, the research program involves development of a series of case studies as part of a three-year client follow-up program. The ICIC program in Kansas City has received support from three major area funders and has been recognized by the national ICIC office as a model program (Lamb 1998). The funders include the Ewing Marion Kauffman Foundation, the Hall Family Foundation, and the Kansas City Greater Community Foundation. Funding for the first year was approximately $125,000 from Kauffman, with the following five years to be funded at a total of approximately $1.5 million, i.e., about $300,000 per year.

The Kansas City Advisor program has been fully staffed since January 1998. The program office employs three professional staff members, each with a significant and varied background. The managing director of the program has experience in military leadership, and extensive operations background in inner-city fast-food and casual-dining restaurants. The other senior staff member has been the CFO of a rapidly growing health-care provider. The junior staff member has had experience with a business incubator and specifically with its micro-loan-financing program. The office has begun to identify and work with a set of high-potential clients, area development initiatives, and business cluster efforts.

The service component embodied in the University Alliance Network currently involves three schools: the University of Missouri at Kansas City's Bloch School of Business and Public Administration, the University of

Kansas (KU) School of Business, and Baker University. A fourth school has indicated interest in joining this group. A sectional meeting of participating and interested schools took place in early September 1998. Of the 14 university service projects completed to date, 12 have involved participants in the newly initiated EMBA program at the UMKC Bloch School. In 1997-98, the Kansas City–based ICIC University Alliance Network also included projects undertaken by the KU School of Business. However, KU only recently completed its first two projects, and evaluation of its efforts awaits the Alliance professor's return from summer break.

The Bloch School of Business and Public Administration's EMBA Program and ICIC

The Bloch School of Business and Public Administration undertook a bold experiment in its 1995-initiated EMBA program (Heimovics, Taylor, and Stilwell 1996). An ICIC–Bloch School partnership served as the initial cornerstone of the Kansas City ICIC program. The Bloch School EMBA program provides a model for service-based learning that the ICIC would like to encourage throughout the country. Exhibit 2 describes the background and history of UMKC, the Bloch School, and the EMBA program.

In its first two years, the EMBA-ICIC program at the Bloch School completed 11 projects (see Exhibit 3). These results appear positive, as judged by evidence of client satisfaction and EMBA student learning. The following summarizes the results of evaluation efforts to date:

- Client satisfaction with the value delivered appears high:
    - All the clients have requested that the projects be given a letter grade of A.
    - Each client was interviewed and surveyed at the conclusion of the EMBA project; these results are favorable.
    - Several clients have lamented publicly that the projects necessarily came to an end at the conclusion of the school year.
    - Anecdotal evidence suggests that the reputation of the EMBA program and the ICIC program have benefited from the activities of the UMKC EMBA-ICIC teams.[4]
    - Four of the five projects from the first year of operation have been involved in follow-on projects, and the fifth is open to participation.
    - As the program entered its third year of operation, it had more potential clients than it could adequately serve.
- EMBA learning appears to be high as evidenced by:
    - Survey feedback

— Facilitated classroom discussions

— The willingness of graduated EMBAs to serve as team mentors

— The eagerness of the first-year class to embark on ICIC-EMBA service ventures.

Factors related to clients, students, and the program itself appear to have contributed to this success.

Client Aspects

The ICIC Advisors endeavor to identify clients who meet the following ICIC criteria: (1) They are located in the urban core or hire a significant number of employees from the urban core, and (2) they have economic growth potential. In addition to these two basic criteria for involvement with the Kansas City ICIC program, other factors are critical from an educational standpoint:

• Fit of the businesses' needs with the pedagogical objectives of the EMBA program. The program seeks projects that (1) permit viewing the organization from the perspective of its interaction with its environment (i.e., a systems perspective), and (2) include strategic and operational components.

• Openness of the client to sharing information.

• Willingness of the client to participate in the multiple roles of client, mentor, and role model.

It is especially important that clients be willing to share information about their operations. At the midyear point, one project suddenly appeared wasteful of the EMBA team members' time and efforts. In this instance, the client waited almost four months before telling the EMBA team that he was strongly considering shutting down the operation that their project focused on. Thus, an industrial market research component of the project had to be shelved, and the team had to switch focus in January/February. In the months following the project's conclusion, discussion and reflection suggested that the data from the proposed study could have (1) yielded potential buyers for the division and (2) been of help to a potential buyer. It was, however, unknown to the ICIC program that this particular owner often "holds his cards close to his vest." Other community executives attempting to mentor him had apparently advised him on other occasions that they could be more helpful if he would be more forthcoming. The team made a brilliant turnaround by applying the conceptual material it had been studying to an analysis of the situation. While the project was not in the end as directly valuable to the client as some of the other projects conducted at the same time, the team learned a great deal. The client later agreed to turn the project into a case study, and one team member — one of our research associates — continues to have interaction with him as the case is being developed.

In addition, clarifying a client's expectations is an important factor contributing to high-quality service experiences. The Advisors and the director spend several hours with each client establishing a company profile, baseline data, and potential focal points, as well as explaining the ICIC program and the EMBA-ICIC partnership. Letters and correspondence precede project implementation. Throughout the project, regular EMBA team meetings and written reports shared with the client, faculty mentors, and Advisors keep the client informed as to its status.

Student Aspects

The Bloch School EMBAs are mature (mid-30s), midcareer (almost all are in significant managerial or executive careers) individuals who have high expectations for themselves and high energy (most are in more than 40-hour-per-week jobs and have families) and are recruited and selected because they demonstrate both potential for leading change and community or professional volunteer involvement. The EMBAs thus offer a sharp contrast to 21-year-old senior students with much less experience. EMBAs demonstrate a broader spectrum of ability in (usually) semester-long projects than do seniors or even mid-20s MBA students. The EMBAs are often the kinds of individuals a business or organization seeks for board membership. They bring to the client knowledge from their first-year EMBA experiences and their expanding second-year EMBA knowledge base as well as their often significant professional backgrounds. They are very capable of rendering mature judgments and sophisticated insights.

Program Aspects

A number of factors related to the design of the overall EMBA program support the ICIC component: (1) the team formation and selection process, (2) the cohort experience, (3) the team training process, (4) the length of the projects, and (5) business faculty and community involvement and support. Each of these aspects is discussed below.

Team Formation and Selection Process: The service-learning EMBA-ICIC teams are the result of a facilitated three-hour process involving class representatives, the EMBA director, a professional business consultant, and the managing director of the Kansas City ICIC Advisors. The consultant also serves as director of executive education, is involved with some aspect of teaching in the first-year EMBA program, acts as a mentor to selected ICIC-EMBA teams, and heads up the group that undertakes the project management training session. Team formation takes place according to four criteria:

1. "Stretching" of the EMBA participants (i.e., learning — an executive with a small, entrepreneurial company is more likely to be assigned to a

nonprofit or area development project than to a company that parallels his or her current employer profile, for example).

2. Background or skills that are expected to be useful to the client (e.g., a CFO of a large multidivisional company may be assigned to a small entrepreneurial company that is struggling to understand its financial position and to plan financing for its future).

3. Compatibility of team members (the EMBAs are a cohort, have operated in teams during the first year, and know one another well by the time the second-year teams are formed).

4. Other relevant factors:

• *Personal:* For example, in the 1997 facilitation process, the class representatives refused to allow the mother of three young children to be involved in a three-person team because they noted that she would have to take on too much responsibility to the detriment of her family life; her team ended up with four members.

• *Conflicts of interest:* A city official could not work on an area development project.

• *Potential schedule conflicts:* A member of a team was newly appointed to a chief operating officer's position and felt she had little flexibility in taking off time during the day other than the previously arranged Fridays and Saturdays scheduled for the EMBA. (The EMBA program leaves most Friday mornings in the second year unscheduled to provide for team meetings with the client.) However, the team's client generally had Friday morning staff meetings. This issue was difficult for the team to resolve and resulted in fewer meetings with the client than occurred in the case of other teams.

There is, of course, no guarantee that all teams will function smoothly. However, observations suggest that the second-year teams function more smoothly than the first-year teams and are proud of their productivity. To date, only one EMBA is known to have complained about insufficient learning. In that instance, the student insisted on being placed with a particular client because she felt her background was suitable. Not surprisingly, at the end of the year she wrote that she "did not learn a great deal because [she had] done much of the same thing before." The client, however, indicated significant satisfaction with the usefulness of the project.

Cohort Experience: The EMBAs are a cohort; that is, they undertake together all learning experiences during the two years. They come to know one another well. During the second year, they come to know the clients and the projects as a class. In some instances, teams draw on the expertise of other classmates to solve problems and issues related to their own clients.

Team Training: The University of Missouri at Kansas City's ICIC-EMBA program is offered by the Bloch School of *Business and Public* Administration. This dual focus gives support to and provides a background for the task of sensitizing EMBAs to the community and the businesses that operate within it. Of particular note in this regard are two learning components positioned earlier in the Bloch School EMBA program (see Exhibit 4). The first is a Washington, D.C., residency that takes the EMBA participants to Washington for a four-day experience that sensitizes them to national issues, many of which have an impact on local businesses. The second is a public sector and business (PS&B) component that occurs over the summer between year one and year two. PS&B is a guided field-learning component that explores specific issues in the Kansas City region and is intended to expose the EMBAs to how Kansas City works. Thus, the EMBAs come to their ICIC client projects sensitized to systemic interactions between companies located in the urban core and the urban environment. In addition, the EMBAs go through an adeptly facilitated processing of their first-year team experience and establish expectations for their new team. Finally, all teams participate in a session on managing consulting projects and client relationships.

Project Length and Intensity: The EMBA-ICIC projects at the Bloch School begin in August/September and conclude in April/May. The program meets every other Friday and Saturday throughout the school year. Nearly every Friday morning (i.e., about 20% of the class time) is held free of scheduled in-class sessions so that teams can spend time with their clients, the project, and their mentors. In other words, the projects represent a significant portion of the entire EMBA second academic year. The students thus have more time to become acquainted with their client organizations than student participants in typical semester-length projects do.

As the above discussion indicates, the second year of the EMBA program was conceived as significant outside-the-walls learning. The entire program thus supports these team efforts during the second year. The Bloch School program has focused on the building of a learning community in which students and faculty share in a common learning journey. Admittedly, faculty remain primarily discipline-specific in their expertise, but they have worked together in four groups to guide the learning of the EMBA cohort through four approximately semester-length "modules." Particularly in the second year, an emphasis on five applied projects (of which three are field based) and a nine-day international residency emphasize the EMBAs' common journey and application of learning, and the program's outside-the-walls orientation — all of which were part of its original design (Heimovics, Taylor, and Stilwell 1996). Given these circumstances, faculty tend to use the term EMBA "participant" rather than "student."

Business Faculty and Community Involvement and Support: Each three- to five-person EMBA team is augmented by at least three individuals external to the client who are available to provide guidance or insight. They include:

- the EMBA director, with 20 years of experience working with service-learning teams;
- another faculty mentor whose expertise appears to match the expressed needs of the client and who is acceptable to the EMBA team;
- a business executive or consultant who might be a member of the Advisors' staff, a former EMBA participant, or another senior person from the business or consulting community.

Mentorship of the projects is thus shared by the university and business communities as well as the contact persons in the client organizations.

Summary/Conclusions

In undertaking outside-the-walls learning in the form of ICIC-related service activities, the Bloch School Executive MBA program of participant projects has confronted many of the issues faced by typical field-research programs and consulting activities.[5] Moreover, as might be expected, such EMBA-ICIC activities must cope constantly with the challenge of providing EMBA participant learning simultaneously with providing service to a client (or client value). Thanks to various factors — the philosophy and content of the ICIC program as well as factors relating to the EMBA program and its participants — the program has encountered considerable success. In the final analysis, however, the quality of any service-related academic program must be measured in that simultaneous value it provides for the community/businesses/clients, on the one hand, and students/faculty, on the other. Furthermore, the impact on the community/businesses/clients is multifold. UMKC's ICIC clients have spoken of the encouragement and enthusiasm that the teams have generated, the different insights they have brought, and the catalyzing influence they have had on internal and external constituencies of the organizations.

EMBA student participants value many outcomes from their ICIC service experience. They speak of an opportunity to think outside the box, to experience a different setting, to practice what they have been learning, to derive satisfaction from making a visible impact on another organization, and to appreciate how their efforts ultimately strengthen their own community. The EMBAs tell us that concepts, especially those related to the Porter model, come alive. They derive immense satisfaction from seeing how their efforts have a value-added impact on their client organizations. Further, they increasingly recognize that *most* of the value created for themselves and their clients is derived from the *process* of their engagement — not from their final "student" products, i.e., highly polished final written and oral reports.

Finally, EMBA student participants have also borne witness to the impact this work has had on their own value systems. They come to understand more fully the importance of the contribution they make as professionals within their own work organizations and as volunteers in their private lives. Through their experiences with their client organizations, they come to see the interplay between organization and community. We find them leaving our EMBA program challenged in their professional and personal lives to take up the mission of strengthening the fiber of the community within which they are embedded. As an alumna put it recently, more than a year after the completion of her ICIC service-learning project:

> I don't look at businesses in the same way since that project. I think of all the things contained in Porter's theory and his concepts. They have stayed with me in a way that they never would have if I had simply taken an exam. My current company is located in the KC suburbs. But, I find myself defending the city's inner core when others make [negative] remarks. I am more aware of the needs of our community. Many people [who take MBAs] would never have the insight I developed as a result of the project. ICIC creates a conscious awareness of the viability and possibilities in the urban core and what the urban core means to the entire community.

As a faculty member in the ICIC program, EMBA director, director of ICIC-KC research, and coordinator of the area University Alliance Network, I have personally derived significant value and satisfaction from this work. I am increasingly aware that constituencies external to higher education are asking that academe demonstrate the relevance of student learning. The constituencies point to their heavy investment in higher education's labor-intensive pedagogy. UMKC's EMBA program is a highly labor-intensive effort by the UMKC faculty. However, the relevance and payoff of the program, and of the ICIC component within it, are immediately apparent. My roles are synergistic and permit me multiple meaningful insights from each perspective and across perspectives.

I have had the privilege of being at the nexus of UMKC's EMBA living learning community. This learning experience is two years in length for each cohort of students. I have participated in teams of faculty partnering with faculty, students with students, students with faculty, and students and faculty with community members to impact the learning of all three — faculty, students, and community members. Recently I wrote to my fellow alums at my alma mater:

> The challenge of the EMBA and ICIC represents the intermingling of a number of threads of my professional development and is certainly one of the

most meaningful chapters in my professional career. The ICIC-KC program has been praised as a showcase. It's been awesome to work with a wide variety of individuals from the business, community, and academic sectors to bring the research, the [University Alliance] Network, and the EMBA projects into being here in the Kansas City area.

There is no one magic key to such results. The experience has required resources, hard work, careful attention to the needs of multiple constituencies, and time from many players. The greatest lesson I have learned is that truly impactful service-learning programs must be embedded in a network of partner players; moreover, the process must simultaneously produce psychic as well as tangible benefits for all those players.

Good business education ultimately involves a partnership between the business and academic communities. Perhaps one could also claim, more generally, that good learning ultimately arises from a partnership between the community and academe. Ultimately, the latter must serve as a good steward of the resources invested by the former, and the former must serve as a recipient of value demonstrated by the latter. Service-related learning, at its best, simultaneously delivers both demonstrated value to the community and learning to students and faculty.

Acknowledgments

The author wishes to express thanks to many individuals who, over the last 20 years, have been responsible for the experiences reflected in this paper. Because they are so numerous, the author thanks these special colleagues (current and past) as members of their respective organizations — the Bloch School of Business and Public Administration at the University of Missouri at Kansas City, including alumni, participants, staff, and faculty of the EMBA program; national foundations that have supported the national and local ICIC efforts; the Ewing Marion Kauffman Foundation, the Hall Family Foundation, and the Greater Kansas City Community Foundation; and the University of Kansas School of Business and the Kansas City Region Small Business Administration. Special thanks to Professor C. Roland Christensen, professor emeritus at Harvard Graduate School of Business Administration, who has given valued encouragement and mentoring, as well as provided a significant role model for both the founder of the Initiative for a Competitive Inner City and this author throughout the duration of our careers.

Notes

1. Porter has been referred to as a "Strategic Seer" (John Dillon, in *Harvard Magazine*, July-August 1996). Porter is the C. Roland Christensen professor of business administration at the Harvard Business School, where he has been since 1973. He is author of 14 books and more than 50 articles. His book *Competitive Strategy: Techniques for Analyzing Industries and Competitors* (Free Press, 1980) has been translated into 17 languages. Two other books, *Competitive Advantage: Creating and Sustaining Superior Performance* (Free Press, 1985) and *The Competitive Advantage of Nations: Creating and Sustaining Nations* (Free Press, 1990), have been referenced widely. He has received several awards for articles and books. He dedicates 25 percent of his time to the Initiative, all without compensation.

2. This paper uses the terms *business, company*, and *enterprise* interchangeably. The focus on business connotes the business school primary focus on for-profit enterprises. However, many business school service-learning programs, including the UMKC-EMBA ICIC program to be described, include nonprofits in the set of organizations served. For example, the UMKC-EMBA ICIC program is committed to serving at least one nonprofit among the set of six to eight projects the EMBAs will undertake yearly. This inclusion of nonprofits at UMKC is in keeping with the UMKC Bloch School's philosophy as a school of business *and* public administration. The Bloch School has a well-deserved regional and national reputation for training and service to the non-profit and public sectors through the Cookingham Institute and Midwest Center for Non-Profit Leadership, both organizationally located in its Public Administration division. The EMBA program, though a Business Administration division program, is philosophically a Bloch School offering and thus focuses on bringing the best of the Bloch School to train the executives, managers, and entrepreneurs who come into the program with the intent of enhancing their leadership skills.

3. Venture capital efforts focus on equity positions in companies with considerable promise. A venture capital company will expect a 30 to 50 percent yearly return on the equity funds invested in a venture. This high rate of return must cover the many failures. Venture capital firms may bring a variety of funding sources to the companies they choose for their investment portfolios. The infusion of actual equity funds may be small. The venture capital firm may take an equity position in return for arranging a line of credit, a traditional loan, or an infusion of funds from a private individual not involved in the fund.

4. To date, this assertion is admittedly based on anecdotal information. However, the ICIC research program at the Bloch School has initiated a study to ascertain whether the recent ICIC activities have any effect on perceived satisfaction with doing business in the urban core. This study is a follow-on of a baseline study undertaken in fall 1997 (cf. "Business Strategies" 1998 and Taylor, Baker, and Krishnan 1998).

5. See, for example, Michael H. Agar, *Speaking of Ethnography* (Sage, 1986); E. Raymond Corey, ed., *MBA Field Studies: A Guide for Students and Faculty* (Harvard Business School, 1990); Lisa K. Gundry and Aaron A. Buchko, *Field Casework: Methods for Consulting to Small and Startup Businesses* (Sage, 1996); George D. Kuh et al., *Student Learning Outside the Classroom: Transcending Artificial Boundaries*, (ASHE-ERIC/GWU, 1996); Maurice Punch, *The Politics and Ethics of Fieldwork* (Sage, 1986); and Edgar H. Schein, *Process Consultation: Its Role in Organization Development, Volume 1* (Addison-Wesley, 1988).

References

Bloom, B.S., M.D. Engelhart, E.J. Furst, W.H. Hill, and D.R. Krathwohl, eds. (1956). *Taxonomy of Educational Objectives: The Classification of Educational Goals. Handbook 1: Cognitive Domain.* New York, NY: David McKay Company.

"Business Strategies for Kansas City's Urban Core: Executive Summary." (April 1998). Kansas City, MO: ICIC Kansas City Advisors and the Bloch School of Business and Public Administration, University of Missouri at Kansas City.

Dean, M. (September 1997). "The History of ICIC." *National Business School Network News* 1(1): 1-6.

Heimovics, D., M. Taylor, and R. Stilwell. (1996). "Assessing and Developing a New Strategic Direction for the Executive MBA." *Journal of Management Education* 20(4): 462-478.

"Jesse Jackson Leads Conference on Investing in Underserved Areas." (July 16, 1998). *Kansas City Star:* b2.

Lamb, M. (1998). *The Kansas City Story.* Boston, MA: Initiative for a Competitive Inner City.

Porter, M.E. (1990). *The Competitive Advantage of Nations: Creating and Sustaining Nations.* New York, NY: Free Press.

——— . (May/June 1995). "The Competitive Advantage of the Inner City." *Harvard Business Review:* 55-70.

——— . (February 1997). "New Strategies for Inner-City Economic Development." *Economic Development Quarterly:*

Taylor, M.L., G. Baker, and R. Krishnan. (1998). "Kansas City Baseline Study: Findings, Insights, and Recommendations." Unpublished internal document.

Exhibit 1

Schools in the Four Cities Where the Initiative Has Inner-City Advisor Programs

Boston, MA:
- Harvard University Graduate School of Business Administration
- Sloan School of Business, Massachusetts Institute of Technology
- Franklin W. Olin Graduate School of Business, Babson College

Baltimore, MD:
- Sellinger School of Business, Loyola College
- Merrick School of Business, University of Maryland-College Park
- Johns Hopkins University, Division of Management
- School of Business, Morgan State University

Kansas City, MO:
- Bloch School of Business and Public Administration, University of Missouri at Kansas City
- Baker University
- School of Business, University of Kansas
- William Jewell College

Oakland, CA:
- Walter A. Haas School of Business, University of California-Berkeley
- McLaren School of Business, University of San Francisco
- Golden Gate University, Graduate School of Business
- San Francisco State University

Adapted and updated from *National Business School Network News,* Vol. 1, No. 1 (September, 1997), p. 3.

Exhibit 2

The University of Missouri at Kansas City,
The Bloch School of Business and Public Administration,
and the Executive MBA Program

The University of Missouri at Kansas City (UMKC)

With approximately 11,000 students, UMKC is primarily a professional-level graduate school with well-regarded programs in a number of areas including medicine, dentistry, nursing, law, business and public administration, as well as liberal arts majors. Some of the programs trace their origins to the last century when the schools were free-standing, but after WWII came under the umbrella of the Kansas City University (KCU), the precursor organization of today's UMKC.

UMKC is one of four campuses of the University of Missouri system. The other three campuses are located in Columbia (the mother campus), St. Louis (primarily undergraduate), and Rolla (with emphasis on science and engineering). UMKC, primarily a commuter school, is located about four miles south of downtown Kansas City, Missouri just south and east of the first planned shopping area in the US – the Country Club Plaza. The primary eastern boundary of the campus is Troost Avenue, long regarded as a major demarcation between the upscale Kansas City areas represented by "The Plaza" and the lower socioeconomic and often heavily African-American populated areas of the city.

The University reaffirmed its mission of taking an active role in the Kansas City community during its last major strategic planning process that occurred during the 1994-96 period. It has also set a goal to increase its status to a more research-oriented institution. A challenge program from the State of Missouri Legislature committed $500,000 into endowed chairs for any of the four UM campuses that could obtain matching funds from outside sources. To date UMKC has established thirteen such chairs, five of which are in the business school.

cont.

The Bloch School of Business and Public Administration

Founded in 1953, the Bloch School evolved to serve a large, mostly seasoned, urban MBA student body. The MBA curriculum was primarily discipline-based and represented the traditional areas of economics, accounting, finance, marketing, organizational behavior/management/human resources, and business law. Courses were generally taught in isolation, although they were sequenced to represent relationships among the business subdisciplines. For example, accounting and statistics were taught before finance.

Following the 1988 inauguration of a new building and the gift from Henry W. Bloch, and in keeping with recommendations from a Blue Ribbon Task Force of business leaders, the school embarked on a new era to emphasize innovative graduate education, including executive education. The business school dean for the last decade has been William Eddy, who has been largely credited with the significant fundraising accomplishments of the school. These include nine chairs or professorships in addition to the 1988 major gift endowment from Henry W. Bloch, one of the Bloch brothers who founded H&R Block, Co. By 1995, 50% of the faculty was new, the result of the addition of chairs and professorships plus retirements.

The Executive MBA Program

An EMBA faculty-planning group undertook a two-year planning effort to design a curriculum for a new EMBA program. The planning group reviewed data from AACS accredited EMBA programs, input from focus groups from the business community, alumni, and prospective students. The final design reflected a fundamentally different structure for delivering the MBA content and learning experiences. The major features of the new EMBA were a) a learning community, b) integrated learning modules, c) skill applications projects, d) significant outside-the-classroom learning, and e) learning residencies. Exhibit 4 captures the basic structure and sequence of the design.

cont.

The program includes the basic disciplinarians that appear in any accredited MBA program. Indeed, the transcript of the EMBA graduates reflects sixteen courses and a total of forty-eight semester credit hours. However, the faculty have worked hard to find ways to integrate material, including reducing redundancies; planning the delivery of across-disciplinary topics to reinforce learning within modules; and designing joint learning experiences that apply or illustrate concepts from multiple disciplines. Each module and faculty group uses different integrative mechanisms as indicated below:

Module 1 – Tools of Competitive Analysis: The faculty team uses a carefully designed major project involving analysis of an industry and two companies within that industry. The project components are used as a major part of the end-of-module assessment for economics, accounting, finance, and statistics.

Module 2 – Management People and Systems: The faculty team uses several cases and experiential exercises at strategic times during the module to illustrate and apply cross-disciplinary concepts.

Module 3 – The Enterprise and Its Environment: The faculty team uses an individual project to connect marketing, strategic planning, and entrepreneurship; cases to capture entrepreneurship, strategic management, and strategic management of technology; and team teaching across two, three, or even four areas.

Module 4 – Strategic Leadership and Change: Uses a set of cases, team teaching, and the continuation of the ICIC-EMBA projects (initiated the prior August).

Connections are made in various ways with the residencies and strategic application projects. For example, the Module 1 faculty has begun to provide assignments during the Residency in Executive Leadership, which replace a previous experiential exercise. The processing of the team interaction as it

cont.

pursues this assignment provides the grist for reflective learning under the facilitation of the residency coordinator. The International Business Residency coordinator links his work with marketing, strategic management, strategic management of technology, and human resources at appropriate times during year two. The Public Sector and Business Application Project (PS&B) links with the Washington D.C. residency through a day in the field devoted to teams undertaking interviews with national figures about the topic areas they will pursue during the coming summer in Kansas City. The PS&B Project links with the ICIC-EMBA project through a) timing of delivery of the final presentations, b) assignment of team members from the first-year teams to the second year, and c) the involvement of the PS&B Coordinator as a mentor to at least one of the second-year ICIC-EMBA project teams. In short, where possible, the deliberate links are made to reinforce allocated concepts and links across otherwise often separated disciplinary areas.

The program is not without its costs. EMBA participants are clearly pushed. They are fully employed in significant, demanding careers and most have families. Unlike most part-time MBA students who are attempting one or two courses per semester, the EMBAs are enrolled in four. About one in twenty opts out in the first module. In addition to the early dropouts, the current experience indicates one or two participants in a cohort of twenty-five to thirty will not complete the program. This completion rate, however, compares favorably with the 25% noncompletion rate generally expected in part-time MBA programs.

Some faculty have never before been involved in a classroom settings where student participants in some instances may have more professional qualifications to help illustrate or apply material than themselves. Others feel the program implementation has challenges and are uncomfortable with fellow faculty members in their classroom during team teaching. Still others, previously using more lecture mode, find the reliance on experiential teaching foreign. Team teaching takes more time—planning time as well as time in the classroom. The EMBAs are demanding. They form powerful bonds in their teams and as a class. They ask for a firm calendar, no surprise assignments, clearly articulated

cont.

instructions in assignments, a reasonably balanced workload from one weekend to another, and dynamic classroom sessions. Indeed, one faculty member has used the term "whining" to describe their demands. Grading is more difficult, especially if it is jointly determined. Invoking assessment from student team members to factor into the grade feels uncomfortable to some instructors. Some faculty charge that the traditional functional area content is "light" and that the list of topics in the regular courses cannot be covered fully in a module that they perceive cluttered with demands to integrate and team-teach. Some faculty refuse to teach in the program.

Overall, however, the program has been well received by the community. Now enrolling its fourth class for fall, 1998, the class is oversubscribed. The learning community has been particularly powerful within the first- and second-year team experiences. The participants are a diverse group across ethnic, age, and socioeconomic origins. The EMBA class draws representatives from the traditional larger companies that usually support EMBA learning experiences but also come from the public sector, nonprofit organizations, and entrepreneurial companies. Faculty have learned new ways of relating to one another. A set of Executive MBA alums who are making an impact in their various companies and organizations in Kansas City now exist in the community and beyond.

Drawn from Dick Heimovics, Marilyn Taylor, and Richard Stilwell, "Assessing and Developing a New Strategic Direction for the Executive MBA," *Journal of Management Education,* Vol. 20, No. 4 (November, 1996), pp. 462-478); and updated from the author's experience as director of the Executive MBA Program.

Exhibit 3

EMBA-ICIC Client Projects

1996-97:

Black Economic Union/18th and Vine: benchmarking study of Kansas City's historic African-American District, which is undergoing development as a destination location, as well as a community involving existing housing projects, retail, and businesses.

Real Estate Development and Management Company: facilitated merger with a smaller company including financial, legal, organizational, computer/accounting systems, and leadership assessment help.

Leading nonprofit multi-unit childcare organization: baseline assessment of the firm's visibility in the community and the perceptions of various constituencies.

Plastics Manufacturing Company: strategic assessment of this plastics molding division of a larger company.

Construction Company: strategic, financial, and organizational assessment, including review of a lease purchase agreement of the company's building and baseline plans for diversification.

1997-98:

18th and Vine: review of the current and anticipated parking needs for the six-block development area. Working with an undergraduate applied math team from Baker University, modeled the parking need projections. Identified a temporary solution to the parking issue that had not been previously considered.

Area Development: worked with the developer of record for a four-block area slated for private and public investment redevelopment. Identified a number of issues regarding the design of the area, the balance of the businesses planned for the area.

Nonprofit Community Development Organization: facilitated the beginnings of a merchants association in one of the most disenfranchised areas of the city.

cont.

Building and Maintenance Company: facilitated review of mission and dialog concerning the multi-general issues involving leadership of the organization, designed new marketing materials, began an operations and organizational human resources manual.

Community Bank: reviewed mission and operations and market and customer information for this African-American-initiated community bank; facilitated dialog among staff to consider organizational and operational issues with the president.

Strip Shopping Mall: established a best practices model for a twenty-three-year-old strip shopping mall which is part of a larger corridor redevelopment undertaken as a partnership between a large multi-unit health care organization campus and other businesses and neighborhoods in the area.

<u>**1998-99 (Planned):**</u>

18th and Vine: review of the complement of businesses in the area, consideration of possible additions, and feasibility study for one.

Health Care Delivery Company: strategic and organizational assessment of this innovative company; assistance in preparing a financing package.

Specialty wholesale coffee roasting and distribution company: review of one or more market diversification opportunities.

Electronic Document Storage Company: review of one or more vertical markets and recommendation of growth plans for this avante garde technology company that does electronic scanning and vectoring of specialty and large scale document projects.

Health Care Clinic: review of the retail and businesses in an economic development area for which the clinic is the designated area developer.

Metal fabrication company for the HVAC Industry: facilitation of movement away from dependency for minority set-aside contracts; assessment of current organizational structure and processes.

Specialty financing firm for health care organizations: review of a vertical market and design of plans for aggressive exploitation of the market.

Exhibit 4

Structure and Flow of the Learning Components of
the Bloch School executive MBA Program

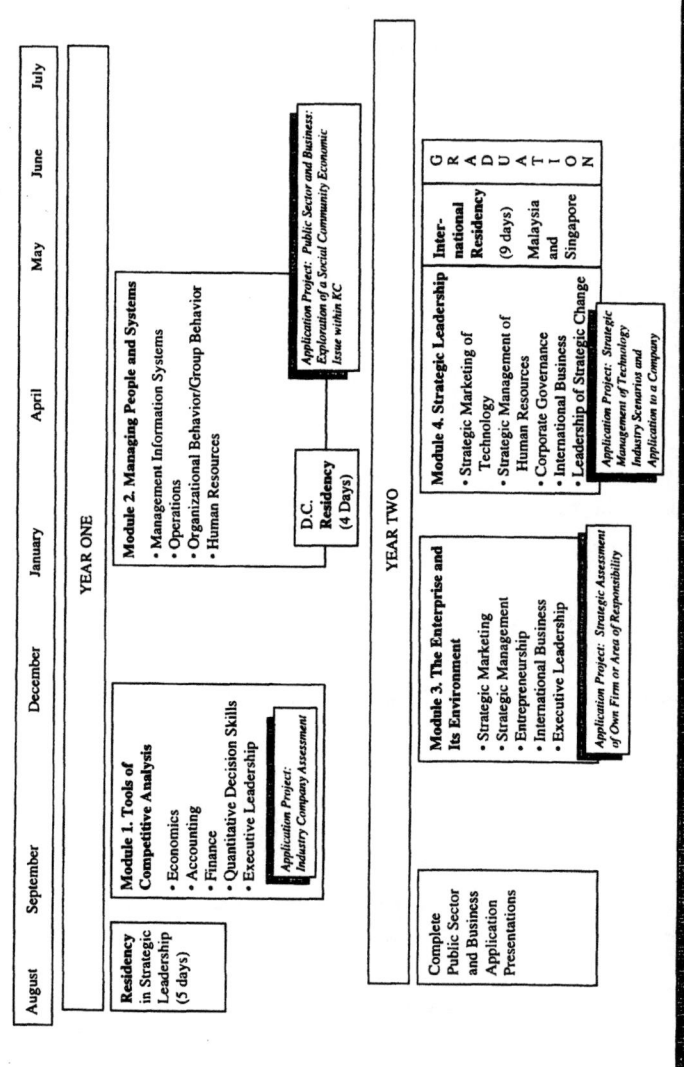

YEAR ONE

| August | September | December | January | April | May | June | July |

Residency in Strategic Leadership (5 days)

Module 1. Tools of Competitive Analysis
- Economics
- Accounting
- Finance
- Quantitative Decision Skills
- Executive Leadership

Application Project: Industry Company Assessment

Module 2. Managing People and Systems
- Management Information Systems
- Operations
- Organizational Behavior/Group Behavior
- Human Resources

D.C. **Residency** (4 Days)

Application Project: Public Sector and Business: Exploration of a Social Community Economic Issue within KC

YEAR TWO

Complete Public Sector and Business Application Presentations

Module 3. The Enterprise and Its Environment
- Strategic Marketing
- Strategic Management
- Entrepreneurship
- International Business
- Executive Leadership

Application Project: Strategic Assessment of Own Firm or Area of Responsibility

Module 4. Strategic Leadership
- Strategic Marketing of Technology
- Strategic Management of Human Resources
- Corporate Governance
- International Business
- Leadership of Strategic Change

Application Project: Strategic Management of Technology Industry Scenarios and Application to a Company

International Residency (9 days) Malaysia and Singapore

GRADUATION

Strategic Organizational Assessment and Application Projects carried out in partnership with the Initiative for a Competitive Inner City as the ICIC-EMBA Projects in teams of three to five EMBAs. Client organizations are businesses, non-profits, and area developments located in the Greater Kansas City urban Core. About seven clients, eight faculty members, and as many business community mentors are expected to work with the 1998-99 ICIC-EMBA program. Projects initiate with team formation in July, project management training and team transitions in September, engagement letters (proposals) in October including the schedule for deliverables (output), periodic written and oral update reports, and final reports scheduled for late April, 1999.

Service-Learning and Management Education

by Daniel R. McKell

This bibliography is divided into three main areas — foundation pieces, education in general, and management education. An asterisk indicates the author's choice for best article or book in each section.

Foundation Pieces

Experiential Education

Dewey, J. (1963). *Experience and Education.* New York, NY: Collier Books.
   Dewey masterfully helps the reader understand the true meaning of education. He essentially narrates his intellectual journey toward developing an educational philosophy that is both pure and simple. The book compares and contrasts educational perspectives and presents arguments for the development of a theory and its foundational principles. Developing the theory allows educators to offer the true fruits of education to their pupils, making education a reality rather than just a name or title.

Kolb, D.A. (1984). *Experiential Learning: Experience as the Source of Learning and Development.* Englewood Cliffs, NJ: Prentice-Hall.*
   Kolb's book integrates and bridges the gaps between the theory and application of learning/education. The book takes the reader through the ideas of past thinkers and provides an integrated framework intended to improve understanding of the learning process. The book covers diverse topics ranging from individual learning styles to knowledge structures to the development of integrity. By focusing the book on development, Kolb provides insights into how and where experiential learning might be applied.

Service-Learning

Jacoby, B., and Associates. (1996). *Service-Learning in Higher Education.* San Francisco, CA: Jossey-Bass.
   Jacoby and Associates have compiled a valuable resource tool for those interested in developing service-learning–based courses or programs. The book introduces foundational principles that, when enacted, provide a sound base upon which to develop the service-

learning orientation. Next, the reader learns about a number of designs currently in use around the United States. Finally, the work offers valuable insights into how to administer, integrate, and institutionalize. Also included in the book is a list of national organizations that support service-learning.

Kendall, J.C., and Associates. (1990). *Combining Service and Learning: A Resource Book for Community and Public Service.* 3 vols. Raleigh, NC: National Society for Internships and Experiential Education.*

Kendall and Associates' three volumes explore and expound on service-learning in what is probably one of the more complete reference guides on the subject. The first volume contains much of the background on many of the principles that lead to effective service-learning. The second volume explores a number of programs already in existence, and uses these case studies to offer practical advice. The third volume is a fully indexed annotated bibliography. All three volumes taken together provide valuable information about service-learning.

Education in General

Experiential Learning

Brookfield, S. (1996). "Experiential Pedagogy: Grounding Teaching in Students' Learning." *Journal of Experiential Education* 19(1): 62-68.

The author discusses the value of student feedback as a way to improve pedagogy, especially as it relates to experiential education. The article explores the why's, how's, and resulting benefits of accessing student reactions to the learning process. Specifically, the article explains the Classroom Critical Incident Questionnaire, a tool for gathering information, and provides implementation ideas for both small and large classes.

Cantor, J.A. (1997). *Experiential Learning in Higher Education: Linking Classroom and Community.* ASHE-ERIC Higher Education Reports, no. 7. Washington, DC: The George Washington University, Graduate School of Education and Human Development.*

Cantor's report will educate and inform future discussions concerning experiential education. The author discusses policy issues and philosophical foundations. The best part of the report, however, contains a set of "best practices" of experiential programs relating to topics such as activity design, student needs assessments, and program evaluations.

Carver, R. (1996). "Theory for Practice: A Framework for Thinking About Experiential Education." *Journal of Experiential Education* 19(1): 8-13.
This article provides a means of understanding the complexity of experiential education. The interdisciplinary nature of experiential education requires a framework that takes into consideration a spectrum of views from various disciplines. The framework is useful to aid evaluation, illuminate previously unrecognized relationships, and facilitate communication across subject areas. The framework consists of identifying program characteristics, contextual influences, and the students' experience, and the relationship among the three variables.

Service-Learning

Fouhey, H., and J. Saltmarsh. (1996). "Outward Bound and Community Service Learning: An Experiment in Connected Knowing." *Journal of Experiential Education* 19(1): 82-89.
This article studies how using community service-learning frameworks has improved the Outward Bound program. The authors use a theoretical framework developed by Delve, Mintz, and Stewart that integrates the thoughts and ideas of Perry, Kolb, Gilligan, Dewey, Levin, and Piaget. The framework highlights the importance of the beginning stages (i.e., exploration and clarification) as a way to enhance cognitive and moral outcomes. Synergistic effects are demonstrated by merging wilderness programs such as Outward Bound with community service-learning.

Leder, D., and I. McGuinness. (1996). "Making the Paradigm Shift: Service-Learning in Higher Education." *Metropolitan Universities: An International Forum* 7(1): 47-56.*
Drawing on their experience at Loyola College, the authors suggest a number of ways to support and enhance service-learning pedagogy. These suggestions focus on facilitating student access, increasing faculty motivation, and involving administrative and institutional support persons in the programs. Some of the specific strategies include semester colloquiums, department associates/mentors, and faculty-development resources.

Price, J.R., and J.S. Martello. (1996). "Naming and Framing Service-Learning: A Taxonomy and Four Levels of Value." *Metropolitan Universities: An International Forum* 7(1): 11-23.

> While service-learning is rapidly gaining popularity throughout higher education, the authors argue for a clear and focused taxonomy to ensure that service-learning becomes all it proposes to be. The article calls for clarity in practice and in mission/purpose. The greater the clarity in these areas, the less confusion regarding experiential education. Increased clarity also provides a useful framework to highlight the structures needed to achieve program objectives. The four-value framework directs inquiry and goal selection as administrators determine which level of value they hope to achieve.

Service-Learning in Management Education

Fleckenstein, M.P. (1997). "Service-Learning in Business Ethics." *Journal of Business Ethics* 16: 1347-1351.

> The author discusses the relative difficulty of teaching ethics in the business school setting, offering service-learning pedagogy as a potential solution to improving ethics courses. The author discusses ideas from Dewey and suggests applications that may help educators overcome factors previously inhibiting success. Two key factors mentioned include ensuring that the service is directly related to the academic field of study and providing opportunities for the students to make significant contributions during the course of the project.

Hogner, R.H. (1996). "Speaking in Poetry: Community Service–Based Business Education." *Journal of Business Ethics* 15: 33-43.

> Hogner takes the reader through the process of developing a service-based business course at Florida International University. He discusses a four-step process by which the course was developed. He also describes course readings to establish a base upon which experience is added. Course outcomes and learnings are provided to show the value of implementing service-learning programs in business education.

Kolenko, T.A., G. Porter, W. Wheatley, and M. Colby. (1996). "A Critique of Service-Learning Projects in Management Education: Pedagogical Foundations, Barriers, and Guidelines." *Journal of Business Ethics* 15: 5-19.*

> Kolenko et al. offer a brief critique of nine service-learning programs in order to identify characteristics of successful service-learning expe-

riences. By identifying elements that need to be incorporated, common obstacles, and key elements of success, the authors hope to improve business ethics courses for teachers and students alike.

Lamond, D.A. (1995). "Using Consulting Projects in Management Education: The Joys and Jitters of Serving Two Masters." *Journal of Management Development* 14(8): 60-72.
Active learning and its related subsets are a common ingredient in many recipes for improving education. This article looks at how one university has used active learning as a way to improve business education. The author takes the reader through the consulting project program, explaining how and why the program has been a success. The ideas may provide a good working model for others to emulate.

Morton, K., and M. Troppe. (1996). "From the Margin to the Mainstream: Campus Compact's Project of Integrating Service With Academic Study." *Journal of Business Ethics* 15: 21-32.
Morton and Troppe narrate the historical roots and progression of Campus Compact, an organization of 517 college and university presidents who have united to support community service in their respective communities. The article contains suggestions for ways to institutionalize service-learning, followed by case examples of successes and failures to illustrate some of the main ideas.

Zlotkowski, E. (1996). "Opportunity for All: Linking Service-Learning and Business Education." *Journal of Business Ethics* 15: 5-19.
The author begins the article by discussing educational reform issues related to business education. Integrating service-learning into business education is identified as a potential cure for many of the stated weaknesses and shortcomings. Benefits of integrating service-learning include developing tolerance for ambiguity, improved people/"soft" skills, and more resolute ethics. The article presents obstacles as well as models for overcoming those obstacles to illustrate the argument for integration.

Contributors to This Volume

Volume Editors

Paul C. Godfrey is an associate professor in the Department of Organizational Leadership and Strategy in the Marriott School of Management at Brigham Young University. He teaches courses in business strategy, implementing business strategy, and business ethics.

Edward T. Grasso is a professor of decision sciences and the coordinator of the management major at Eckerd College. He frequently leads student groups throughout the world as part of the international education program at Eckerd.

Authors

David M. Boje is a professor in the Management Department, in the College of Business Administration and Economics, at New Mexico State University and is a codirector of the university's Center for Strategic Decisions.

Gaylen N. Chandler is an associate professor in the Department of Management and Human Resources at Utah State University. He is also the director of the MSS/HRM program.

Sue Campbell Clark teaches in the Business Department at the University of Idaho.

James H. Davis is an associate professor in the Management Department at the University of Notre Dame.

Forest L. Frueh works with Larry Michaelsen at the University of Oklahoma.

John Hobbs is an instructor in the Division of Marketing and is the coordinator of Applied Business Programs in the Michael F. Price College of Business at the University of Oklahoma.

James M. Kenderdine is an associate professor in the Division of Marketing in the Michael F. Price College of Business at the University of Oklahoma.

Amy Kenworthy-U'Ren is an assistant professor of management at Bond University in Australia.

Christine H. Lamb is the assistant dean of the College of Business at Montana State University.

James B. Lee works at Montana State University.

Daniel R. McKell was a graduate student in the Master of Organizational Behavior program at Brigham Young University; he works in human resources development at Intel Corporation.

Larry K. Michaelsen is the David Ross Boyd professor of management in the Michael F. Price College of Business at the University of Oklahoma.

John G. Michel is an assistant professor in the Management Department at the University of Notre Dame.

James Post is a professor in the Management Policy Department at Boston University. He is also the director of the DBA program.

Grace Ann Rosile is an associate professor in the Management Department, in the College of Business Administration and Economics, at New Mexico State University.

Judith Samuelson is the director of the Initiative for Social Innovation Through Business at the Aspen Institute. She is located in New York City.

Robert L. Swinth is a professor of management in the College of Business at Montana State University.

Marilyn Taylor is the Arvin Gottlieb/Missouri chair in strategic management, in the Henry W. Bloch School of Business and Public Administration, at the University of Missouri in Kansas City. She is also currently the director of its Executive MBA program.

Karen L. Vinton works at Montana State University.

Sandra Waddock is an associate professor of operations and strategic management in the Wallace E. Carroll School of Management at Boston College.

Series Editor

Edward Zlotkowski is professor of English and was founding director of the Service-Learning Project at Bentley College. He also is senior associate at the American Association for Higher Education.

About AAHE's Series on Service-Learning in the Disciplines

The Series goes beyond simple "how to" to provide a rigorous intellectual forum. *Theoretical essays* illuminate issues of general importance to educators interested in using a service-learning pedagogy. *Pedagogical essays* discuss the design, implementation, conceptual content, outcomes, advantages, and disadvantages of specific service-learning programs, courses, and projects. All essays are authored by teacher-scholars in the discipline.

Representative of a wide range of individual interests and approaches, the Series provide substantive discussions. supported by research, course models in a rich conceptual context, annotated bibliographies, and program descriptions.

Visit Stylus Publishing's website (www.styluspub.com) for the list of disciplines covered in the Series, pricing, and ordering information.